WIVES AND STUNNERS

Also by Henrietta Garnett

FAMILY SKELETONS

ANNY: A BIOGRAPHY OF ANNY THACKERAY RICHIE

HENRIETTA GARNETT

WIVES AND STUNNERS

The Pre-Raphaelites and Their Muses

MACMILLAN

First published 2012 by Macmillan
an imprint of Pan Macmillan, a division of Macmillan Publishers Limited
Pan Macmillan, 20 New Wharf Road, London N1 9RR
Basingstoke and Oxford
Associated companies throughout the world
www.panmacmillan.com

ISBN 978-0-230-70940-9

The acknowledgements on page 317 constitute an extension of this copyright page.

1 3 5 7 9 8 6 4 2

A CIP catalogue record for this book is available from the British Library.

Typeset by SetSystems Ltd, Saffron Walden, Essex
Printed and bound by CPI Group (UK) Ltd, Croydon, CR0 4YY

For John Drane
with love from the author

'But to the Eyes of the Man of Imagination,
Nature is Imagination itself. As a man is, So he Sees.'

WILLIAM BLAKE

'You will conclude, and quite rightly, that we are in
an age in which nature was poetic, love affairs passionate,
while hair, skirts, railways, families and incomes
extended far and wide.'

QUENTIN BELL, *Blunderhead* (unpublished), 1966

Contents

Introduction

A wife is a married woman. A 'stunner'* is nineteenth-century slang, coined by Gabriel Rossetti, generally referring to a woman of exceptional beauty, glamour and charisma. She might be propriety personified, but she is the kind of woman, from any social class, who turns the heads of complete strangers wherever she goes. She is, in fact, a star. A stunner might be a wife, but a wife is not necessarily a stunner.

The influence of the stunners on Pre-Raphaelite painting was profound. These women informed the paintings they modelled for, were worshipped by the artists for their beauty and charm, and introduced a new concept of female beauty to the Victorian public. Women such as Elizabeth (Lizzie) Siddal, Mary (Maria) Zambaco† and Jane Morris became a cult, inspired some of the most important painters of the nineteenth century, and set new trends in fashion and culture.

While the accepted definition of a wife is correct, the interpretation of what a wife was in English nineteenth-century terms is very different from our twenty-first century understanding of the

---

* The modern reader might be bewildered by William Makepeace Thackeray's statement in *The Newcomes* that 'the cook is a stunner for tarts', but this should be interpreted as meaning that the cook is brilliant at cooking tarts, which, knowing Thackeray, were probably jam ones.

† Although the Greek name is Maria, she was usually known as Mary, while Maria Spartali was always called Marie.

word. Until 1870, when the Married Woman's Property Act was passed, as soon as a woman signed her marriage certificate, she was signing away not only her worldly goods but also herself. From that moment she became the property of her husband and since, in the eyes of the law, a married couple were regarded as one person, she had no legal identity of her own. Her money automatically became her husband's. She had no right to make a will. In the case of separation, or, more rarely, a divorce, a wife had no access to her children by that marriage except through the benevolence of her husband. Her husband was entitled to consign her to an institution or asylum even against her will.

After 1870, a wife, like her unmarried sisters, had the right to own any money she earned independently, to inherit up to £200, and to inherit property bequeathed her by her next of kin, although her husband still owned any property she had possessed in her own name before her marriage. This form of female emancipation worked both ways: a woman's husband remained liable to maintain their children, but now she was equally liable to maintain those children with anything she earned. It was not until 1882 that the act was amended so that a married woman was allowed to own and control her own property without any reference to her husband. By now, she was regarded as a separate identity, no longer her husband's property. A wife was also liable for any debts she might incur, although how she could have incurred them under previous conditions, as a person who did not exist in her own right, is open to debate. However, even if her legal power was limited, the influence of a wife, like that of the stunner, could be immeasurable.

Wives and Stunners is a group biography, telling stories of related events in the lives of the Pre-Raphaelite artists and the relationships they had with the women who were variously their wives, mistresses, models and muses. I have deliberately concentrated on Euphemia Gray and her marriages to John Ruskin and, subsequently, John Everett Millais; Dante Gabriel Rossetti and Elizabeth Siddal and Rossetti's later affair with Jane Morris; the marriage between William and Jane Morris; and the marriage of Edward and Georgiana Burne-Jones, allowing the subplot of Annie Miller's affair with Holman Hunt to emerge as it occurs in the primary narrative. I have also included the impact of the Anglo-Greek Ionides family and the influence of their stunning daughters, without which no study of the Pre-Raphaelites and their muses would be complete.

The year 1848, when my story opens, was a fascinating time to be young, ardent and alive. It was the year of revolution in Europe: various Italian states rose against the Austrian occupation and Venice declared itself a republic.* In Austria, Metternich was overthrown. In France, the Second Empire was established and Louis-Philippe fled to England. In England, matters were not so clear. It was a time of both political unrest and intense respectability. The year 1848 was the year of the last Chartist petition in England. Thomas Carlyle had meant to go to the protest meeting at Kennington Green, but had got drenched in a thunderstorm on his way to the London Library, lost his brolly in the throng of demonstrators in Piccadilly, and then stayed at home in Chelsea. Various young men, John Everett Millais, William Holman Hunt and William Michael Rossetti among them, went as spectators to the demonstration at Kennington Green, where the sun was shining, but none of them stayed for long. These three young men were more interested in the aesthetics of the meeting than the politics. The authorities had called in the Duke of Wellington to arrange civic protection for the expected hundreds of thousands of protesters. Extra constables, police and other forces had been mobilized and the Royal Family exiled to Osborne on the Isle of Wight out of harm's way. In the event, only an estimated fifteen thousand protesters turned up.

---

* Two years previously, in 1846, Mr Alfred Bird invented custard powder, which, in my view, should have caused a revolution in England. It failed to and has been guzzled up in prisons, schools, canteens, hospitals, lunatic asylums and other dismal institutions ever since with a deleterious effect on its consumers.

While 'the spirit of revolt had run like wildfire from kingdom to kingdom and capital to capital of Europe: Paris, Vienna, Naples, Berlin, Dresden, Milan, Venice, Palermo, Frankfurt, and Carlsruhe, all had experienced the revolutionary shock, and none had been able completely to withstand it. Now came the turn of London, the greatest capital of all – the greatest prize that the world could afford to revolutionary adventure – the most magnificent prey to the bands of the plunderers who moved about from one point of Europe to another, committing robberies under the name of revolution. London withstood the shock, and escaped without the slightest injury.'[1] It was not merely a triumph for Wellington but also a testimony to the nature of the pragmatism of John Bull. While it was clear that the Chartists had much cause for their grievances, the average Englishman did not wish to be robbed or to have his suburban villa vandalized. The English preferred to live in peace and prosperity if they could and, understandably, having been horrified by the Reign of Terror in France, thought a revolution more trouble than it was worth. 'Thus,' in the words of *The Times*, 'the great demonstration was brought to a ridiculous issue by the unity and resolution of the metropolis, backed by the judicious measures of the Government, and the masterly military precautions of the Duke of Wellington, though no military display was anywhere to be seen', and the petition fizzled out in the seasonal showers on that Monday, 10 April 1848.[2]

The year 1848 was the year which saw the publication of the Marx-Engels *Communist Manifesto*** and John Stuart Mill's *Principles of Political Economy*,† both of which became standard texts for natural scientists and economists of the period and are still referred to and

---

* The *Communist Manifesto* stated 'The history of all hitherto existing society is the history of class struggles', and predicted how capitalist society would evolve into a socialist and then a communist one.

† John Stuart Mill, 1806–73, was opposed to unlimited state control and, with Jeremy Bentham, advocated utilitarianism. He was highly influential in liberal politics.

read widely today. The English moral climate hadn't been quite so puritanical since the days of Cromwell, demonstrating itself most clearly in the aspirations of the newly emerged middle classes. The women in black bonnets and shawls, their gowns of bombazine, and the gentlemen in black frock coats and black silk top hats, lent a new sobriety to the city streets. It was hard to believe that some of the older of these earnest folk had once been Regency bucks. The year 1848 was also the year of the formation of the Pre-Raphaelite Brotherhood, known as the P. R. B.

The English have always been crazy about clubs, sets, groups and circles: the Cannibal Club, the Hellfire Club, Samuel Palmer and the Ancients, to name but a few. All club members appear to be under the illusion that they are unique. The Pre-Raphaelites were no exception.

In some respects, the Pre-Raphaelites were precursors of the Bloomsbury Group: in their sexual imbroglios, their dedication to their art, their bohemian lifestyle and their influence on popular culture, dress, interior design, literature and politics. Both sets of friends not only produced work which changed public perception of aesthetics, but also, because of the drama and intricacy of their relationships, they have become part of our modern mythology.

As much as taste in hemlines varies, so does fashion in literature, politics and art. Just as sartorial fashion changes, so that a female who enjoys wearing a mini-skirt and bobbed hair, may, at a later date, delight in a floor-length dress and grow her hair as long as she can, so does the perception of the viewer of a work of art. It comes as a shock to reflect that, across the English Channel in 1863, Edouard Manet was painting *Olympia* in the very year that Rossetti had begun work on the posthumous portrait of Lizzie Siddal in *Beata Beatrix*. In the beginning, the Pre-Raphaelites' painting was reviled by the public. Their models were considered to be hideous and scraggy and, by the standards of mainstream mid-Victorian taste, they were. Yet, towards the end of the nineteenth century, Pre-Raphaelite painting enjoyed an immense popularity and the women who modelled for them were generally esteemed as beauties. The later work of Burne-Jones evolved into Symbolism, for which he was much admired in Europe, but as art became more 'modern', Cézanne's still lives of apples superseded portraits of stunners, and public enthusiasm for Pre-Raphaelite art slumped. For most art lovers from the early to late twentieth century, who embraced Fauvism, Cubism, Dadaism and all the other isms leading to postmodernism, the Pre-Raphaelites would have been anathema and made their toes shrivel in their shoes.

In the mid-1960s, when the fashion for avant-garde 'beautiful people' insisted on long hair and extravagantly long and swirly skirts for women, and velvet suits with the trousers cut like jeans for men, who also sported long locks, the tide appeared to have turned. But this taste was more evident in the nightclubs, picnics in Hyde Park and fashionable parties of the time than it was in galleries and auction rooms. Of course, there were a few exceptions; there always are. Notable art dealers such as Christopher Gibbs, Jeremy Maas, the late Charlie Thomas and the art collector and musical composer Andrew Lloyd Webber were among the perceptive few who could profit from their perception. In recent years, there have been many popular exhibitions of Pre-Raphaelite painting, notably at Tate Britain, The Royal Academy, The National Gallery, Manchester City Art Gallery, The Walker Art Gallery, The Victoria and Albert Museum, The Fitzwilliam Museum, Leighton House and Nottingham Art Gallery. The Pre-Raphaelites have also been the subjects of many recent studies and biographies, which I have listed in the Select Biography, as well as earlier ones. People of sufficient interest and creators of merit always resurface, even if they suffer from periods of obscurity. The re-emergence of the Pre-Raphaelite Brotherhood and the wives and stunners who inspired them is, quite apart from my own obsession with the nineteenth century, why I have been impelled to write about them.

HENRIETTA GARNETT
London, April 2012

Sonnet XVIII
GENIUS IN BEAUTY

Beauty like hers is genius. Not the call
Of Homer's or of Dante's heart sublime, —
Not Michael's hand furrowing the zones of time, —
Is more with compassed mysteries musical;
Nay, not in Spring's or Summer's sweet footfall
More gathered gifts exuberant Life bequeaths
Than does this sovereign face, whose love-spell breathes
Even from its shadowed contour on the wall.

As many men are poets in their youth,
But for one sweet-strung soul the wires prolong
Even through all change the indomitable song;
So in likewise the envenomed years, whose tooth
Rends shallower grace with ruin void of truth,
Upon this beauty's power shall wreak no wrong.

DANTE GABRIEL ROSSETTI

1

THE FORMATION OF THE P. R. B.

'The visionary vanities of half a dozen boys'

D. G. ROSSETTI

They were very young and very poor; a bunch of seven idealistic art students at the Royal Academy, then the only serious art school in England. Johnny (John Everett) Millais, who had just turned nineteen, was the most talented. Having entered the school as a prodigy at the age of eleven, the youngest student ever to have been admitted, he was still the darling of the Academy, known by his fellow students as 'The Child', a nickname which continued well into his adult life. He was as narcissistic as he was handsome, but his friends forgave him his absurd vanity when they recollected that his main preoccupation was, like their own, with aesthetics. Gabriel Dante Rossetti (who signed his work Dante Gabriel), whose own sultry looks were the epitome of Romanticism, was the most imaginative and endearing. At this stage, he had no technique, couldn't apply himself to any discipline and was torn between the persuasions of poetry and painting. With his impetuous manners, outrageous demands, sheer charm and irreverent humour, he infuriated and fascinated them all. William Holman Hunt, who, with Millais, had somehow stumbled on the lost secret of reproducing the brilliant colours of the quattrocento they all agreed were so divine, was the most earnest and took himself doggedly seriously. He would have been in danger of being dull if it hadn't been for

his wild notions and still odder theories, which no amount of poverty or discomfort could prevent him from putting into practice.
His ardent single-mindedness was often mistaken for eccentricity
and led to his friends nicknaming him 'Mad'. The others were
James Collinson, piety personified, who was in love with Rossetti's
sister Christina and made them all laugh by his constantly dropping
asleep even in the most vivacious situations; the sculptor Thomas
Woolner; Frederick George (Fred) Stephens, who finally became
an art critic; and Gabriel's younger brother, the prematurely bald
William Michael, as solid in his affections as a mahogany side-
board, who worked for the Inland Revenue and wasn't an artist at
all. Eventually, William Michael became a good art critic, a bad
poet and the chronicler of the Pre-Raphaelite movement.

None of them were very clear about how they were going to
express what they meant, but they all had a healthy appetite for
rebelling against the order of the day, which they regarded as
singularly stuffy, the established artists of the Academy turning out
pictures the colour of bitumen, a dingy brown pigment impregnat-
ing the canvas; the subjects classical clichés.

These seven students were borne along by a gust of enthusiasm,
reflecting the spirit of revolution in the wind. It didn't matter that
they had little knowledge of the world, were poor and proud and
somehow reckless at the same time. With the exception of Millais,
whose appearance was conventional – apart from the way he had
of parting his curly hair, at this period, in the centre, the parting
running all the way down the back of his head – they dressed in
velvet and wore their hair long, hoping to look artistic but not
quite achieving the effect they desired. Gabriel, who was always
running out of 'tin', as they called ready cash, camouflaged the
holes of his trousers by dabbing black paint on his skin. He and
his brother, William Michael, shared one evening jacket between
them, which they wore in turns to go to the opera. At this point
they all loved each other dearly, vowed everlasting friendship and
formed what became known as the Pre-Raphaelite Brotherhood.

Naturally, it was to be a secret society. They published a

magazine and called it *The Germ.* Somehow, they persuaded a good-natured friend, John Tupper, who happened to be a printer, to publish it for them. A lively and, in many ways, fascinating journal, it ran to only four issues. It was beautifully printed and illustrated, but was a commercial failure, leaving the Brotherhood in debt to Tupper to the tune of thirty-two guineas. Yet underlying their extravagant claims, they were extremely serious and worked immensely hard. They believed that art had become corrupted and that the only way forward was to go back to the painters of the fourteenth and fifteenth centuries, which they considered the sublime moment in the history of art.

The first meeting of the group was held at Millais' parents' house on Gower Street, London W1. Like all their gatherings, it was an informal occasion even though they were serious about the issue. Amid teasing, much laughter and generally letting off their rollicking spirits, they declared the Brotherhood to have four definite purposes: 1) to have a genuine idea to express; 2) to study nature attentively, so as to know how to express it; 3) to sympathize with what was direct and serious and heartfelt in previous art, to the exclusion of what was conventional and self-parodying and learned by rote; 4) and, most indispensable of all, to produce thoroughly good pictures and statues.

Between them, led by Hunt and Millais, they had hit on a method of painting which involved laying colour on a background of lead white mixed to a tacky, malleable consistency with linseed oil. Colour – rose madder, gamboge yellow, cobalt blue, viridian green – was applied with a minute sable brush, generally used only for watercolours. The painting was to be executed *en plein air*, the painter and the canvas exposed to the vagaries of light and the prevailing wind, as well as midges, nettle patches and other hazards. The painting was to be as true to life as was physically possible. No one could have dreamed of a more tortuous or time-consuming method of painting. The result was a brilliancy of colour combined with a startling realism, their understanding of truth disarmingly literal and very much in harness with the recent invention of photography, a craze which was not only catching on with surprising swiftness, but which was also to change for ever the way in which people perceived things. Nothing could have been more ambitious, more demanding or more exhausting.

They would abandon shades of bitumen, be true to nature down to the most exacting detail, and paint in the purest and brightest of colours, avoiding strong contrasts of light and shade. Curiously, none of them, except for Holman Hunt, had read John Ruskin, who had been propounding views similar to their own in the first volume of his series *Modern Painters,* and who later became their champion. They signed their paintings P. R. B., which might well have puzzled the public, but they didn't care and it amused them. Some wag said that it might be interpreted as 'Please Ring the Bell' and somebody else said it could stand for 'Penis Rather Better'.

Much later, in 1868, Gabriel wrote to Ernest Chesneau: 'The idea that Ruskin had by his writings founded the Pre-Raphaelite school is a mistake which seems almost universal, but it is none the less completely wrong. In fact I believe that of the painters who produced the school not one had read a single one of the admirable books of Mr Ruskin and certainly none of them knew him personally. It was not until after several annual exhibitions of their paintings [at the Royal Academy] that this great writer generously made himself their advocate in the face of the furious attacks of the press.'*

Very much of their generation, they were immensely literary and were inspired by the Bible, Arthurian myth and legend, ballads, Thomas Malory, Geoffrey Chaucer, William Shakespeare, John Keats, William Blake, whose poetry was then generally considered the wanderings of someone deranged, Alfred Tennyson, Robert Browning and William Makepeace Thackeray, whose work they read voraciously in instalments of *Fraser's Magazine.* More

---

* Also quoted in *A New and Noble School: The Pre-Raphaelites* by Quentin Bell (p. 43).

outlandishly, the haunting tales of Edgar Allan Poe, Friedrich de la Motte Fouqué's *Undine, Aslauga's Knight* and *Sintram and His Companions*, with Dürer's engraving of *Knight, Death and the Devil* as its frontispiece (an illustration which was to have 'catastrophic' results[*] on one of Millais' subsequent paintings), and later, when it was published in 1854, Charlotte M. Yonge's *The Heir of Redclyffe*,[†] all figured among their favourite reading.

The Heir of Redclyffe is a highly moral novel which concerns the story of Guy Morville, the heir of a baronetcy, and the family seat and estate of Redclyffe. Passionate and bedevilled with a hot temper, Morville is fundamentally good, generous and honourable. His inimical cousin Philip prevents his marriage to Amy by spreading unfounded suspicions about Guy's honesty while he, Philip, carries on a clandestine affair with Amy's sister, Laura. Guy's good name is finally redeemed and he and Amy marry. They honeymoon in Italy, where they find Philip seriously ill with a fever. Guy nurses Philip back to health, then catches the fever himself. It proves fatal and he dies. By now, Amy is pregnant and when the child proves to be a daughter, Philip, who is now repentant, inherits the Redclyffe estate and marries Laura. The widowed Amy and her disinherited daughter, Mary Verena, lead a saintly existence hallowed by Guy's love, while Philip and Laura, though repentant, are soured by their initial disingenuousness.

The following passage from de la Motte Fouqué's tale of *The Two Captains* could have been written with Rossetti expressly in mind: 'Branches half teasing, half caressing, already brushed [Heimbert's] cheeks, magic birds growing from the bushes sang joyously; over the silky turf of the ground on which Heimbert kept

---

[*] Ruskin's verdict on Millais' painting *Sir Isumbras at the Ford* (1857), Lady Lever Art Gallery, Port Sunlight, Liverpool.

[†] de la Motte Fouqué's *Sintram* is the favourite reading of the chief protagonists, Guy and Amy, in *The Heir of Redclyffe*. When Louisa May Alcott came to write *Little Women* (1868), the heroine, Jo March, is discovered up in the garret munching apples and in tears over *The Heir of Redclyffe* . Jo and her three sisters were equally fond of reading *Sintram*.

his eyes fixed, glided snakes of brilliant gold and green with golden coronets, and jewels blossomed from the carpet of moss; when the snakes touched them, there was a silvery tinkle.' These were tales of fair damsels and brave knights, of courtly love and the power of good over evil. Having imbibed them young, such writings had an immense effect on Rossetti and directly affected both his painting and his poetry.

Gabriel Rossetti and his three siblings were remarkably well read and, a result of their Italian heritage, were bilingual in Italian. All of them, including the much neglected Maria, the elder sister who became an Anglican nun,* were published authors. Their father, Gabriele Rossetti, a political refugee from Italy, was an immensely cultured man, a slightly cracked poet and scholar and the first Professor of Italian Language at London University, which had opened ten years previously in 1838. At home, they generally spoke Italian. Visitors to the small, relatively spartan house in Charlotte Street were mainly friends of their father's, Italian political refugees. Their dinners were usually Italian, consisting of, to English notions of the day, outlandish farinaceous foods such as polenta, gnocchi and macaroni. With their father, too, they shared a passion for the poet Dante. Gabriel, in particular, became obsessed by Dante. Many of his paintings refer to the story of Dante's own obsession with Beatrice; Gabriel's translation of *La Vita Nuova* remains refreshingly vivid. From their mother's side, the young Rossettis may have inherited their ability to write. Their uncle, John Polidori, had been a companion and doctor to Byron on his travels through Switzerland and Italy when, inspired by Mary Shelley's success with *Frankenstein*, he wrote a short Gothic romance, *The Vampyre*, the first English story about a vampire.†

---

*   Maria Rossetti was the author of *The Shadow of Dante* (1871) and translator of *The Day Hours and Other Offices as Used by the Sisters of All Saints*, an English translation of the Monastic Diurnal for her order, which remained in use until 1922.

†   Polidori travelled with Byron to Switzerland in 1816 and was present on the

The sculptor Thomas Woolner was also a poet. His most famous poem, *My Beautiful Lady*, was illustrated by Holman Hunt and originally appeared in the first issue of the Pre-Raphaelite magazine, *The Germ*. Although, like many Victorian poets, his work is largely unread now, his other poems, including *Of My Lady in Death*, *Pygmalion*, *Silenus* and *Tiresias*, enjoyed considerable popularity at the time. Genuinely gifted and with an unusually sensitive ear for language much admired by Tennyson, he was the source of inspiration for Tennyson's *Enoch Arden* and *Aylmer's Field*.

Given the fact that the average educated Victorian was far more inclined to read poetry and the Classics than his modern counterpart, the Pre-Raphaelites were exceptionally well read, even for their time, and clearly this affected the subject matter of their painting. Obsessed by the notion of being true to nature, they were simultaneously impelled to execute *genre* paintings – paintings which told a story, illustrated a scene. As well as their depictions of biblical subjects, Millais' *Ophelia*, *Ferdinand Lured by Ariel* and *The Order of Release*, Hunt's *The Eve of Saint Agnes* and *The Two Gentlemen of Verona*, and Rossetti's myriad paintings illuminating the works of Dante, are but a few of the examples of how their knowledge of and feeling for literature affected the work of the Brotherhood.

---

famous occasion when Byron first met Shelley at the Hotel d'Angleterre at Sécheron on the shores of Lake Geneva (Lac Léman). Soon after, the Shelleys, together with Mary's half-sister, Claire Claremont, spent a few days with Byron who, with Polidori, had taken up residence at the Villa Diodati. During a wild storm which lasted the few days the Shelley party were at the Villa Diodati, they decided to write ghost stories. Mary took four days of stormy weather to write *Frankenstein*. Shelley didn't finish his attempt, nor did Byron, although he had earlier referred to vampires in *The Giaour*, in 1813. Claire Claremont, who had had a brief liaison earlier in London with Byron, which he regretted, did not take part in this literary pastime. In 1817, she gave birth to his daughter, Allegra. The Rossettis' uncle, Polidori, subsequently ran up debts he was unable to meet and consequently shot himself. Afterwards, Gaetano Polidori, the Rossetti siblings' grandfather, would not have his name mentioned in the house. Later, Shelley mania became an obsession with the Rossettis and their close friend and associate, the painter Ford Madox Brown.

It was their models who exemplified their notion of beauty. At first, however, they couldn't afford to hire models. Instead, they painted each other, friends, family and fellow artists. Rossetti painted his sister Christina as the Virgin Mary in his *Ecce Ancilla Domini!* Christina also sat for Holman Hunt as Christ in his painting *The Light of the World*. Certainly, Christ's eyes, as portrayed by Holman Hunt, have a distinct resemblance to Christina's. Elizabeth (Lizzie) Siddal also posed for Hunt, who painted her abundant auburn hair for his Christ figure. A stickler for accurate representation, Hunt nevertheless painted this picture using unusual disciplines. It wouldn't have been possible for him to have painted much of it by actual moonlight, however much rumour spread this myth around; the myths and legends bound up with the Pre-Raphaelites are so intricately braided that it requires immense patience to disentangle fact from fiction. Yet, there is a more convincing account by Hunt's contemporary, the poet and painter William Bell Scott, closely associated with the Brotherhood:

> I found him . . . in a small drawing-room . . . with an elaborate arrangement of screens and curtains so as to get the dark effect he wanted. The lay figure held a lighted lantern, and Hunt, painting by good daylight in the farther part of the room, peeped into the mysterious gloom by a hole. The arrangement had a bogey effect, and the amount of exercise made it the pursuit of difficulties certainly. He was at that time, however, a Hercules, though not a giant, and after an economical dish of savoury fish and ginger beer which my long walk made excellent, evening coming on, we crossed the street and jumped into a wherry, the management of which he was quite accustomed to, and he pulled me up to Hammersmith and back again . . . He was determined to carry out his accurate method of representation even when the subject was so removed from the realities of life that an abstract treatment, a rendering of 'the idea in his mind,' as Raphael is reported to have preferred, would have emancipated him from the slavery of painting

lamplight in daytime,* and rendering moonlight by artificial means. The omnibus groom, taking his horses home at one o'clock in the morning, used to see him working at the open window from nature when real moonlight was to be had.[1]

It is doubtful that Christina ever sat by moonlight. It is more likely that she gave Hunt chaperoned afternoon sittings, probably not changing her dress, for it was her beautiful, contemplative gaze which he wished to reproduce on canvas. Lizzie, on the other hand, while straining to be respectable, would not have hesitated to comply with any of Hunt's requests, had the model's fees been forthcoming; Lizzie could not afford to refuse. Christina's reputation was priceless; her fees non-existent.

Public reaction to the Pre-Raphaelites' early work was mainly one of shock and horror. The critics were violent in their disapproval. The Chartist menace might have evaporated, but the vexed question of religion was equally disturbing. The Oxford Movement, led by John Henry Newman (who famously converted to Catholicism), John Keble[†] and Edward Pusey,[‡] initially

---

* Holman Hunt's granddaughter, Diana Holman Hunt, has this to say regarding Hunt's obsession with light, which is of sufficient wit and perspicacity to quote in full: 'I think there was always something abnormal about his eyesight and that perhaps this was why he finally lost it: he was not only obsessed by light but even made an attempt to depict supernatural light. To this end, he tested the "character of intensified moonlight" using a lens and found to his surprise "that the focus transmitted was not of silvery tone, but of warm sunlight" giving both a real and unreal effect. At least one contemporary critic understood him and wrote: "The eye, when dazzled by effects of light, sees colours which do not exist outwardly and physically, but only inwardly and within the mind's consciousness." In fact, what some might now call "psychedelic colours".' (*My Grandfather, His Wives and Loves*, Hamish Hamilton, 1969, p. 19.)

† John Keble (1792–1866) was one of the leaders of The Oxford Movement. He was Vicar of Coln St Aldwyns and an immense influence on the prolific author Charlotte M. Yonge, whose novel, *The Heir of Redclyffe* (1853), proved such an influence on the second generation of the P. R. B.s.

‡ Edward Bouverie Pusey (1800–82) was another eminent leader of The Oxford Movement. His sermon *The Entire Absolution of The Penitent* (1846),

aroused profound hostility. High among the movement's aims was to restore traditional Catholic teaching within the frame of the Church of England. This eventually had a profound influence on the Anglican Church, but at the time, the notion of reintroducing ritualistic customs such as burning incense, candlelit ceremonials, candles lit upon the altar and the wearing of Eucharist vestments, all smacked of 'popery', which the ordinary member of the Church of England found a travesty and an affront.*

For the Victorians, Christian religion was central to their everyday lives, culture and way of thinking. Although most of the middle classes went to church, held family prayers and read the Bible assiduously, these were days riddled with anxiety. Thomas Carlyle published *Sartor Resartus* in 1833 and *The French Revolution* in 1837. In 1843, Ruskin published his first volume of *Modern Painters* followed by the second volume in 1846. Not only was the reintro-duction of Catholic practices alarming, but also, still more awful, was the prospect of a Godless abyss as conjured by Alfred Tenny-son in *In Memoriam* and the questions raised by contemporary scientists.†

The young men who formed the Pre-Raphaelite Brotherhood may not explicitly have been aware of these tensions, but since such tensions found their expression in the literature and architec-ture of the day and formed the basis of much contemporary public discussion, the Brotherhood could not have been totally unaffected.

---

advocating the Roman Catholic practice of penitence, caused furore within the Church of England.

* *The Perpetual Curate* (1864) by Mrs Oliphant is a good example of a contem-porary fictional account of the effect of Anglican ritual on dyed-in-the-wool Church of England parishioners.

† Naturally, Darwin springs to mind. Although his *Origin of Species* was not published until 1859, the theory of evolution was already very much in the wind. It's interesting, but possibly not significant, that the geologist Charles Lyell, whose own views supported those of Darwin, was Gabriel Rossetti's godfather. It may be more significant to note that while Darwin's discoveries upset the ecclesiastical apple cart, he himself never abandoned his faith in God.

Indeed, while the two Rossetti brothers, Gabriel and William Michael, were professed non-believers, their younger sister Christina was strongly associated with Tractarianism* while the elder, Maria, eventually became an Anglican nun.

The subject matter of many of the Pre-Raphaelites' early work was biblical: Holman Hunt's *The Light of the World*, Rossetti's *Ecce Ancilla Domini!* and *The Girlhood of Mary Virgin*, together with Millais' *Christ in the House of His Parents*, all depicted biblical figures in a manner so realistic that the consequential intimacy was decidedly shocking. Millais depicts the child Christ in his father Joseph's carpenter's shop. Jesus has just pierced his hand with a nail (the blood was painted from a drop of Millais' own to ensure the colour was right). Christ's cousin, John the Baptist, has brought a basin of water to wash the wound. His mother Mary kneels beside Jesus, apprehensive and supplicating. Joseph's rippling muscles are those of a real workman. In the background, sheep are visible, painted from real sheep's heads which Millais bought from the local butcher. The wood shavings on the floor are almost tangible. Because of the degree of realism with which Millais had depicted Mary, the public perceived Millais' portrait of her as a blasphemous interpretation. Charles Dickens was notoriously outraged:

> In the foreground of that carpenter's shop [he wrote in his own magazine, *Household Words*, in the June 1850 issue], is a hideous, wry-necked, blubbering, red-headed boy in a bed-gown; who appears to have received a poke in the hand, from the stick of another boy with whom he has been playing in an adjacent gutter, and to be holding it up for the contemplation of a kneeling woman, so horrible in her ugliness, that (supposing it were possible for any human creature to exist for a moment with that dislocated throat) she would stand out from the rest of the company as a Monster in the vilest cabaret in France, or the lowest gin-shop in England.

---

* So called after *Tracts for the Times*, leaflets which were freely distributed and which outlined the principles of The Oxford Movement.

Subsequently, Millais avoided painting religious subjects. For the first time in his life, the infant prodigy was deeply shaken.

Carlyle, whom Hunt much admired, made short shrift of Hunt's painting *The Light of the World*. Hunt was as shaken by Carlyle's objection as Millais had been by Dickens's.* But, unlike Millais, Hunt did not give up the ghost. *The Light of the World*, which depicts Jesus in the moonlight, holding a lantern and knocking on a door overgrown with ivy, later became one of the paintings most loved and venerated by the Victorians. It is, perhaps, significant that there is no latch on the door so that all may enter,† the kind of symbolic detail which featured so much in Pre-Raphaelite paintings.

Rossetti suffered torments of self-doubt. Earlier, he had impulsively written to the painter Ford Madox Brown, and begged for lessons. Brown, although older and much less insular than any of the Brotherhood (he had been born in Calais in 1823 and had studied art in Bruges and Antwerp), took Rossetti's request as an impertinent tease from a young whippersnapper. He marched round to the Rossettis' house with a 'stout cudgel', with which he intended to teach Rossetti a lesson. On meeting Gabriel face to face, he was so disarmed by Gabriel's charm and evident sincerity that he agreed on the spot to give him lessons. He put Gabriel to painting studies of old glass bottles and empty jam jars. After a short time, Gabriel found this tedious and the lessons lapsed, but a friendship was formed that lasted for the rest of Gabriel's life. Gabriel then turned to Hunt. Hunt, who had a predilection for teaching and was good at it, agreed to give him lessons and the two of them shared a studio at 7 Cleveland Street, Fitzroy Square, just around the corner from Rossetti's parents' house in Charlotte Street.

---

* William Holman Hunt's *Pre-Raphaelitism and the Pre-Raphaelite Brotherhood* (Macmillan, 1905, p. 355); see also Holman-Hunt, *My Grandfather*, 106.

† 'Behold, I stand at the door, and knock: if any man hear my voice, and open the door, I will come in to him, and will sup with him, and he with me.' (The Holy Bible, Revelation 3:20.)

It was not a happy arrangement. Rossetti was in despair over the seeming impossibility of painting *The Girlhood of Mary Virgin*. He couldn't afford fresh flowers and so the lily held by the Virgin was painted from an imitation one made of wool. At least it wouldn't fade. He fell into trances, moaned, refused to eat and made himself thoroughly objectionable, sometimes creating the most fiendish din. He frightened the child who came to sit for the angel, by revealing 'his irritation beyond bounds, storming wildly ... and stamping about, until the poor child sobbed and screamed with fright'.*

Hunt, who was a manic-depressive, was no easier to live with than Gabriel. He, too, was having difficulties with his own painting, *Rienzi* – for which Millais and his brother, as well as Gabriel, posed, though not altogether willing models. They lived in turmoil, often going without meals as work was of the utmost importance. Naturally, they frequently quarrelled but then made it up again.

In 1849, Rossetti did the unforgivable. They had all agreed that they would show their P. R. B. paintings at the 1849 Royal Academy Exhibition. Without saying a word, Gabriel took his painting to the confusingly called Free Exhibition (the artists were required to pay a fee for their paintings to be exhibited, which ensured that they were). Hunt and Millais were outraged. In the end they forgave him but, at the time, it caused a distinctly unpleasant rift. Millais never again felt the same towards Rossetti: in his view, although Rossetti was not exactly a scoundrel, he was not to be relied on and clearly no gentleman.

The reception of Rossetti's work, *The Girlhood of Mary Virgin*, was mixed. 'Every allusion gives evidence of maturity of thought', wrote the critic in *The Atheneum*, who had the expectation that 'Mr Rossetti will continue to pursue the lofty career which he has here so successfully begun.' But, the following year, *The Atheneum* was vitriolic in its damnation of *Ecce Ancilla Domine!*, denouncing

---

*   Ibid.

Rossetti for 'ignoring all that has made the art great in the works of the greatest masters'. Like Millais and Hunt, Rossetti's faith in himself was shaken. It may have been this reaction that started his lifelong dread of exhibiting his work. In the event, *The Girlhood of Mary Virgin* was bought by the Marchioness of Bath for eighty guineas. Gabriel's aunt, Charlotte Polidori, was companion to Lady Bath at Longleat, that magnificent house in Wiltshire. It certainly helped to have a well-connected aunt.

The members of the Brotherhood lived from hand to mouth, careless of propriety, fending for themselves on a daily basis, imprudent, ambitious and rich only in the optimism of youth. Millais stayed at his parents' house and had a studio there. His parents had always been supportive of him, moving to London in order to send him to the Academy when he was a boy, and having every faith in his remarkable ability.

Gabriel, whose bad behaviour became as legendary as his charm, moved out of the studio in Cleveland Street, leaving Hunt starving. At one point, Hunt found half a crown hidden down the back of a chair, which literally saved his bacon, though only temporarily. What would have happened to him does not bear thinking about had not the painter Augustus Egg turned up out of the blue, admired *Rienzi*, and found a buyer for it. By now, however, Hunt's landlord had had enough. He threw Hunt and his few possessions out into the street.

A reconciliation took place between Hunt and Rossetti. With the money they had both earned by selling their paintings, they decided to go to Paris and, possibly, Belgium to see what their continental contemporaries were producing. Until then they had only seen a few monochrome prints, and not particularly good prints at that. They returned with their ardour renewed, an enthusiasm for Hans Memling* and a coffee pot *éxtraordinaire* which

---

* Hans Memling (1430–95), a German painter who moved to Flanders and whose seminal work is best remembered for his portraits and treatment of religious subjects.

produced the blackest and most bitter of coffees and which was regarded as something of a lucky charm at the P. R. B.'s meetings.

*

Walter Deverell was not actually one of the Brotherhood, but a young, talented painter very much in sympathy with and closely associated with them. He had known and been friends with Rossetti and Millais since he had first met them at the Academy. For a brief time, Deverell and Rossetti shared lodgings at Red Lion Square in High Holborn. Walter's father, who was Secretary-Assistant to William Dyce at the Government School of Design, strongly disapproved of his son's career as a painter. The Deverells were not rich and his father may have feared, with reason, that Walter would fall on hard times. Walter himself possessed a singular charm as well as beguiling, delicate, good looks. He had such impetuous high spirits that it was difficult to believe how perilously balanced his health was. The poet and painter William Bell Scott thought he had a 'great but impatient ability, and of so lovely yet manly a character of face, with its finely formed nose, dark eyes and eyebrows and young silky moustache, that it was said ladies had gone hurriedly round by side streets to catch another sight of him'.* He lived with his parents and his younger sister and brothers.

Sometime during the winter of 1849–50, Deverell spotted Lizzie Siddal through the window of a milliner's shop where she worked in Cranbourne Alley in the then seedy district of Leicester Square. Like actresses and artists' models, bonnetmakers were considered, not altogether justly, to be of questionable virtue. Anxious not to offend her, Deverell persuaded his mother to act for him, to see her parents and to lend respectability to the notion that he should paint her. Mrs Deverell found the Siddals absurdly genteel with ideas which, at the time, would have been considered

---

* William Bell Scott, *Autobiographical Notes of the Life of William Bell Scott*, 2 vols p. 308.

above their station, and pretensions to being descended from landed gentry. They clung to vague notions of being disinherited of property they believed to be rightly theirs, including a title certainly never found in *Debrett's*. Lizzie's father, a cutler who lived over his shop in Southwark, was sufficiently optimistic to take the matter to court. However, the suit was expensive and cost the family money they could ill afford. In reality, they were a family of respectable working-class Dissenters.

Lizzie, who was just nineteen, was the embodiment of the Pre-Raphaelites' conception of a stunner. She was unfashionably tall, unnervingly thin, with a long, pillar of a neck, heavily lidded eyes the colour of agate, sensual lips and bundles of glorious copper-coloured hair. While Lizzie may have been the antithesis of the general mid-Victorian idea of female beauty, she exemplified the Pre-Raphaelite concept of it.

Deverell began to paint her as Viola in *Twelfth Night*, using a small shed in his parents' garden as a studio. In the final version of the painting, Lizzie is seated on the left, gazing adoringly at Count Orsino, a self-portrait of Deverell. Rossetti was the model for the melancholy fool, Feste – ironically so, as it later turned out. The public, apart from their disapproval of the new school of painting, may well have been shocked by the extensive amount of leg shown by Lizzie in the guise of Viola. For although the naked model exposed her entire body, a scantily cross-dressed female figure wearing a doublet, hose and jerkin was considered more erotic. The fact that the subject was inspired by Shakespeare, commonly read by Victorian women and children in Bowdlerized form, lent the painting a spurious respectability.

In July 1850, the reviewer in *The Critic* wrote:

> The head of Viola is beautifully intended, but not physically beautiful enough, owing, as we fancy, to inadequate execution; and her position is in perfect accordance and subordination to the pervading idea ... Mr Deverell has here, for the first time in a form at all conspicuous, entered on art boldly and

with credit to himself; his faults are those of youth and his beauties will doubtless mature into the resources of a true artist.

Clearly attracted to Lizzie (and she, from her own account, to him), Deverell queered his own pitch by rushing round to Holman Hunt's studio, where Rossetti was also working. He 'bounded up, marching, or rather dancing to and fro about the room, and, stopping emphatically, he whispered, "You fellows can't tell what a stupendously beautiful creature I have found. By Jove! She's like a queen, magnificently tall, with a lovely figure, a stately neck, and a face of the most delicate and finished modelling ... I got my mother to persuade the miraculous creature to sit for me for my *Viola* in Twelfth Night, and to-day I have been trying to paint her; but I have made a mess of my beginning. To-morrow she's coming again; you two should come down and see her; she's really a wonder; for while her friends, of course, are quite humble, she behaves like a real lady, by clear commonsense, and without any affectation, knowing perfectly, too, how to keep people respectful at a distance." '

When he met her, Rossetti asked her to pose for him on the spot. Hunt was equally taken by her and later painted her as Sylvia. Like many other girls in her position, Lizzie had daydreams about becoming a lady. She was taking a huge gamble by modelling. At first she enjoyed the carefree atmosphere of the studio, soaked up Gabriel's immense knowledge of literature, and basked in the homage of the artists. She also started to write poetry in the manner of border ballads and took up painting. Ruskin affirmed that she was a genius, but then Ruskin frequently got things muddled where pretty girls – notably Kate Greenaway* – were concerned. Lizzie was suddenly in demand and when, two years later, Millais painted her as Ophelia, the obscure shop girl found

---

* Kate Greenaway (1846–1901) was a talented and popular prolific children's writer and illustrator. Ruskin's enthusiasm for her drawings knew no bounds.

she had become the embodiment of a cult. Algernon Swinburne worshipped her; the feminist and landscape painter Barbara Bodichon made the astute comment, 'Although she isn't a lady, her mind is poetic.' Like most of the Brotherhood's subsequent muses, Lizzie was to find that the very men who had put her on a pedestal, which made her seem more unobtainable than she was, were so closely bound together that the fraternity was tantamount to being impenetrable.

*

It was an era of intensely close male love and companionship, which the modern reader might be forgiven for mistaking for homosexuality. The mistake would be a perfect one. The nature of Tennyson's exalted feelings for Arthur Hallam and the unconscionable grief he felt at Hallam's death, which found expression in *In Memoriam*, one of the most remarkable laments ever written, might be considered excessive, even self-indulgent today. It is very much a measure of the sentiment of the time and is a reflection of what Tennyson actually felt. The poem is a model example of what men of similar circles felt for each other and how they expressed their feelings, without fear of being misinterpreted. *In Memoriam* mirrors very closely the feelings felt by members of the Brotherhood at that period of their lives.

Paradoxically, in spite of being the innovators of a new school, these seven young men were also very much of their time in adhering to the notion that art represented the highest ideals of civilization. What bound them together so strongly and lent their affections the semblance of the Knights of the Round Table was a mutual pledge, a crusade to further the cause of their art.

Initially, it was precisely because of this allegiance that the women who inspired them, some of whom became their wives, nearly all of whom were stunners, were so important to the movement, whatever their origins. 'All the members of the P. R. B. belonged to the middle or lower classes of society,' William Michael Rossetti later recorded. Most of the women came from even humbler backgrounds, with the exception of Effie Gray, the Greek Pre-Raphaelite painter Marie Spartali, and her cousin Mary Zambaco, the medallist and sculptor. Their role as muses to the artists was the key which could open the door to a different, more elevated way of life. It was not without its hazards, since artists' models, like actresses and shop girls, were closely associated in the public imagination with loose living and prostitution. If, as in the case of Lizzie Siddal, the wish for respectability was of paramount importance, then marriage was the only solution. This understand-able desire of the women to better themselves appealed to one of the strangest traits not only of the P. R. B. but also of a certain strata of mid-Victorian society – namely, to reform, improve and transform the so-called 'ugly duckling' into a swan. These girls of humble origins must be refined out of recognition, taught to aspirate their H's, wear clean linen, be articulate, and be socially presentable. If this now seems unacceptably arrogant, it should be borne in mind that this was what these women wanted. Such a degree of reform requires a measure of complicity and a corre-sponding degree of intimacy between the reformer and the person to be reformed. The very nature of the relationship between artist and model creates a singular intimacy involving comparative degrees of collaboration and mystery – mystery being an essential component of both the inspired and the inspirer. Those women who belonged to the higher echelons of society, who were 'ladies' and not in need of social reform, shared this distinctive bond with their socially inferior, equally inspiring sisters.

As Vernon Lee put it in her controversial roman-à-clef, *Miss Brown*:*

> There is no doubt that to certain temperaments not given to respect for social distinctions or Religious institutions, or even the kind of moral characteristics held to be worthy of respect

---

* Vernon Lee was the nom de plume of Viola Paget (1856–1935), a prolific author and formidable blue-stocking. Her novel *Miss Brown* (1884) caused great pain to those Pre-Raphaelites upon whom her novel was based.

by ordinary folk, there is something actually venerable in some
kinds of beauty: the man respects the unknown woman as a
goddess and respects himself for having discovered her
divinity.

Vernon Lee is equally interesting about the relations between
artists and muses:

> The situations seemed changed: instead of his being a mere
> possible, but by no means probable, instrument of a change
> in her life, she was the predestined instrument for the consum-
> mation of his life. Anne Brown should live for the world and
> for fame; and Walter Hamlin's life should be crowned by
> gradually endowing with vitality, and then wooing, awakening
> the love of this beautiful Galatea whose soul he had moulded,
> even as Pygmalion had moulded the limbs of the image which
> he had made to live and to love.

It should, on the other hand, be remembered that, according to Ovid, the Cypriot sculptor Pygmalion satisfied his sexual
desires, to a point, in creating images of the women who inspired
his art. These were only sublimated when he reached perfection
in his chiselling away at the image of the most beautiful woman
his mind's eye could invent. He fell in love with his creation,
Galatea, as cold as the marble he had carved her in, kissed her
repeatedly and took her to bed. It was only after an ardent prayer
to Venus, which she granted, that his ideal form of Galatea could
come to life. Kissing her again, he had the strangely erotic
sensation of her cold stone body being warmed by the breath of
life, and then made love to her. What happened to Galatea
afterwards is lost in the mists of time, rendered a mystery by the
vagaries of the gods.

2

EFFIE AND THE RUSKINS

Born in the Highlands in 1828, the eldest of fifteen children of whom only seven survived, Euphemia Chalmers Gray was an exceptionally pretty child with auburn hair, grey eyes and a clear complexion. Her liveliness and sense of humour, combined with an eagerness to please, made her immediately attractive. Moderately well off, her father, George Gray, was a Writer to the Signet – a member of an old established Scottish society of solicitors with the sole right to prepare warrants and crown writs. He adored his daughter. Euphemia, known as Effie, shared an uncommonly close bond with her mother, Sophia. After an idyllic early childhood which persuaded Effie ever afterwards that her parental home, Bowerswell, near Perth, was an unparalleled earthly paradise, it was decided that she should be sent to boarding school. There she would acquire those accomplishments considered fitting for a young lady and make suitable friends, which would qualify her to help with the instruction of her younger siblings. Fortunately, her parents didn't send her to one of the numerous fashionable seminaries which turned out paper-pattern misses with pretensions to gentility but scant education. She was sent to Avonbank, an exceptionally good school in Stratford-on-Avon.

In the summer of 1840, Mrs Gray took Effie south as far as London, where she left her with the Ruskins, friends and distant cousins of her husband's, at their suburban, semi-detached villa in Herne Hill until Effie could continue her journey under an escort provided by Avonbank. Meanwhile, Mrs Gray continued on to

Germany where she joined her husband for a short holiday. It was the first time Effie had been away from home and it was the first time she had been separated from her mother. She was just twelve years old.

The connection between the Grays and the Ruskins was fraught with unlucky associations. John James Ruskin and his wife Margaret were first cousins. Coming from a less prosperous branch of the family (her mother was the landlady of the King's Head Inn at Croydon), Margaret Cox, four years older than John James, found a position as housekeeper to her uncle, John Thomas Ruskin, who lived at Bowerswell. An excellent manager, Margaret was 'a tall, handsome, finely made girl',[1] a singularly determined character with scarcely one vestige of humour. John James Ruskin, if not romantically in love with her, grew to value her shrewd pragmatism and proposed. Their engagement was a long one. Reputedly a manic-depressive (some said he was mad), John Thomas Ruskin had lost his fortune, and, horrified by the prospect of his son's marriage, he slit his own throat with a razor in September 1817.

It was Margaret who discovered him lying on the floor and bleeding to death. She tried to staunch the flow of blood with her bare hands and sent for the doctor, who stitched up the fearful injury, Margaret assisting as best she could. Two days later, however, he was dead. Margaret never overcame the traumatic circumstances of his death. She refused to visit Bowerswell ever again and developed a violent antipathy to Scotland and to all things Scottish. Shortly after John Thomas's death, Mr Gray bought Bowerswell. Eleven years later, on 7 May 1828, Effie Gray was born in the very same room as the one in which John Thomas Ruskin had died.

Despite Mrs Ruskin's abhorrence of Scotland, relations between the Ruskins and the Grays continued on affable terms. They corresponded regularly. Mr Ruskin became an exceptionally well-to-do sherry merchant; Mr Gray administered a trust fund left for Mr Ruskin's nephews; Mrs Gray sent Mrs Ruskin plants for her garden and, when Effie was two years old, Mrs Ruskin sent her a doll.

Margaret Ruskin was thirty-eight by the time she gave birth to her only child, John, in 1819. Deeply religious, she determined to dedicate him to God and vowed he would become a bishop. He was supervised by his doting mother with a vigilance considered extraordinary even by nineteenth-century standards: 'Mrs Ruskin, with all her passionate devotion to her son, seems to have had no idea of making a little child happy. The baby's education was terribly consistent, he was steadily whipped when he was troublesome or when he tumbled downstairs.'[2] On one occasion, when he was a very small child, entranced by the glitter of the tea kettle, he begged to be allowed to touch it. Mrs Ruskin indulged him. The kettle was boiling hot. His hands were scalded. She thought it would teach him a lesson. But it would be a mistake to think that his mother did not love him: her love was terrible, both obsessive and possessive. She taught him the Bible rigorously, with daily readings which she made him memorize and then, when they eventually came to the end of that great Book, he was made to go back to the beginning and repeat the process all over again. This early familiarity with the Bible left a distinctive mark on Ruskin's subsequent resonant prose. A precocious and observant boy, his early years were not so much unhappy as solitary. Nearly fifty years later, he summed up his situation when he wrote, 'I had nothing to love.'[3]

Nothing could have been more different from the young John Ruskin's disciplinarian upbringing than Effie's carefree childhood in the Highlands. But while she romped with her younger brothers and sisters and raced breathless up the wild hills of Kinnoull, she had been brought up to have excellent 'drawing-room' manners. Staying with the Ruskins at Herne Hill, Effie appeared to be more demure, more docile than she actually was. During the few days between her mother's departure and Effie leaving for Avonbank, she evidently endeared herself to all the family. 'After you left me in London,' she wrote to her mother, 'I enjoyed myself very much indeed. Mr Ruskin took me to see all the sights. I was very much pleased with the Zoological Gardens and with Westminster Abbey.'[4]

Effie did well at school. She made friends, was liked by her teachers, the three Misses Ainsworth,* and won prizes. 'My dear Mamma ... I got the general attention, the history, and the French ... The general attention is Lamb's tales from Shakespeare, the History is a card of Honour as I was not lucky enough to draw the prize; and the French is, *"Contes à ma Fille"*.'† In the same letter, she expressed delight about going up to London at the beginning of her holidays, but concern over her clothes. 'What am I to do about a bonnet for London – my size I have is so small I can scarcely get it on ...' The bonnet may have been too small, but her frocks would last until she could have new ones made in London and luckily she had 'a light fawn-coloured *Mousseline de laine* nearly new.'[5]

The matter of dress was to occupy Effie all her life. She was deeply concerned with fashion; with the question of frills, fichus, flounces and the all-important shawl.‡ Pink was her favourite colour

---

* The three Misses Ainsworth succeeded the original owners of Avonbank, Miss Byerly and her younger sister Miss Jane Byerly. Both the Miss Byerlys retired in 1840 '& the following Midsummer they handed the school over to their carefully chosen successors, the three Misses Ainsworth'. [CSW] It was Miss Jane Byerly who accompanied Effie to Avonbank from the Ruskins' home at Herne Hill in 1840. Effie remained fond of the Miss Byerlys and maintained her friendship with the Misses Ainsworth throughout her adult life.

† *Contes à ma Fille* by Jean Nicolas Bouilly (1763–1842). *Contes à ma Fille*, published in 1809, was written for his daughter and is a collection of thirty-two moral tales 'mostly about young people who each have some fault of besetting sin, but who after one untoward adventure are cured of it for life. A certain elegance and intelligence redeems it – and them – from complete silliness.' [CSW]

‡ Shawls, particularly Paisleys, were highly popular at this time. There was a particular aspect of etiquette connected with shawls: in those days of strict chaperonage, there was little chance of physical contact between young, unmarried men and women. When young ladies left a party, their favoured gentlemen vied to 'shawl' them – i.e. to drape their shoulders tenderly with their

for a gown, especially when made of glacé silk with an overskirt of black lace. Lace was a consuming passion which she continued to nurture long after it had gone out of fashion. In 1840, when she was only twelve, Effie's bonnet was likely to have had a deep, close-fitting brim which would have concealed her face from the side view, and to have been fastened with coloured ribbons tied beneath the chin. By the 1840s, girls' frocks had regained their natural waist line, and were cut with full, fairly short skirts, often with several tucks used for both decorative and practical purposes on the hemlines, the frilled white pantalettes showing beneath.

Effie spent a brief holiday again with the Ruskins at Herne Hill in the summer of 1841. A prosperous London suburb south of the Thames, Herne Hill was still a rural district, pleasantly wooded. The Wandle and Effra streams ran openly through what was then a not overly populated stretch of the Norwood hills. The Ruskin house, 26 Herne Hill, was a substantial semi-detached three-storey villa with a large garden and an orchard of pears, apples and plum trees. Inside, the rooms were well appointed, the library was extensive since Mr Ruskin was inordinately fond of poetry, and the walls were hung with an eclectic collection of paintings including Samuel Prout and J. M. W. Turner. It was all very fine and comfortable. The household consisted of Mr and Mrs Ruskin, who went out of their way to be kind to Effie, and their adopted niece, Mary. It was a predominantly female establishment. Effie had already met John on her previous visit, but it was only now that she attracted his attention.

He was a tall young man of twenty-two with a nervous yet penetrating gaze. His hair was a pale russet, his eyes blue, his eyebrows unusually shaggy. His thin lips were scarred where a dog had bitten him in early childhood. He was conservative in his dress and habitually wore a blue neckerchief up to his chin, a high-

---

shawls as they said goodnight. But at twelve years old, Effie was too young to wear a shawl and would have to anticipate the charm of such opportunities for flirtation for several years to come.

buttoned waistcoat and a tapered frock-coat with a brown velvet collar. His bearing was self-consciously deliberate, his manners fastidious, his charm undeniable and his enthusiasm for the subject in hand contagious.

Effie could not know then what agonies he had suffered from an unrequited love for Adèle Domecq, the second daughter of Pedro Domecq, Mr Ruskin's Spanish partner in the sherry business. The Domecqs lived in Paris, where John had met Adèle and her four sisters for the first time in 1833 when he was fourteen and Adèle was a year older. Adèle couldn't take him seriously and her mocking rejection was a constant torture to him during the four years he remained in love with her. In 1837, when John was eighteen, he went up to Christ Church, Oxford, accompanied by his mother. Mrs Ruskin took up residence on the High Street, his father joining them at weekends while, as was required of an undergraduate, John lived in rooms at college. Throughout his time at Oxford, the young Ruskin spent the evenings in the company of his mother. This bizarre arrangement, ostensibly to guard Ruskin from the evils of the Oxford Movement and the influence of Newman, in whom Ruskin showed little interest, did not prevent him from making lasting friendships, notably with Henry Acland and Henry Liddell. Acland became an influential medical practitioner who was to play a significant role in diagnosing Lizzie Siddal's mysterious malaise; Liddell became Dean of Christ Church and the father of Alice, for whom Lewis Caroll famously wrote *Alice in Wonderland* and *Alice Through the Looking-Glass*, and to whom both Caroll and Ruskin were attracted when she was still a child. But none of the distractions at Oxford, not even his carrying off the prestigious Newdigate Prize for poetry, deflected John's passion for Adèle. When, in 1840, he learned that Adèle was engaged to Baron Duquesne, he collapsed. He coughed blood, was diagnosed as tubercular, and his doctors believed him to be dying. Ruskin believed his doctors. His only hope, they said, was to go to the mountains. In October, he went to Switzerland with his parents. They stayed abroad for ten months, returning in June

1841, shortly before Effie made her second visit to Herne Hill. The sojourn in Switzerland and Italy may have effected a cure for Ruskin's tuberculosis, but his heart remained broken.

Effie also had every reason to be unhappy. Shortly before her arrival at Herne Hill, she had been staying with friends at Shottery, near Stratford-on-Avon when she learned of the death of her six-year-old sister, Sophia Margaret, from scarlet fever.* 'My dearest Papa,' she wrote on 5 July, 'you cannot think how sorry I am at hearing the news – Miss Ainsworth told me in the kindest manner possible – I suppose Mamma is in great distress. Give her my very kindest love & all the children and my hand is shaking so I cannot write any more.' It is likely that her parents didn't want Effie to risk infection and so were relieved to send her on to the Ruskins. Nor would Mr or Mrs Gray have wanted to leave home so soon after their bereavement. Effie could not have returned to Bowerswell without a companion. The journey was long and made by sea, the voyage generally rough and disagreeable.

Effie was an observant child and could not help noticing John's despondency. One day, she suggested he should write her a fairy story. He didn't finish it until the following September, but the result was a delightful tale, *The King of the Golden River*, a fable that demonstrates the victory of good over evil. It was published in 1851 with illustrations by Dicky Doyle and immediately became a bestseller and a Victorian children's classic. It is the story of the two wicked elder brothers, Hans and Schwartz, who insult South-west Wind, Esquire, with disastrous results and cruelly mistreat their younger brother, Gluck. The kind-hearted Gluck wins the day with the connivance of the King of the Golden River while his two brothers are turned into 'TWO BLACK STONES, round which the waters howl mournfully every day at sunset; and these

---

* Sophia Margaret Gray (10 September 1834 – 8 August 1841) should not be confused with her sister, also named Sophia Margaret Gray (28 October 1843 – 15 March 1882). This younger Sophia, usually called Sophy, played a crucial part in the final months of Effie's first marriage.

stones are still called by the people of the valley, The Black Brothers.' Unlike any of his other work, *The King of the Golden River* was written purely for entertainment.* With hindsight, there is a poignant irony that it should have been the thirteen-year-old Effie who was instrumental in inspiring it.

By the end of July 1842, Effie left the Ruskins to stay with friends before returning to Avonbank. Within a fortnight she learned that her two surviving younger sisters, Jane and Mary, had also died of scarlet fever. This time there was no question that Effie must return home. She went back to Bowerswell in the company of Miss Thomas, a friend of the Miss Byerlys.

Effie spent the next two and a half years at Bowerswell. She helped her mother run the house and became an excellent house-keeper. She continued her education with lessons from a Miss Thomson, who had originally been engaged to teach Effie's younger sisters. Effie's brother George, a year her junior, was spending a year in Wiesbaden studying German.

The family home had always thronged with Effie's younger brothers and sisters. Now there was only her eighteen-month-old brother Andrew and the new baby, Sophy, and Bowerswell was a subdued household. It is indicative of Effie's character that her father, in his misery, made her his close companion and confidant.

*

In September 1841, Ruskin stayed at Leamington in the care of Dr Jephson. His health was still delicate. Jephson, who was a great believer in the benefits of iron, was generally considered rather a quack, which appealed to the Ruskins' quirkiness. It was while

---

* In 1851, the publishers' advertisement to the first edition carries the following statement: '*The King of the Golden River* was written in 1841, at the request of a very young lady, and solely for her amusement, without any idea of publication. It has since remained in the possession of a friend, to whose suggestion, and the passive assent of the Author, the Publishers are indebted for the opportunity of printing it.' There is no mention of *The King of the Golden River* in the Bowerswell Papers, but Effie's childhood meeting with Ruskin is confirmed.

Ruskin was at Leamington that he wrote *The King of the Golden River*. 'Not much done today,' he wrote in his diary on 15 September 1841 '. . . a little of Phemy* Gray's fairy tale. Poor thing – she wants something to amuse her just now.'

In the autumn of 1845, the Ruskins moved from Herne Hill to a much larger house in nearby Denmark Hill. It stood in seven acres of ground, with an extensive flower garden, a large kitchen garden where 'the trailings and climbings of deep purple convolvulus . . . bloomed full every autumn morning round the trunks of the apple trees',[6] an orchard and two paddocks. They kept cows, chickens and pigs. Mrs Ruskin delighted in supervising the gardens and smallholding, particularly the pigs, which she not only reared but also served roasted with apple sauce made with apples from the orchard, to her husband's frequent dinner guests. Of course, there were servants. In their newly acquired affluence, for Mr Ruskin had prospered in the sherry trade, they employed men servants as well as the female staff they had employed at Herne Hill. The Ruskins were good employers and their servants were very much part of the family. George Hobbs (whose real name was John, but who was called George as there were already two Johns in the household) was employed as John's personal manservant.

John became inordinately attached to his parents' new house: '. . . the breakfast-room, opening on the lawn and farther field, was extremely pretty when its walls were mostly covered with lakes by Turner and doves by Hunt; the dining and drawing rooms were spacious enough for our grandest receptions . . .'[7] His own workroom, above the breakfast room, was mainly occupied by an enormous long writing table, bookshelves, globes and fossils and carefully displayed work in progress – for John was always anxious

---

* As a child, Euphemia Chalmers Gray was called Phemy. Later, at Ruskin's instigation, she was called Effie. This diminutive stuck, even though some people who had known her since childhood continued to call her Phemy. For the sake of clarity, I have called her Effie throughout.

for his work to be appreciated even before it had been completed. The room was well lit with views overlooking the paddock and the trees beyond. It was perfect in every way for the avid reader, writer, artist and draughtsman John had become. For as long as the house at Denmark Hill remained the family home, this room remained John's chief workplace, a shrine to the testimony of his beliefs in the importance of art and his passionate views on architecture and social reform. That John was passionate in his views cannot be denied and it was partly this passion which made this complex man so attractive. He also possessed considerable charm. Certainly, the young Effie Gray found him compelling.

By the time Effie left Avonbank, in 1844, she was thoroughly accomplished, being proficient in French and history, for which she had won school prizes. She was a graceful dancer, an excellent pianist and had a very clear and beautiful-toned voice. She was extremely pretty, intelligent and had engaging manners. It was small wonder that, when she was seventeen and visited Denmark Hill with her father in 1846, John Ruskin fell in love with her. Mr and Mrs Ruskin were appalled. Ruskin's earlier affair with Adèle Domecq had had disastrous consequences and his parents were understandably anxious that history might repeat itself. More importantly, they were ambitious for their son and wanted him to make an advantageous marriage; Effie simply wasn't good enough. Charming she might be, but she wasn't rich enough or sufficiently well connected and, worse still, she came from Bowerswell where Mrs Ruskin had suffered so much and which she consequently loathed. The visit was not a happy one. The Ruskins were distinctly inhospitable to Effie and her father, who left precipitously, Mr Gray piqued and out of sorts; Effie acutely embarrassed.

Her pride might have taken a drubbing, but she was young, spirited and her sense of self-esteem was not easily quenched. After all, she was generally popular with both sexes and had already turned several heads both in Scotland and at Ewell, where her father's friends, the Gadesdens, lived at Ewell Castle by the banks of the Hogsmill River. Vivacious and witty, Effie was becoming quite a flirt. Later, it was said of her that by the time she was nineteen she had had twenty-seven proposals but had turned them all down. Shortly after her return to Scotland that spring, she became very attracted to Willie MacLeod, an officer in the 74th Highlanders and a close neighbour. He was dashing and a terrific dancer. There was even talk of an unofficial engagement. Another contender for her affections was an eligible young man with the splendid name of Prizie Tasker. Effie, in high spirits and good health, riding over her beloved hills of Kinnoull, was bent on having fun.

John's parents had underestimated him. They knew him to be an uncommonly obedient, doting son, but they hadn't banked on his indomitable will. When Adèle had spurned him, Ruskin became ill. Now he was determined to win Effie. He was not to be thwarted. Mrs Ruskin, who was every bit as obstinate as her son, somehow managed matters so that it appeared to Effie that Ruskin had become engaged to Charlotte Lockhart, the granddaughter of Sir Walter Scott and his heiress, who stood to inherit Scott's baronial folly, Abbotsford. Charlotte was in every way a far better catch for Ruskin than Effie ever could be from his parents' point of view. There is no doubt that Ruskin was, for a time, under Charlotte's spell. He referred to her as 'a Scottish fairy, White Lady, and witch of the fatalist sort . . .' Believing that since Charlotte was 'on the tapis', Effie was no longer a threat, Mrs Ruskin invited Effie back to Denmark Hill in April 1847. She wasted no time in making it clear to Effie that Ruskin was committed to Charlotte. But Effie wasn't easily fooled. She didn't entirely believe in Mrs Ruskin's story, and in John's alleged feelings for Charlotte.

> Mrs R told me of J's *affaire* the first night I came but I did not
> tell you as I thought she perhaps did not wish it to be known,
> but she did not tell me who the Lady is & J never hints of her,
> he is the strangest being I ever saw, for a lover, he never goes
> out without grumbling & I fancy the young lady cannot be
> in London. Mrs R says 'If my John gets her he will have
> a treasure as she is very elegant & high bred.' Mrs R tells me

she has never seen her & that she is in a higher rank of life than they are but she knows her quite well by character.[8]

In the event, Charlotte turned John down.

Despite Mrs Ruskin's reservations, and in her dour way, she couldn't help becoming fond of Effie. In the evenings she played the piano, mainly Mendelssohn, and the Ruskins were entranced. For her birthday, John wrote her a poem which began 'Thorn, and meadow grass, sweet sister . . .' Although it addressed her as 'sister', it praised her beauty and expressed a concern and tenderness beyond purely fraternal sentiment:

> *Thorn, and meadow grass, sweet sister,*
> *Twine them as I may,*
> *Deemst thou a darksome garland,*
> *For thy natal day?*
> *Thou thyself art fairer, sister,*
> *Than all the flowers of May,*
> *Had I brought thee buds and blossoms,*
> *Shamed were I and they,*
> *Think not of thy grace, sweet sister,*
> *Nor their colours gay,*
> *Since their utmost glory, sister,*
> *Is to pass away.*
>
> *Grasses of the field, sweet sister,*
> *And the wreaths they bind,*
> *Though they deck the depth of summer,*
> *Dread no winter wind,*
> *Through the thrilling frost, sister,*
> *Through the sleet storm blind,*
> *These to earth and all her creatures,*
> *Are for ever kind.*
> *And let us remember, sister,*
> *With a quiet mind,*
> *Even thorns are fair, sister,*
> *With the heaven behind.*

May that happy path, sister,
Ever more be thine,
Through the mighty shepherd's pasture,
And by streams divine,
May all earthly sun, sweet sister,
On their journeying shine,
Though perhaps there may be, sister,
Shadows upon mine,
Kindly he for all, dear sister,
Will the end design,
Who for both our sakes, sister,
Brooked the spear and spine.

JOHN RUSKIN, 'Birthday Poem for Effie', 1847

Mr Ruskin and John took her out and about. Everywhere she went, Effie made a tremendous impression. Deeply concerned with the matter of dress – her appearance mattered a good deal to her – she was always well turned out and never complained of the tedium of standing as still as a statue while being fitted for a new gown by Miss Rutherford, her dressmaker in Pall Mall. Her father sent her the money to order an enchanting pale blue silk dress with a matching shawl of barège, a fine gossamer-silk and wool fabric. John took her to the opera to listen to Jenny Lind singing *La Sonnambula*, to visit the artist Richmond,* and to see the new portrait of the Royal Family by Winterhalter on display at St James's Palace. Young, eager, perfectly mannered and very pretty, Effie won the hearts of the Ruskins' friends who were older and

---

* This was probably George Richmond, 1809–96, brother of the lesser known Thomas. In 1848, shortly after Effie's marriage to Ruskin, George Richmond painted a watercolour of Effie in profile, playing the piano. In 1851, Thomas Richmond exhibited an idealized full-length portrait of Effie at the Royal Academy. Effie described it as being 'the most lovely oil painting but much prettier than me. I look like a graceful Doll but John and his father are delighted with it.' In a letter to John, Mr Ruskin wrote, 'Tom, I regret to say, cannot hold a candle to George – it is second rate or lower.' It was commissioned by Mr Ruskin, who paid £20 in wine for it.

more sophisticated than the company she was used to at Ewell or when staying with her parents' friends, William Gardner and his wife.

As the summer went on, London became excessively hot. By the beginning of June, Mr Ruskin went so far as to suggest that Effie would be cooler in a crinoline without the weight of her flannel petticoat. She ordered one from Miss Rutherford. Mr Ruskin was right. The crinoline cage kept the weight of Effie's petticoats off her legs and was a strangely liberating sensation, like walking in an airy bell. Sir Walter and Lady Trevelyan, whom Effie dismissed as 'a nice little woman very quiet and pretty', came to lunch. Mr Ruskin took a box at the theatre and John and Effie accompanied him. When Effie went to spend a week with her father's friends, the Gardners in Paddington, she felt disillusioned. 'I like the family here on the whole very well,' she wrote to her mother, 'but after being with the Ruskins it makes one particular.'

Gradually, it became clear that Effie had captured John's fancy. Charlotte Lockhart faded from the picture.* In spite of everything Mrs Ruskin could do, John was not to be denied. Mr Ruskin wrote Mr Gray a long-winded and thoroughly tactless letter deploring the possibility of an attachment between his son and Effie. He explained the history of John's attachment to Adèle and its effect on his health. Referring to Charlotte as 'a young Lady who has engaged his affections', he gave the game away by saying:

> The only young Lady we have had about us since from whom any thing was to be feared I will admit is your own Daughter and because both Mrs Ruskin and myself were persuaded that no young man of taste and feeling could long look upon her with indifference we felt called upon immediately to consider all consequences.[9]

---

* Charlotte Lockhart (1827–58) married James Hope, grandson of the Earl of Hopetown, in August 1847.

In typical Ruskin fashion, he was adamant that marriage between John and Adèle had been out of the question because the Domecqs were Roman Catholic, rather than admitting to Adèle's scornful rejection of John.

Mr Gray's reply was remarkably restrained. Ignoring the insinuations about Effie's scruples or, rather, the lack of them, he defended her without losing his temper and suggested that Effie went to stay with his friends the Gardners. Effie went.

The Gardners tried to give her a good time, but after life at Denmark Hill with the Ruskins, Effie found them dull and unsophisticated. Their son, 'Snob' Gardner, was keen on Effie, but she didn't respond. A short visit to the Gadesdens at Ewell Castle was not much better, even though she couldn't help enjoying the effect she had on the young men. But she found the parties, dances, gatherings of young people and the fascinating question of dress and what to wear oddly dull. It was as though an invisible curtain of dust was suspended over everything. Surprisingly, she was missing the Ruskins and life at Denmark Hill.

All her life, Effie was a stickler for propriety. Ironically, considering her name is inextricably linked with one of the greatest nineteenth-century domestic scandals, she cared very much what people thought of her. In June 1847, she wrote to her mother about 'the extreme impropriety of my travelling alone homewards . . .'[10] and followed it with another to her mother, declaring '[I] think more than ever how improper it would be for me to be going about by myself', before plunging into the details of the all-absorbing topic of dress. She had just been to Miss Rutherford who had made her an adorable gown in the latest fashion, with 'flounces smocked to the waist thence fine with folds across the body and very short sleeves . . .' Significantly, she goes on to say 'the dress [sic] are worn very low both in front and in the back you would be amazed at some of the ladies and John Ruskin says that those whom he has the highest respect for follow the prevailing fashion which has the Queen for its leader'.[11] John's opinions, even on the seemliness of décolletage, were beginning to influence her. John, too, was planning to go north that autumn to visit his friend William MacDonald at his shooting lodge, Crossmount. In the same letter to her mother, Effie warned her, 'you need not expect to see him at Bowerswell. He cannot come for various reasons and as you know Mrs Ruskin would be miserable every moment she was at Perth or under our roof which would be much worse, it is extraordinary to me how a woman of her powers of mind and extreme clearness of understanding can be so superstitious.'[12]

In spite of her initial humiliation, Effie had enjoyed her stay with the Ruskins and had been sad to leave. John, too, was depressed and went to stay with Dr Jephson again at Leamington. His parents became alarmed. They remembered only too well how Adèle's rejection of John had made him ill, and feared a repetition. To her own surprise, Mrs Ruskin realized that she had grown fond of Effie, and there is every reason to suppose she believed she could train Effie into being the docile wife she wished for her son. She hadn't reckoned on Effie's spirited, independent nature, but then Effie had managed to subdue that aspect of her character during her visit, only finding an occasional outlet in her letters to her mother.

The older Ruskins gave in and gave John their consent to his marriage to Effie. Her own parents had no objection. On the contrary, they were positively enthusiastic. The Ruskins were old connections; John was already well known and respected in his field. When he paid a brief visit to Bowerswell that October, he appeared uncommonly fond of her, but he didn't propose. Effie was a trifle aloof. She didn't want him to think that she was running after him. Her pride was stung and with reason. It wasn't merely the memory of how Mrs Ruskin had used Charlotte Lockhart to keep John out of bounds. Not long before, Mr Gray had lost a good deal of money. He had made what, at the time, seemed to be sound investments in the French railways. Because of the political crisis looming in Europe, however, the venture went bust and Mr Gray suffered a severe reversal of fortune. Since the

Ruskins were considerably richer than the Grays, even before Mr Gray's failure, compounded by the fact that the Ruskins abominated the railways, this was a source of acute embarrassment to Effie. Although it's unlikely that either of them would have discussed her father's finances, John was already aware of Mr Gray's predicament.

By November 1847, John wrote to Effie asking her to marry him and she accepted. Their engagement lasted six months. They planned to spend their honeymoon in the Lake District and then travel to Chamonix and possibly Venice with his parents. Effie had never been abroad before.

During this time, John wrote Effie innumerable declarations of love. There is nothing unusual about a fiancé writing ardent letters to his betrothed. The only surprising thing about John's letters is that he had never made these feelings known in any way before. It was as though he was in love with the idea of being in love with Effie. Already, by 9 November, he was writing, 'My own Effie – my kind Effie – my mistress – my friend – my queen – my darling – my only love . . . I never will be jealous of you – and I will keep that purer form of jealousy – that longing for more love – within proper limits – and you will soon find out how to manage this weakness – and perhaps to conquer it altogether . . .'[13]

At the same time, he made it perfectly clear what he wanted from a wife. He hoped that with her interest in history, she would be his perfect partner, helping him in his work. He envisaged spending a considerable amount of time in the Gothic cathedrals of northern France and imagined himself scrambling about on the roof while Effie stayed in the aisle below, 'making for me such written traditions of the place as were most interesting . . . Keen sighted as you are, I think you would soon find gt [sic] delight in deciphering inscriptions – interpreting devices – & unravelling aenigmas [sic] . . .'[14] He made it clear that he was dedicated to his work and detested wasting time going out into society. Admittedly, he could imagine being proud of her beauty when, 'nicely dressed' with 'just a bud of orange blossom in her hair', he would see everyone gazing at her at the opera and think, 'Yes – you may look as much as you please, but she is mine now, mine, all mine.'[15] Their fingers would touch, out of sight, and she would turn to him with a look of rapture before the curtain came down, Ruskin having only the haziest notion of the opera.

He waxed lyrical about his fantasies of her: 'You are like the bright – soft – swelling – lovely fields of a high glacier covered with fresh morning snow – which is lovely to the eye – and soft and winning on the foot – but beneath, there are winding clefts and dark places in its cold – cold ice – where men fall and rise not again.'[16] Even so, he told Effie how much time he would spend working at the British Museum and etching in his old study in his parents' house at Denmark Hill. Effie could be under no illusion about how important his work was to him and how much he hoped she would become involved with it.

If Ruskin resembled anyone in literature, it was Dr Casubon in George Eliot's *Middlemarch*, though this wasn't written until 1871 and Effie can hardly be blamed for not being aware of the awful warning it contained against marrying anyone like Dr Casubon. In any case, she wasn't remotely like Dorothea. Revealingly, Ruskin wrote how much he grudged the time spent in waiting. He had mistaken her age by a year. 'If I had known – or thought – of the truth – I shouldn't have waited an hour – I could feel bitter – comfortless regret at having lost the precious intercourse of your girlish beauty.'[17]

For her part, Effie declared, 'You will indeed be a kind husband to me. Many trials we shall probably have but not from want of love on either part . . . You who are so kind as a son will be a perfect lover as a husband . . . I shall see your coat brushed and mend your gloves and keep you from wearing white hats, and in order to compromise the matter with you I shall promise never to wear an excessively Pink Bonnet . . .'[18] Socially ambitious, clever, and charming, she was determined to get her own way and generally succeeded. She wanted a husband and she wanted to live in the luxury Ruskin could afford. She knew she would have to change Ruskin's aesthetic habits, but she hadn't banked on him trying to reform her. Both of them had seriously underestimated each other.

By February 1848, it became clear that political unrest was growing increasingly turbulent in Europe. In France, there was another revolution. Louis-Philippe abdicated in favour of his grandson, then fled with his queen to England. Revolutions sprang up like wildfire all through Europe; there were revolts in Vienna and the Austrians occupied the province of Lombardo-Veneto in Italy. The Ruskins' planned visit to Chamonix was now out of the question. It was a bitter disappointment to John who longed to show his beloved alps to Effie on their honeymoon.

A further dampener on the wedding was Mr Gray's financial losses on the Boulogne railway. It was now impossible for him to make any marriage settlement on Effie. John was sympathetic; his father was not. Mr Ruskin wrote a vituperative letter ranting against the dangers of speculation and prophesied bankruptcy and failure. He protested, understandably, that Mr Gray should have told him of the disaster earlier. Mr Ruskin then settled £10,000 on Effie with the understanding that John would have the income and Effie an allowance of £100 a year from that. He also offered to pay for their travel expenses, since travel was essential to John's work. It was generous of him, but it meant that both John and Effie were dependent on him and it gave Mr Ruskin the sense that he could in some degree control and criticize how the money was spent. Neither he nor Mrs Ruskin went to their son's wedding.

John and Effie were married by the Minister of Kinnoull, the Reverend Touch, in the drawing room at Bowerswell at four o'clock in the afternoon on 10 April, two days before the Chartist demonstration on Kennington Common in London. Effie's two little sisters, Sophy and Alice, together with her cousin Eliza Jameson, were her bridesmaids. Later, Mrs Gray wrote to Mrs Ruskin that both John and Effie 'bore up with the greatest firmness throughout the trying ceremony'. Shortly afterwards, the young couple left for Blair Atholl with George Hobbs, Ruskin's valet, while the rest of the party made merry back at Bowerswell. The journey to Blair Atholl took several hours, the weather was freezing cold and, to make matters worse, John had a bout of flu. They didn't get to the inn at Blair Atholl until after ten at night when it was pitch dark.

Their marriage, notoriously unconsummated, has been the subject of intense speculation. Mary Lutyens, Effie's most prestigious biographical editor, claimed that Ruskin was horrified by discovering that Effie had pubic hair, which he thought a deformity. Later, Lutyens realized she had simplified things. It is a perfect mistake to try to simplify anything where Ruskin is concerned. Ruskin may have advocated simplicity, but he himself was one of the most complex, fascinating men of his day. When he married Effie, he was twenty-nine and on the brink of an illustrious career as a pre-eminent art critic, draughtsman, writer on social reform and prolific man of letters. He was charismatic, intense and strangely vulnerable for a man about to make his mark. Effie was only nineteen and extremely pretty in the foxy way so appreciated by the Victorians. Aspects of her character, reflecting her changing moods, could fleetingly make her seem like a vixen, too. But, that night, they were both tired, worn out by the strain of the wedding ceremony and the discomfort of the journey to Blair Atholl. Both of them were nervous, both were virgins and certainly Effie was ignorant. 'I had never been told the duties of married persons to each other and knew little or nothing about their relations in the closest union on earth,' she wrote to her father just before her marriage finally broke up.[19]

None of this was unusual. Most brides in Effie's social circle were ignorant of sexual matters. The subject was taboo. Their mothers didn't tell them, and if the daughters did catch on, they kept quiet. It might seem strange that none of the girls at Avonbank shared any speculations they might have had, that Effie remained completely in the dark as to how her mother was continually pregnant (her last child was born in 1855), or that, growing up in the Highlands, her observations of nature had not informed her. On their wedding night, when John, tired, nervous and with a heavy cold, slipped off her nightdress, he 'had no difficulty in abstaining'. Later, he said that her appearance disgusted him. She may have been menstruating. She may have had an unappealing body odour. What is clear is that the doctors who later were to examine her to discover whether she was a virgin, found nothing abnormal about her. What is not clear is what John expected. During their engagement, he had written to Effie, 'There are moments when I think you have been a foolish girl to marry me – I am so nervous and weak, and – dreamy – and really ill and broken down to most men of my age, that you will have much to bear with and to dispense with . . .'[20] When he was up at Oxford, he had looked at erotic drawings of 'naked bawds' which were more likely than not to have exaggerated aspects of female anatomy. It is more than possible that it was the difference between the romantic notion and the reality of the sexual act which appalled him. Later, he made it clear that he had enjoyed masturbation from an early age. In order to be eligible to John, Effie had to be chaste. If he was to consummate the marriage, she would no longer be the pure virgin who so appealed to him. Besides which, he valued her beauty, didn't want her slender body disfigured by child bearing and, despite his prurience for nubile beauty, actively disliked babies and small children. His rejection of her was probably a mixture of all these reasons. During their honeymoon, they seem to have reached some kind of understanding that since they intended to travel a good deal, and because John didn't want children yet, they wouldn't have sexual relations until Effie was twenty-five. Years later, in a letter to her father, Effie corroborated this but added, 'After I began to see things better I argued with him and took the Bible but he soon silenced me and I was not sufficiently awake to what position I was in.'[21] There was nothing particularly strange about their actual wedding night not being consummated. They were tired and nervous, apprehensive and overwrought. What was ultimately disquieting was that although they continued to share the same bed throughout the six years of their marriage, John never overcame his initial distaste.

It has been speculated that Ruskin perceived Effie's bush as the Medusa, her pubic hair translated into writhing snakes. This is possible.* Certainly, Ruskin had a lifelong horror of reptiles and a revulsion of Effie's sexuality: any confusion between the two could only have been petrifying to him. What is true, although neither of them could guess at it then, is that after their marriage was over, Ruskin developed a distinct sexual taste for little girls, for example, Rose la Touche and Alice Liddell, and was briefly attracted by Effie's younger sister, Sophy Gray. None of these children then had pubic hair. Although it is extremely doubtful that Ruskin ever saw them undressed, it is possible that he liked to imagine their lack of sexual hirsuteness.

> *What thus snaky-headed Gorgon-shield*
> *That wise Minerva wore, unconquered virgin,*
> *Wherewith she freezed her foes to congealed stone,*
> *But rigid looks of chaste austerity,*
> *And noble grace that dashed brute violence*
> *With sudden adoration and blank awe!*
>
> JOHN MILTON, *Comus*

---

* See Phyllis Rose, *Parallel Lives*, p. 281: 'Freud's brief essay *Medusa's Head* suggests a psychoanalytic approach to Ruskin's alleged fixation on pubic hair. To Freud, the bizarre imagery of the mythic Medusa's head, surmounted by snakes instead of hair, expresses a man's horror at seeing a woman naked and perceiving that she has no penis. His castration anxieties aroused, he fastens attention on her pubic hair and transforms it (symbolically) into an over-abundance of the thing whose absence so terrifies him. Hence the imagery of hair as snakes, to express the alarming aspects of female sexuality. It might be noted that in his later years Ruskin frequently mentioned the Medusa and was obsessed by visions of snakes. See *Standard Edition of the Complete Psychological Works of Sigmund Freud*, edited by James Strachey (London, Hogarth Press), vol. 18:273–74.' (Fascinating though Rose's comments are, I am impatient and can't help feeling that this is speculation.)

Impossible as it is to know for certain how anybody sees anything with the organic eye, what they may retain in their mind's eye is anybody's guess, to say nothing of the significance of their vision.

3

MARRIED LIFE

No one reading Effie's honeymoon letters to her parents would have guessed that there was anything wrong. They spent two days at Aberfeldy where 'the weather was lovely, the air like crystal and the sky as bright as could be'. When they got to the inn, the landlady recognized Effie from a previous visit and was friendly. John and Effie both took pleasure in directing how their dinner should be cooked. It consisted of ham and eggs, new potatoes and small fresh trout. 'John and I are as happy as two people can possibly be and he is exceedingly kind and thoughtful. Your concerns are the only thing wanting to make our happiness complete,' she added, referring to her father's financial straits, 'but I hope you too may be made happier soon.'

Effie had hoped that with John's help, Mr Ruskin might be persuaded to contribute to the expenses of her brother George's education and future training. Very close to her own family, she had assumed Mr Ruskin would naturally be willing to help. He refused and wrote another of his bombastic letters to Mr Gray. He took credit for having provided for Effie and made it clear that he wasn't going to do the same for the rest of her family. Since Mr Gray's financial fiasco, George could no longer hope to follow family tradition and be called to the bar. But he might succeed in the City. Mr Ruskin made things worse by saying that John and Effie were to move in the highest circles and could not possibly include George in their scheme of things. As a penniless hanger-on, George was socially unacceptable. Mr Ruskin had a point, but he could have made it more tactfully. The Grays, who by nature were happy-go-lucky, found Mr Ruskin's attitude shockingly unsympathetic. This was the first sign of any severe rift between the families.

When, after an enjoyable though sexless interlude in the Lake District, John brought his bride back to London, they were met by Mr Ruskin at Euston station. Mr Ruskin had been to the trouble and expense of relining and repainting his carriage in order to welcome Effie. At Denmark Hill, the gardener gave her a vast bouquet of orange blossom, geraniums, the cineraria so beloved by the Victorians, myrtles and various heathers, done up in lacy paper and white satin ribbons. The domestic servants, dressed up with 'their neat caps of white net and ribbon and green and stone-coloured *mousselines* up to the neck with their muslin aprons', were all standing by the door to welcome the bridal pair. At dinner, 'a band of Germans came and played delightful music before the windows all time of dinner and it was a great treat. We spent the evening very happily.'

Until they found a house of their own, it was agreed that John and Effie should make their home at Denmark Hill with John's parents. This suited John better than it did Effie. Having spent so much of her girlhood away from school with her parents, she had learned to a fine art how to keep house and accounts, manage servants, and be responsible for creating an ambiance desirable for a husband, a family and the reception of friends and those who might be useful in furthering her husband's career. None of these skills, which she longed to put into practice, could flourish while she and John stayed at Denmark Hill.

John, who was embroiled in the writing of *Modern Painters*, allowed her, somewhat reluctantly, to accept as many invitations as she could. Mr Ruskin was all in favour. Effie might not have been the dazzling catch he had envisaged for John, but even he had to admit that she was an immense social success. It seemed as though she was going to pave the way for John to frequent those ranks of society to which Mr Ruskin, as a man in trade, could not belong. 'I hope they will contrive to be happy and take a due share of Society and solitude – Effie is much better calculated for society than he is – He is best in print.'[1] Only just a month before their wedding, John had written Effie a letter expressing his horror of society, and which betrayed his integral hypochondria. 'Remember the real frets – that late hours – & excitement of all kinds are just as direct and certain poison to me as so much arsenic or hemlock and that the least thing excites me.'

Unlike John, Effie was intensely sociable and remained enamoured of society all her life. Absorbed by the question of dress and how to contrive the most desirable of outfits without too much extravagance, she also took pride in her husband's appearance. Although he protested and was happier to stay at home engrossed in his writing and designs, John took pleasure in being immaculately turned out. Just under six foot, his figure was slight. His clothes were well tailored, expensive and distinguished. At five foot six, Effie was considered tall by her contemporaries. She wore her wavy auburn hair parted in the middle and gathered up and braided round her head. Her nose was straight, her gaze penetrating, her right eye very slightly drooping. Above all, it was her animation, her laughter and sparkle that made her so attractive. Her evening gowns were enviable, invariably of glacé silk draped with lace, her gloves of the finest kid, her bonnets of lace worn with black mantillas. Together, they made a strikingly handsome couple. With Mr Ruskin's connivance, for at this date he had Effie's well-being at heart, they made sure that she and John attended the most fashionable parties, concerts and private views in town. Effie beguiled London society with her charm, youthful vivacity and impeccable manners. She swiftly made sure of her '*grande success* on my first appearance in public', which she felt to be her wifely duty and, in a letter to her parents, added, 'it is only to show you how entirely pleased Mr & Mrs R. are with John's wife, which I know will gratify you . . .'[2]

*

Early in May, John took Effie to breakfast with the elderly poet
Samuel Rogers, who kept one of the most hospitable tables in
town. John had known him since he was sixteen and was anxious
for Effie to make a good impression. Rogers was a strong supporter
of Turner, John's ruling passion, who had illustrated a magnificent
edition of Rogers' poem, *Italy*, together with paintings by Thomas
Stothard and Samuel Prout. Balding, with a long nose, a shrewd
smile and hooded lizard-like eyes that didn't miss a trick, Rogers
had been holding court with the literary and artistic élite for the
last fifty years in his fine house in St James's Place. Effie was
instantly taken by the beauty and splendour of his apartments.
In the drawing room the latest books and periodicals were spread
out in a spiral pattern on the table. The walls were hung with
magnificent paintings and 'the room [was] covered with articles of
virtu of the rarest kind'.[3] Rogers showed the young Ruskins and
his other guests portfolios of letters to him from such dignitaries
as Charles James Fox, Edmund Burke and Richard Brinsley
Sheridan, and others he had collected by George Washington,
John Dryden and Alexander Pope.

The breakfast itself was the picture of elegance, with a great
bouquet of cut flowers and shining cut-glass dishes filled with
preserved fruit and white rolls. Two men servants handed round
coffee and tea. Effie was amused when Rogers cut the crusts off
her roll, saying that the crumbs were to be fed to the birds who
flew over from the palace to be fed. After showing the company
his Giotto, he patted her on the cheek and admired her good taste
before they left. She had scored another success. On leaving
Rogers, John took her to call on J. M. W. Turner in his miserable
lodgings in Chelsea. The fire was out and the room 'bare and
miserly', but Turner immediately made them at home and produced wine and biscuits for them to drink each other's health.
Then he showed them his paintings. Effie was bowled over by
what she called '*The Old Téméraire*'. She declared that she would
pawn all she had to own it, but he had already been offered

£1,000 for the 'Steamer drawing a wreck through calm water and such a sunset as you never see in any pictures but his own'.[4]

The social whirl continued and Effie enjoyed it to the hilt. Old Lady Davy, the widow of Sir Humphrey, took a special fancy to her and invited them to dinner where the guests included the Marquis and Marchioness of Lansdowne; the heiress Miss Burdett Coutts, who was distinctly ugly, dressed in pale green satin, her shining black hair dressed with diamonds and roses; Lady Frances Hope, a stout young woman in a white barège dress, a black lace shawl and lots of ornaments; and Mr Lockhart, the father of John's earlier flame, Charlotte. The Marquis took Effie down to dinner. It was an elaborate affair with course after course: soup was followed by turbot, then roast mutton and chicken and tongue and castles made of jellied consommé with plovers eggs making the turrets. There was duckling and asparagus, and desert consisted of pineapple, ices and preserves. Effie got on famously with the Marquis who told her how much he loathed the railways and entertained her with descriptions of France. After dinner, more guests joined them. The conversation was lively and a Miss Lyttleton played the piano.

In spite of turning up his nose at society, John was proud of Effie. 'I am happier every day with John . . .' she wrote to her mother, 'he really is the kindest creature in the world and he is so pleased with me, he says he thinks we are quite a model couple . . . we are really always so happy to do what the other wants that I do not think we shall ever quarrel.'[5]

When they weren't invited to dinner, John and Effie went to the opera. One night they heard Jenny Lind in Donizetti's *La Figlia de Reggimento*; on another occasion, they saw Giulia Grisi singing Bellini's *Norma*. Effie's great triumph that season was to secure an invitation for them to dine at Lansdowne House in Berkeley Square. It was a magnificent house designed by Robert Adam with a large garden which ran the length of the square, enclosed by high walls with a green in front. They were greeted by footmen in a livery of fawn and scarlet and with powdered hair. It was all very splendid, the walls hung with fine paintings in antique frames and vast glittering mirrors. Lady Davy was there and Mr and Mrs Sartoris. By that time, Adelaide Sartoris, an internationally famous opera singer, had retired and grown enormously fat.* Effie didn't admire her or pay her any attention, which was a pity, since Mrs Sartoris was a fascinating and highly intelligent woman who might have proved a good friend to Effie. They ate one of the finest dinners Effie had ever tasted, while overlooked in the dining room by antique statues of ancient gods and goddesses.

The young couple evidently made a good impression, for, shortly afterwards, they were invited to a great 'rout' at Lansdowne House, the last party of the season. There were more than six hundred guests, the ladies in elaborate evening dresses, wearing flowers and diamonds in their hair. The rooms were decorated with flowers and the lights from the golden chandeliers were reflected in the numerous sparkling mirrors. Effie wore a beautiful voluminous dress of white tarlatan 'sewed at the edge with a wreath of flowers in white floss silk with double berthe to match and it looks like silver at night over white glacé silk with large bouquets of pale green gauze ribbon and a wreath of green different kinds of leaves'.[6] She must have looked very lovely indeed.

John took Effie down to Reading on their way to Oxford for the College Commemoration. They went to have tea with John's friend, Miss Mitford, authoress of *Our Village*, who lived in a little cottage at Swallowfield near Newbury with a charming garden filled with flowers.† Miss Mitford was sixty, vigorous, amusing and

---

* Adelaide Sartoris, née Kemble (1816?–78), was a niece of the actress Sarah Siddons and sister of Fanny Kemble. She was an internationally acclaimed opera singer, known particularly for her performance in *Norma*. She married the wealthy businessman, John Sartoris, and was the author of *A Weekend in a French Country House*, republished in 1909 with an introduction by Anne Thackeray Ritchie. The painter Lord Leighton was deeply attached to her.

† Mary Russell Mitford (1787–1855) was an essayist and playwright, best known for *Our Village*, a series of sketches of rural life which first appeared in 1826. A close friend of Elizabeth Barrett Browning, it was Miss Mitford who gave the poet her dog Flush.

all the more interesting to Effie on account of her romantic past. On leaving, Miss Mitford pressed a bunch of flowers from her garden into Effie's hand. Afterwards the Commemoration was rowdy and disorganized, the ladies sitting separately from the men, making a colourful bevy in their summer dresses. After listening to Haydn's *Creation*, John burying his head in a book all the while, Effie met Sir Thomas Acland, the father of John's close friend Henry, and they sat under the trees drinking tea and listening to the band.

Her enjoyment was cut short by Mr and Mrs Ruskin's decision to join them at Salisbury. It was a disaster and the beginning of the end of Effie's good relations with her in-laws. They stayed in Salisbury at the White Hart Inn. John was eager to study the cathedral. Almost immediately, he caught a bad cold. Never can the common cold have been the cause of so much contention. Since the wedding, it appeared that Mrs Ruskin had reconciled herself to Effie with the best grace she could muster. But now that they were installed at the White Hart, Mrs Ruskin, understandably anxious about her son's health, was insensitive to the point of downright rudeness towards Effie. As Mrs Ruskin saw it, nobody understood John's need for nursing as she did. She felt that she was infinitely more familiar with her son's pattern of ailments than anyone else. Effie saw things differently. Mrs Ruskin fussed over John like a broody hen. She gave him constant injunctions not to sit near damp towels, not to read the papers before they had been dried, and smothered his chest with a poultice of tea-papers.* Effie thought that he was being mollycoddled. She noticed that when-ever his parents asked him how he was, he began to cough, but if she was alone with him and didn't mention his cold, then he stayed quiet. The trouble started when Mrs Ruskin wanted to dose him with a blue pill which she firmly believed would be effective Effie

* Tea-papers were made from sheets of brown paper soaked in boiling tea and then mashed like *papier mâché* to form a poultice. This was supposed to draw the phlegm from the chest and seemed to work fairly well.

disagreed. John had to choose. He chose to take his mother's medicine. He didn't get better. Then both his parents caught his cold. John retired to bed in a separate room. For Effie, the last straw was Mr Ruskin making uncalled-for innuendos about their sleeping apart, implying that John had been too weak to respond to Effie's sexual demands. To rub salt in the wound, John didn't hide his contempt but openly sneered at her. They all left abruptly for Denmark Hill. John stayed in bed, cosseted by his mother and making arrangements for a tour of the Gothic cathedrals in Normandy, which he planned to visit with Effie.

Matters in France had calmed down on the political front. On 7 August 1848, John and Effie, together with Mr Ruskin and the valet, George Hobbs, sailed to Boulogne. The crossing was choppy and Effie, who was always a bad sailor, suffered dreadfully down in the overcrowded cabin. When they got to France, John, Effie and Hobbs caught the train to Abbeville and Mr Ruskin returned to England. John's obsession, at this point, was the nature of French Gothic architecture and its preservation, as opposed to the contemporary notion of restoration, to which he was violently opposed. Eventually, his studies resulted in *The Seven Lamps of Architecture*, which proved an immediate success. Now that John and Effie were finally together on their own – George naturally in attendance – without the inhibiting presence of her in-laws, this was Effie's first chance to prove herself the ideal wife John had outlined in his love letters to her during their engagement.

He had been specific about the chilly, dismal nature of hours spent transcribing texts from tombstones in ancient churches. He had warned her that if she didn't accompany him on these excursions, she would be bored and lonely, secluded in whichever hotel they were staying at. What John hadn't realized, however, was the nature of Effie's imagination. Intelligent, well educated and eager, Effie was incapable of envisaging the squalor, inconvenience and poverty of post-Bourbon revolutionary France. She had never been abroad before. She was totally inexperienced. She was only just twenty.

Anyone with a modicum of common sense might be forgiven for thinking that a newly-wed couple who spent so much time looking at Gothic gargoyles might have put two and two together, as far as the subject of sexual activity goes. But for the young Ruskins nothing was obvious; the most ordinary things in life remained shrouded in obscurity.

At first it was an adventure. It was all so strange and foreign. Effie found the way the country people looked and dressed fascinating: 'the faces of the people, their smooth hair and picturesque caps, with scarlet petticoats and yellow or red garters'.[7] John left the hotel very early with George to sketch the complicated traceries of St Vulfran's Church and Effie spent the mornings reading *The Count of Monte Cristo* by way of improving her French, although she didn't rate Dumas as highly as Balzac. By the time they had left Abbeville for Lisieux, the novelty had worn off. The hotel was filthy, the food inedible, the churches freezing. John was too engrossed in his work to attend to her so that, if she didn't go out to the gloomy old monuments, she either had to stay in the hotel or amuse herself as best she could. She found her expeditions with John exhausting and was frequently reduced to nearly fainting. Even so, she wasn't altogether daunted and spent hours waiting for him in lugubrious corners. John was impressed. 'She is also a capital investigator, and I owe it to her determined perseverance – and fearlessness of dark passages and dirt in the cause of – philosophy – or curiosity – that I saw the other day the interior of the Abbaye St Armand, certainly the most exquisite piece of wood painting for rooms, I ever saw in any country.'[8]

In Rouen, Effie learned in a letter from her father that her Aunt Jessie had died in childbirth, and that his financial affairs were going from bad to worse as a result of a further drop in railway shares. Effie came close to collapse, felt very low and was constantly in tears. John pitied her but found it hard to show sympathy. He admitted that 'I felt it by no means as a husband should – but rather a bore – however, I comforted her in a very dutiful way – but it may be as well – perhaps on the other hand, that I am not easily worked upon by these things.'[9] He professed no guilt and pretended none. What he said was true and that was that. It was not so much that John was alienated by her distress as that he was incapable of understanding it. For him, love was an imaginary affair. Apart from the most obvious gratifications of confirming their union with sexual intercourse, it was perhaps at this point that the consequences of the lack of physical relations between them began to inhibit their communications. Had they been more intimate, it might have been easier for John to demonstrate his concern for Effie, if only by look and gesture, those small attentions which she valued so much. Effie was worn out, wretched and far from her family, and her hair began to fall out in handfuls.

In spite of her misery, Effie did her best to rally. If John couldn't show compassion, he couldn't hide his fervour over the reckless destruction of the cathedral at Rouen which, surprisingly, given the post-revolutionary economic climate, workmen were frantically tearing down in the name of restoration. He spent every daylight hour measuring, recording and sketching the Gothic remains, and he stayed up late into the night writing up his notes. By the time they left via Paris, where John bought Effie a false hair piece to pad out what remained of her own, they were both exhausted.

During their absence, Mr Ruskin had taken the lease on a small furnished house for them in Park Street in the centre of Mayfair. They moved into it in November. Mrs Ruskin had engaged servants for them. Effie was delighted with the house and found the furnishings very much to her taste. Mr Ruskin had also been to some trouble to arrange for them to have their own brougham, which was dark blue and lined with fawn damask. The stage seemed set for a new era in their lives. The house was three doors down from old Lady Davy, who had taken such a fancy to Effie the previous summer. She and Effie were constantly together and Lady Davy, who was a sociable woman, made a point of introducing the young Ruskins to her distinguished friends, Henry Milman, soon to become Dean of St Paul's, Thomas Macaulay and the historian Henry Hallam. Like most newly married couples, the Ruskins delighted in having their friends round to dinner. They tended to invite old friends such as Lord Somers, who had been a friend of Ruskin's at Oxford, the Pagets and the Richmonds. Effie devised delicious menus: sole with shrimp sauce, pheasant, tartlets, custard with very fine pancakes, and desserts of choice fruit, nuts and sweetmeats. John was always particular about what he ate and insisted on dessert (then considered a luxury) every day, and did not 'want any change in our usual style if any one dines with us so that our table always looks very nice'.[10] When, years later in 1876, Anny Thackeray and her widowed brother-in-law, Leslie Stephen, went to dine with Ruskin at Brantwood, his house in the Lake District, the dinner produced for them was simple and excellent. They were given homemade wheaten bread and oat cakes, trout from the lake and strawberries from the garden. The strawberries were the most delicious Anny had ever tasted. The wine, too, was noble.[11]

Ruskin has this to say about his views on food:

> Cookery means the knowledge of Medea and of Circe and of Helen and the Queen of Sheba. It means the knowledge of all herbs and fruits and balms and spices, and all that is healing and sweet in the fields and groves, and savoury in meats. It means carefulness and inventiveness, and willingness, and readiness of appliances. It means the economy of your grandmothers and the science of the modern chemist; it means much tasting and no wasting; it means English thoroughness and French art and Arabian hospitality; and, in fine, it means that you are to be perfectly and always ladies – loaf givers.[12]

Their domestic happiness was short-lived. They spent Christmas with John's parents at Denmark Hill and the day after Boxing Day, Effie fell ill. She had a fever and was racked by a bad cough. She was still in bed when the news came from Scotland that another of her aunts, Lexy Jameson, had died in childbirth.

On New Year's Day, the Ruskins gave a large dinner party and although Effie didn't feel at all well, she went downstairs in the evening. By 4 January she was worse. The Ruskins' doctor, Dr Grant, prescribed laudanum, spa water and an emetic called ipecacuanha, none of which she was used to and which, unsurprisingly, made her feel sick. Even though she could only manage to take small quantities of beef tea, Mrs Ruskin insisted she should come down to dinner. Unlike John and Effie, who had dinner at 1 p.m., the Ruskins dined in the evening, stayed up until midnight and entertained almost every night. Mrs Ruskin found Effie in tears when she should have been changing for dinner; she lost her temper and there was a row which neither of them forgot. Dr Grant, who had been invited to dinner, was shocked at Effie's appearance; she nearly fainted during the evening. But Mrs Ruskin couldn't bring herself to believe in the seriousness of Effie's condition and seemed to take her illness as a personal affront. Both Mr and Mrs Ruskin took the line that Effie hadn't co-operated with Dr Grant's treatment and that she had only herself to blame. Effie wrote to her mother, begging her to visit at Park Street, to where she and John returned on 6 January.

It was the first time Mrs Gray had seen her daughter since the wedding. She found her worryingly thin, ill and changed. Over Christmas, the Ruskins had proposed making the journey to Switzerland, which had been planned for Effie's honeymoon, in the spring. Effie went back to Bowerswell with her mother at the beginning of February 1849. As soon as she left, John returned to Denmark Hill. The Ruskins continued their preparations for the foreign tour, but the fashionable house in Park Street was left expensively empty except for the servants, who also needed to be paid.

*

At Bowerswell, Effie's younger brothers and sisters had caught whooping cough. Effie herself was still ill with a persistent cough. She remained feverish and developed blisters in her throat. Then on 1 March, her seven-year-old brother, Robert, a great favourite in the family, died. Effie was still unwell. She decided not to go to Europe with the Ruskins but to stay at Bowerswell. It seemed a sensible idea and the Ruskins may have been relieved, even if it wasn't in accordance with their notion that a young couple should be together and be seen together. John intended the trip to Switzerland to be a working holiday, and even Mr Ruskin conceded that when immersed in work John could be demanding: 'It may be his pleasure but to be with him is other people's toil.' The Ruskins left for Switzerland on 18 April. The separation between John and Effie lasted nine months.

Very slowly, Effie began to grow stronger. When she went to see the gynaecologist, Dr Simpson, in Edinburgh while on a visit to her uncle, Simpson made a vague diagnosis suggesting her illness was the result of 'a nervous ailment'. Unaware of her virginity, he had nevertheless divined part of Effie's problem even though it didn't explain why her frustration should express itself in her present symptoms. By the early summer she was riding again and going out for long walks over the hills of Kinnoull.

From Switzerland, John wrote her a barrage of love letters which, even then, must have seemed bizarre. Despite his rejection of her and his disgust of her body – a declaration which cut Effie to the quick and which she later described as 'villainous', he could write: 'Do you know, pet, it seems almost a dream to me that we have been married: I look forward to meeting you: and to your next bridal night: and to the time when I shall again draw your dress from your snowy shoulder: and lean my cheek upon them, as if you were still my betrothed only: and I had never held you in my arms. God bless you my dearest.' It was as if separation from Effie had made him forget the reality of their marriage, as if he was addressing a mythical being who haunted his dreams. In this respect, the tone of his letters to Effie from Switzerland resemble the love letters he had written to her during their engagement, when the reality of their marriage was still to come and so had been a fantasy. Even now that they were married, he could only envisage seducing her as if she were his betrothed, not making love to her as his wife.

In June, Effie wrote suggesting how much happier they would be if they had a family. On 24 June, he replied from Chamonix:

I have been thinking of you a great deal in my walks today, as of course I always do when I am not busy, but when I am measuring or drawing mountains, I forget myself – and my wife both; if I did not I could not stop so long away from her: for I begin to wonder whether I am married at all, and to think of all my happy hours, and soft slumber in my dearest lady's arms, as a dream. I got a letter on Friday; that in which you tell me you are better – thank God; and that you would like a little Alice of our own. So should I; a little Effie, at least. Only I wish they weren't so small at first that one hardly knows what one has got hold of.[13]

Shortly afterwards, he admitted, 'I have your precious letter here: with the account so long and kind – of all your trial at Blair Athol – indeed it must have been cruel my dearest: I think it will be much nicer next time – we will neither of us be frightened.'[14] It was the tenderest letter he ever wrote to her and the only time he ever entertained the idea of having a child by her.

And then, quite bafflingly, Ruskin wrote to Effie's father, implying that Effie was of unsound mind:

If she had not been seriously ill, I should have had fault to find with her: but the state of her feelings I ascribe now, simply to bodily weakness: that is to say – and this is a serious and distressing admission – to a nervous disease affecting the brain. I do not know when the complaint first showed itself – but the first that I saw of it was at Oxford after our journey to Dover: it showed itself then, as it does now, in tears and depression: being probably a more acute manifestation, in consequence of fatigue and excitement – of disease under which she has long been labouring. I have my own opinion as to its principal cause – but it does not bear on matter in hand.[15]

The letter went on for several pages, attempting to analyse the causes of disagreement between Effie, John and his parents during the marriage, but naturally never divulging the lack of any sexual relations. Coming immediately after a long-winded communication from Mr Ruskin railing against Effie's inability to fit in with their life at Denmark Hill and justifying his wife's attitude, Mr Gray, who adored his daughter, showed remarkable restraint when he merely suggested that, generally speaking, young married couples got along much better without interference from their elders.

As the summer wore on, Effie's health improved and she began to go out and see her friends. But her long absence from her husband gave rise to unpleasant gossip. Effie, who cared very much what other people thought of her, insisted that when John came back from Switzerland, he should be seen to come and fetch her back to London. He demurred. They had a tiff but, in the event, Effie had her way. As a result of being married to such a contrary man, Effie was developing a certain steeliness in her character. She wouldn't have survived without it, even if it cut both ways.

She wasn't sure what lay in store for her back in London and dreaded further contretemps with the Ruskins at Denmark Hill. While she was waiting for John's arrival, Effie had a brainwave. She and John should go to Venice. She knew he was fascinated by the architecture, which even then was threatened by constant flooding and impending sinking, to say nothing of the damage caused by Austrian troops in the recent siege. It would be an adventure and she would be free of her in-laws. They would go with John's valet, George, the only inmate of Denmark Hill with whom she got along, and she could take Charlotte Kerr, a friend from Perth, as her companion and chaperone. John listened to her proposal and liked it. The political situation had calmed down: Daniele Manin, the Venetian revolutionary and herald of the

unification of Italy, had capitulated and again Venice was occupied
by the Austrians. A week after leaving Bowerswell, they set off
from London in style, in two carriages, John and George in one;
Effie and Charlotte in the other, with an enormous quantity of
books, clothes and luggage.

*

John and Effie took rooms in the Hotel Daniele on the Riva
degli Schiavoni, close to St Mark's Square. As soon as they got
to Venice, Effie knew that she had made the right decision: John
was inspired by the light, the colours, the grandeur and jostle, the
sudden sight of a rat in the Grand Canal. He was immediately
absorbed in writing what was to be *The Stones of Venice*, spending
most of the day measuring, sketching and recording the buildings.
He had been given a letter of introduction to Rawdon Brown, an
eccentric bachelor who had lived in Venice for many years. John
and Effie both took to him at once. His knowledge of the place
was exhaustive and invaluable to John. He provided Effie with just
the kind of gay, gossipy erudition she delighted in. He made her
welcome in his palace on the Grand Canal, which he had filled
with Venetian treasures, and took her, together with Charlotte, out
and about. While John was immersed in his work, Effie and
Charlotte were free to explore the magical city and accept a flood
of invitations to parties, balls, soirées and the opera which came
from the occupying Austrians. John protested that he was too busy
and very seldom went out with them. 'Operas, drawing-rooms,
and living creatures have become alike nuisances to me,' he wrote
to his father. 'I go out to them as if I was to pass the time in the
Stocks.'

   Under the Austrian occupation, Venice was a glittering, dazzling, highly cosmopolitan society. Effie loved it. She was much
admired for her wit and beauty, enjoyed airing her French,
German and Italian, and was in heaven dancing the night away in
the arms of handsome officers. Luckily for her, Charlotte was an
impeccable chaperone. If they stayed at home, Charlotte and Effie

practised their dancing while John shut himself away with his books. Apart from occasional picnics and dinners with Rawdon Brown, Effie and John were now leading a semi-detached marriage. 'I could hardly see less of him than I do at present with his work, and think it is much better if we follow our different occupations and never interfere with one another and are always happy,'[16] she wrote. She had never been happier since the beginning of their marriage. It seemed that at last the couple had found a modus vivendi which, however unconventional, suited them both. If Venice itself and Venetian society played a part in Effie's newfound radiance, the fact that she was free from the interference of her parents-in-law was a divine deliverance.

As winter set in, it grew icy cold. Italians have a curious way of denying winter exists and the Venetian way of keeping warm in their vast damp palaces was to carry around an iron saucepan of burning coals. It was dirty, smelly and not efficacious. Effie's upbringing in the Scottish Highlands was providential and her humour and resourcefulness made their regime convivial. They took to playing shuttlecock and battledore to keep warm in their enormous ill-heated apartment, Charlotte and Effie racing about in their immensely wide skirts. John cut an extraordinary figure, capering after the shuttlecock dressed in his tailored suit and neckcloth, his legs slicing the air like the blades of a pair of scissors.

It was in 1850 that Effie first met the Austrian officer Charles Paulizza. It was Paulizza who had planned and carried out the bombing of Venice and who had devised the fiendishly ingenious aerial shelling of the city. If it strikes the modern reader as politically unacceptable that the Ruskins fraternized with the occupying forces, it should be emphasized that Ruskin, like many modern tourists, was not in the least interested in the present. He dwelt almost exclusively in the past. He was concerned not with people, but with painting and architecture. Effie was not in the least interested in politics. Hoping to mend her marriage, she was out to enjoy herself as best she could. When she bought exquisite Venetian lace at bargain prices and Ruskin picked up 'curiosities' for a song, they didn't pay the occupied Italian population of Venice any more thought than many a modern tourist does when buying souvenirs in Third World countries today.

Charles Paulizza was immensely attractive, with a long curling moustache, fair hair and blue eyes, and sported a grey military cloak lined with scarlet. Effie and Charlotte both agreed that he was the most handsome man in Venice. Besides which, he played the piano, spoke a variety of languages, wrote poetry, enjoyed sketching, had been decorated by the Emperor for bravery, had the most beautiful manners and, to cap it all, was an excellent dancer. Very soon, it became clear that he was devoted to Effie. He went with her and Charlotte to the opera to hear Donizetti. Effie didn't enjoy the music as much as she would have liked because it was so cold at the theatre she couldn't concentrate. But she did enjoy Paulizza's attentions. They played chess and met around town and at friends' houses. John appeared to like Paulizza, too, and encouraged his friendship with Effie. When, during a spell of heavy snow, she became ill with a fever, her throat troubling her again, Paulizza offered to nurse her, suggesting that she should be leeched and offered to leech her himself. At first, Effie was horrified by the impropriety of the suggestion, but when he insisted, 'John & I could hardly help smiling when we looked at our handsome friend with his long curling moustaches and striking dress . . . John only laughed & seemed highly delighted with the novelty of the thing.'[17]

Effie, who was diplomacy personified, showed great tact when she took Rawdon Brown's advice and consulted a Dominican friar, whom they always called the Padre, who was a brother at the monastery on the island of San Servolo. This didn't prevent Paulizza continuing to visit and sending Effie unguents of linseed and almond oil while Rawdon Brown sent pots of Scottish marmalade and body-brushes to stimulate her circulation. The Padre sent bottles of fresh milk.

John's attitude to Paulizza has been the source of much speculation. Effie's brother George was persuaded that John wanted to compromise Effie and that Effie knew it. There may have been an element of truth in George's insinuations, but it was much truer of John's attitude to Effie's relations with her subsequent admirers. In Venice, John and Effie were happier than they had ever been, or ever were to be. As it was, Effie insisted on Charlotte's chaperonage and managed her affairs so that she wasn't the subject of social scandal. Nevertheless, she did ask Charlotte not to mention Paulizza in her letters back home. Effie was more concerned about tongues wagging in Perth than she was by Venetian innuendo. Towards the end of March, John had finished work on the first volume of *The Stones of Venice*. Effie was loath to leave Venice and dreaded returning to Denmark Hill, but she had no choice but to go back to England.

4

THE RUSKINS AND THE PRE-RAPHAELITES

By the end of April 1850, the Ruskins were back in Park Street. The one consolation for Effie was that they were in time for the beginning of the London season. While she set about resuming relations with the denizens of Mayfair, John set off every morning for Denmark Hill where he immersed himself in his books and collection of paintings and fell once more under the indomitable thumb of his mother. Effie cantered in Rotten Row, ordered yards of silk to be made up into new gowns, bought lace from Swan and Edgar,* the department store in Piccadilly, accepted invitations to parties and, at the suggestion of Lady Davy, was presented at court by Lady Charlemont, a friend of Lady Davy's and one of the Queen's ladies-in-waiting.

Instead of going to her dressmaker Miss Rutherford in Park Lane, Effie's maid, Melina, sewed her court dress, which was much admired when she got to the palace. The occasion was a shambles. The long trains of the ladies' frocks were trampled underfoot and the floor strewn with torn lace and fallen flowers. One of the ladies got hysterics in the fearful crush and had to be carried out. When Effie was presented to the Queen, Effie found her red in the face and fearfully stout. Effie remained elegant and composed; John

---

* Swan and Edgar were established at 10 Piccadilly in 1812.

was proud of her. For Effie, her first visit to court was a significant triumph, a confirmation of her position in society.

That summer, she went out a great deal and made a good many influential friends: the Cheyney brothers who were old acquaintances of Rawdon Brown and had a palazzo in Venice as well as being landowners in Shropshire; the widowed Richard Ford who lived with his daughters a few doors away in Park Street; and the Prussian ambassador, the Chevalier de Bunsen, amongst others. Effie was fun and she was popular. The most influential person she met that season was Lady Eastlake, the formidable wife of Sir Charles, then President of the Royal Academy.

Elizabeth Eastlake was twenty years Effie's senior. Just under six foot tall (her nickname in London circles was Lofty Lucy), Lady Eastlake was the daughter and sister of eminent gynaecologists, and was emphatically clever and undeniably magnificent. The author of works on Goethe and *A Residence on the Shores of the Baltic*, she translated Gustav Waagen's *Treasures of Art in Great Britain* and was, at that time, the only female contributor to *The Quarterly Review*, then edited by Frank Gibson Lockhart, the father of Ruskin's earlier inamorata, Charlotte. A gifted amateur painter (many of her works are now in the Tate Gallery), she was 'a striking-looking woman with penetrating black eyes and a fine intelligent face'. Lady Eastlake was like a breath of fresh air and she and Effie immediately became close friends. Their intimacy may partly have been accounted for by the difference in their age, for Lady Eastlake had married late in life, never had any children, and always addressed Effie as 'Dear Child' in her letters. Unfortunately, John didn't get on with the Eastlakes. He could never make friends with people who didn't share his point of view and nobody could have been more opposed to his sense of aesthetics than Sir Charles and Lady Eastlake.

*

While Effie was occupied by the season, going out to dinners and parties almost every evening, John gave more sedate dinners at his parents' house in Denmark Hill. His friends were almost exclusively literary or connected with the art world. A close friend was the poet Coventry Patmore, who had married John's old tutor's daughter. It was through Patmore that John became involved with the young group of Pre-Raphaelite painters. Ruskin had been in Venice when Holman Hunt had shown *Rienzi* and Millais *Lorenzo and Isabella* at the Royal Academy. But he did go to the Academy exhibition in 1850, where he saw Hunt's *Claudio and Isabella* and Millais' *Ferdinand lured by Ariel* and *Christ in the House of His Parents*. He certainly read the openly hostile reviews, but it wasn't until the following May that he saw Millais' *Mariana*, *The Return of the Dove to the Ark* and *The Woodman's Daughter*, all exhibited at the Academy. *The Woodman's Daughter* illustrated a passage in Coventry Patmore's poem of the same title.*

Since the Pre-Raphaelites had begun to exhibit, they had all been down on their luck. Hunt and Millais, keen fans of the poet Coventry Patmore, like the rest of the Brotherhood, knew perfectly well that Patmore was a friend of Ruskin's. Between them, and with the help of Woolner, who knew Patmore personally, they got Patmore to approach Ruskin who then wrote to *The Times* in their defence:

> I wish them all heartily good speed, believing in sincerity that if they temper the courage and energy which they have shown in the adoption of their system with patience and discretion in pursuing it, and if they do not suffer themselves to be driven by harsh and careless criticism into rejection of the ordinary means of obtaining influence over the minds of others, they may, as they gain experience, lay in our England the founda-

---

* *She went merely to think she helped; / And, whilst he hack'd and saw'd, / The rich Squire's son, a young boy then, / For whole days, as if awed, / Stood silent by, and gazed in turn / At Gerald, and at Maud; / He, sometimes in a sullen tone, / Would offer fruits and she / Always received his gifts with an air / So unreserved and free, / That half-feigned distance soon became / Familiarity.* – 'The Woodman's Daughter', Coventry Patmore.

tions of a school of art nobler than the world has seen for three hundred years.

Ruskin's letter to *The Times*, dated 7 May 1851, was a triumph and, for the Pre-Raphaelites, proved a turning point in their careers. With Ruskin's championship, their path to success was cleared. To mark their appreciation, Hunt and Millais got together and wrote to Ruskin, giving Millais' address at the house of his parents. Not long afterwards, John and Effie called on Millais in Gower Street.

This meeting was a key moment in the lives of all three of them. Ruskin was intrigued by the young painter, by the work in his studio in his parents' house and by his intrinsic intelligence, however untutored. It may have been precisely this aspect of Millais' potential brilliance that attracted Ruskin. That he was a genius, there could be no doubt. Merely by swivelling one's eyes around the sketches, finished and unfinished, the canvases stacked against the wall, one work in progress on the easel, Millais' quality was evident. Ruskin couldn't help wondering how much he might be able to refine it, draw it out, realize it to the full. Effie, too, was impressed. The view, admittedly, was uninspiring. From the windows of Millais' studio could be seen nothing but oblongs of sky interrupted by a panorama of the chimney pots of Bloomsbury. But the occupant was more affecting: tall, so slender as to justify his own description of being as thin as a paper-knife, with a clean-shaven, youthful face, a mop of curly hair, a charming smile and a penetrating gaze. Effie heard him expounding his views on art to her husband in excited tones that rattled on at the speed of a railway train. His surprisingly neat appearance had the effect of making him seem younger than he really was – twenty-one, only a year younger than Effie. The Ruskins left the studio with its props, its lay figure, palettes, brushes, decorative feathers, bizarre pieces of armour and the smell of coal and turpentine, both struck by their separate yet similar impressions.

To be taken up by such a fashionable and influential couple as the Ruskins was more than Millais had dreamed of. Moreover, they all got along famously. The Ruskins asked him to breakfast and dinner and it didn't matter that John couldn't persuade young Millais to view Turner with the same reverence that he did. Millais listened but remained unconverted, enjoying the good things for breakfast and the tilt of Effie's nose in profile. Even if he didn't agree with everything Ruskin expounded, Millais was enthralled by him. It transpired that the Ruskins were returning to Italy for John to write the second volume of *The Stones of Venice*. This time they were going to travel with a party of distinguished friends as far as Switzerland before going on by themselves to Venice. They asked Millais to join them. He declined. He had already arranged to spend the summer painting in Surrey with his bosom friend, Holman Hunt. So Millais went down to Ewell to paint the background for *Ophelia* and the Ruskins went abroad.

5

EN PLEIN AIR

There is a Willow growes aslant a Brooke,
That shewes his hore leaves in the glassie streame:
There with fantasticke Garlands did she come,
Of Crow-flowers, Nettles, Daysies, and long Purples,
That liberall Shepheards give a grosser name;
But our cold Maids doe Dead Mens Fingers call them:
There on the pendant boughes, her Coronet weeds
Clambring to hang; an envious sliver broke,
When down the weedy Trophies, and her selfe,
Fell in the weeping Brooke, her clothes spread wide,
And Mermaid-like, a while they bore her up,
Which time she chaunted snatches of old tunes,
As one incapable of her own distresse,
Or like a creature Native, and indued
Unto that Element: but long it could not be,
Till that her garments, heavy with their drinke,
Pul'd the poor wretch from her melodious lay,
To muddy death.

WILLIAM SHAKESPEARE, *Hamlet* (Act 4, Scene 2)

Ewell in Surrey had long been a favourite haunt of both Millais and Hunt. Hunt had a benevolent uncle and aunt who lived in a farmhouse nearby and Millais was familiar with the Lemprières, family friends who also lived in the district. Between them, they were also acquainted with the local vicar, the Reverend Sir George

Glynn, who had earlier asked Hunt to paint the old village church before it was pulled down to make way for a new one. Early in July 1851, Millais and Hunt rented a poky, dark and uncomfortable cottage near Kingston.

It was beautiful weather; the Surrey countryside, then unspoiled, was lush and pastoral. In the meadows, hay-making had already begun. Hunt swiftly found an appropriate spot to serve as the background for *The Hireling Shepherd*. It was only after trudging for several days along the banks of the Hogsmill, a tributary of the Thames, that Millais discovered the ideal stretch of river for the background of *Ophelia*, but when he did, it was perfect. Beside a hay field, the river widened into a pool where Ophelia could later be painted, floating to her muddy death. The banks were overhung with willow, dog roses, river daisies, forget-me-nots, mint, meadowsweet and willowherb or 'long purples'. The light on the dappled water, shaded by the trees, was just what he had in mind. The greenness, a running joke among the band of young painters, and the varieties of green – viridian, jade, emerald, malachite, sage and beryl, were everywhere, running in and out of complimentary colours. Constable had been one of the first English painters of the nineteenth century to paint grass and leaves indisputably green as opposed to muddy brown and different shades of ochre, an act of daring for which he was much criticized at the time. Millais set his easel up in Six Acre Meadow alongside Church Road, near Old Malden.[1]

They both set to work in earnest, rising at six and setting out soon after breakfast, parting at a stile in the directions of their chosen sites. Millais found painting the background *en plein air* for Ophelia more arduous than any other work he had yet attempted. Sitting hunched on the riverbank, his legs crossed tailor-fashion, tormented by flies, frequently in danger of tumbling into the water and shaded against the sun by the smallest of umbrellas, he often worked for more than eleven hours at a stretch. Eating nothing at midday, drinking only water from the stream, his regime reduced him to exhaustion. Further exasperations included a pair of swans who had decided to nest exactly where he wanted to paint and then, when the hay had been harvested, the farmer decided that the meadow was the ideal pasture for his most ferocious bull. To cap it all, Millais' chosen method of painting, on a ground of wet white, the colours mixed on a heavy white china palette, was possibly the most laborious ever devised. Yet he persisted, as did Hunt, who was painting in a field four miles off. When they returned to the cottage in the evening, their landlady produced nothing but lamb chops for their supper night after night so that Millais finally declared, 'I have taken such an aversion to sheep, from so frequently having mutton chops for dinner, that I feel my very feet revolt at the proximity of woollen socks.'[2]

What never seemed to strike either of the painters as anomalous was that, whereas they insisted that the quality of light was all important, swore by being true to nature and clung to the importance of painting their subjects in all the discomfort of being *en plein air*, they divided the actual execution of their work into two main stages. The backgrounds, they painted out of doors in all the variegated lights afforded by nature. The people depicted in the foregrounds were painted later, back in town where the light, dimmed by soot, pea-soupers and chimney pots, could scarcely have been more different, although the light in the city was by no means more dependable than that in the country. How any of the Pre-Raphaelites reconciled this incongruity was never satisfactorily explained. Later, it transpired that their most influential critics appeared to be on a line of rough agreement. Ruskin, who loathed the tameness of the Surrey countryside, deplored the fact that Millais had chosen it for the scene of Ophelia's drowning. 'Why the mischief should you not paint pure nature, and not that rascally wire-fenced garden-rolled-nursery-maid's paradise? . . . I have only one quarrel with you – that you will mottle your flesh as if it was brick wall seen through a diminishing glass – or worsted worm. I believe your hands and faces could be verily imitated – all but the drawing of the mouths and eyes – with small stitches of coloured worsted. The expression is glorious.'[3]

By the time Millais set about painting *Ophelia*, *Hamlet* had become thoroughly absorbed into English culture. If Shakespeare had set it in Denmark, it was a Denmark as imaginary as the Court of Athens in *A Midsummer Night's Dream*, both paeans to the English pastoral scene. Likewise, when Hunt showed *The Light of the World* to his hero, Carlyle, he dismissed it as 'a mere papistical fancy', before going into a towering tirade and pronouncing it to be 'a poor misshaped presentation of the noblest, the brotherliest, and the most heroic-minded Being that ever walked God's earth. Do you ever suppose that Jesus walked about bedizened in priestly robes and a crown, and with yon jewels on his breast, and a gilt aureole around His head?'[4]

Hunt was by no means the first artist to have transformed Jesus into a golden-haired, somewhat effete paragon of Anglo-Saxon beauty. Indeed, if Carlyle had been privy to the fact that Christina Rossetti and Lizzie Siddal had both modelled for the image of Christ, he might well have been even more vituperative. Yet it is possible that Carlyle's outrage had effect. Not long afterwards, Hunt set off to the Holy Land, determined to paint what he saw as the real thing. Yet neither of those great men, Ruskin and Carlyle, not afraid to mince their words, mentioned the subject of light.

When Millais' close friend from his Royal Academy days, Charlie Collins, joined him and Hunt for a time at Ewell, they moved to more congenial quarters at Worcester Park Farm, originally built as a hunting lodge for a mistress of Charles II. It was approached by a glorious avenue of elms where rooks and wood pigeons nested. Their new landlady was a vast improvement and so was her cooking. The painters warmed to her family and enjoyed playing with the children. Millais, who had been looking forward to Charlie's visit, was disappointed and exasperated. Charlie was sadly altered, had developed an irritating religious fervour, and had grown melancholic. While Hunt was a devout Christian, and Millais supposed that he himself was too, they didn't discuss the matter much except in terms relevant to art. From time immemorial, the Bible had been one of the prime sources of inspiration for all the arts in Western civilization and still, in the nineteenth century, belief in the tenets of Christianity was largely taken for granted. But Charlie Collins's continually professed ardour was both a bore and an embarrassment: it took the form of a combination of supercilious silence, a propensity for prolonged prayer and an abstinence from pastry. One wet night, their landlady served them up a delicious blackberry pudding but Charlie refused it. Millais, generally the most tolerant of men, lost his temper. Charlie left the room in tears. Hunt, who had been suffering the common trials of an artist, namely lack of inspiration, left the table.

As things turned out, Hunt's difficulty had been in not knowing what to do with the background for a proposed painting he was working on alternately with *The Hireling Shepherd*. It was indeed a puzzle, for the incomplete sketches so far indicated a wall, possibly a door, certainly a door-knocker, and some strands of wizened ivy, together with the outline of a naked man (like Millais, Hunt made preliminary studies of his subjects in the nude, the better to achieve anatomic plausibility) tentatively knocking on the door. It was then that the two friends struck upon the notion of the brief reference to Christ knocking on the door in *Revelation*. Certainly, it would serve the purpose of providing the unfinished sketches with a ready-made story, understandable to Everyman.

It was an unforgettable period in their lives. The luxury of being able to work long hours uninterrupted except by the hazards of the nature they were so keen to paint, followed by evenings of intense discussion about the theory of the art which so absorbed them, was a source of intense stimulation and sealed the intimacy of the friends. Quite often, they spent part of their evenings reading poetry aloud. Tennyson, Keats and Coventry Patmore were favourites. Sometimes they were joined by Millais' brother William, a landscape painter, as well as by other visitors who would take the train down for the day. These included Millais' father, Coventry Patmore, Dicky Doyle, Ford Madox Brown and William Michael Rossetti. Then the atmosphere of intensity, which unsurprisingly occasionally reached absurd heights, would relax amid howls of laughter mingled with serious discussion and sometimes music, for both William Millais and his father played the flute and sang delightfully.

It was an exclusively male society, not unusual for the time when, certainly before marriage, the sexes were generally segregated unless chaperoned. It was not so much that the young men didn't care for women as that they didn't know many girls of their own age. Class played a part in their attitude since it was, like religion, an immensely important and unquestioned factor in their society. They took it for granted that flirting with field girls they met in the lanes could only be pleasurable for all parties. Nor were they wrong. Hunt took his flirtations more seriously than Millais. But then Hunt was painting Emma Watkins in *The Hireling Shepherd*, whereas Millais had only a blank space on his canvas.

Hunt had met Emma when she and her sister were walking across the field where he was painting. It struck him then that Emma would be ideal as the buxom, wanton shepherdess in his painting. He made enquiries, met her mother and they agreed that Emma, who was engaged to marry a sailor, should later go to London to sit for him in his studio. It didn't occur to Hunt that she could have posed then and there on a tussock in the field. Somehow, the young artists seemed to have got it into their heads that nature was one thing, the human figure quite another.

Millais wasn't the only one of the group of friends to find Hunt's attitude to women bizarre. Flirting with field girls was one thing, but what none of them could grasp was his avowed intention to reform and marry Annie Miller, a slum girl who worked in the bar of the Cross Keys, a pub in Lawrence Street, Chelsea. She might have red-gold hair, but it was lice infested. She might be what they called 'jolly', but her language was foul. His friends laughed amongst themselves and treated the matter as a joke, not bothering to consider Annie's feelings, but regarding the subject as yet one more example of 'Mad' Hunt's eccentricity. Even so, it was obvious that there were to be storms ahead if Emma

Watkins, despite being engaged to a sailor, was going to put in an appearance in London.

The weeks sped by and summer rolled into autumn. The weather remained lovely, but by October the mornings were chilly and frosty. One morning at Ewell, after breakfast, a local man brought Millais a dead water rat. Millais was delighted and began to paint it swimming close to the riverbank where Ophelia was going to drown. After four hours of painting the rat, whisker by whisker, he decided it looked exactly like a drowned kitten. He persevered, but there was something about the rat that defeated him. When Hunt's uncle and aunt came to lunch, Millais asked them what they thought of the 'varmint'. Try as they might, they couldn't identify it. The trouble was that Millais had painted it out of all proportion so that it was more the size of a drowned sheep than a water vole. After a great deal of laughter, Millais painted the wretched creature out.

When it began to snow early in November, Millais had an open shed or shelter made for him, so that he could go on painting without damaging his canvas. Hunt was so impressed that he had one made too, while Charlie Collins went on with a picture he never finished in a hut he had found. By now, they were all painting walls. It was a mania which briefly obsessed them. Microscopic views of brick hung about with ivy served for the background of *The Light of the World* which Holman Hunt had been steadily engaged in, and Millais was painting *Two Lovers Whispering by a Wall* to illustrate Tennyson's *Circumstance*, while, unknown to them, up in London, Rossetti was at work on an immense expanse of brick wall, the bricks delineated by pale oblongs of Portland cement, for his unfinished canvas, *Found*. Even Ruskin, then in Venice with Effie, was obsessed by the subject of the wall:

> It matters little if it be of brick or jasper: the light of heaven upon it, and the weight of earth in it are all we need . . . and it is a noble thing for men to . . . make the face of a wall look infinite, and its edge against the sky like a horizon; or even if

less than this be reached, it is still delightful to mark the play of passing light on its broad surface and to see by how many artifices and gradations of tinting and shadow, time and storm will set their wild signatures upon it; and how in the rising or declining of the day the unbroken twilight rests loud and luridly on its high lineless forehead, and fades away untraceably down its tiers of confused and countless stone.[5]

By which time, with the constant rhythm of Ruskin's biblical prose, the reader might be forgiven for having forgotten that he was writing merely about a wall instead of his wife.

And then the painters were back in London with the work they had completed during their months at Ewell. Hunt found lodgings down by the riverside in Chelsea and Millais went back to Bloomsbury to fill in the space he had left for Ophelia.

6

LIZZIE BECOMES OPHELIA

Lizzie Siddal had agreed to sit for Millais as Ophelia. She was beginning to wake up to her position as model, the focal point of attention of the group of young men who were all so keen to paint her, and to appreciate it. It was certainly very different from working for Mrs Tozer, making bonnets, trimming hats with feathers, lace and ribbons for the ladies who came to the shop in Cranbourne Alley off Leicester Square. The hours at Mrs Tozer's had been long, hard and gruelling. Even so, Lizzie had been popular, stitching buttons and baubles alongside her friend Jeanette at Mrs Tozer's. Jeanette had an Irish gentleman friend, Mr Allingham, who was a poet, and Lizzie had enjoyed aspects of the bonnet shop: the gossip and the company.

The money had been steady and regular, and her father was thankful for her contribution to the family household on the other side of the river in Southwark. Twenty-four pounds a year was not to be sneezed at, even if the hours were long and her fingers, in spite of all the thimbles in the world, were as rough as brambles. The money was only slightly less than a lady in reduced circumstances, obliged to work as a governess, would get. But the governess, even if she subsisted on thirty pounds a year, would 'have it all found' – that was to say, her board and lodging would be provided. Lizzie couldn't possibly have been a governess. Except for a penchant for reading whatever came her way – she had read some verses by Tennyson printed on an old sheet of newspaper used to wrap a pound of butter in – she was not educated.

But she was clever and eager to learn. Her father couldn't understand why the young men wanted to paint his daughter. Clever she might be, but lovely never. Scraggy was more like it, nothing but skin and bone, like something from the knacker's yard, and she had all that outlandish red hair tumbling about her. Even so, she had an air. He could see that she held herself even better than his wife, her mother.* To him Lizzie modelling for men surely wasn't right at all. How could one tell how far they went and, in any case, he prided himself that no matter the slenderness of their income, he and his wife had done their very best by their children.

Lizzie didn't care what her father thought. She was excited by the prospect of making an entirely new life for herself, by the admiration she aroused, and was eager to climb the social ladder and leave behind her past, especially her family. At least, if her family background was mentioned, and it was bound to be, she would make it sound more interesting than it really was. Instead of being poor, genteel and, as she thought, deadly dull, she would portray herself as a victim of extreme hardship and suffering, which would make her more romantic, more desirable in the eyes of the band of artists who were to transform her life. Their adulation of her was intoxicating. Openly, before her and amongst themselves, they declared her a beauty and called her a stunner. Lizzie, who had never been thought of as a beauty before, felt much as the ugly duckling must have done on turning into a swan. They seemed to like and respect her and to enjoy her company as much as she did theirs. She was happier than she had ever been before. Moreover, she was earning good money, more than she had at Mrs Tozer's, even if it wasn't so regular.

For her costume as Ophelia, Millais had rummaged around in various junk shops and finally had found a cast-off dress of old

---

* Later, Lizzie was diagnosed as having a curvature of the spine. It is less painful for the sufferer to hold the back very straight. If the curvature is pronounced, it may lead to severe pulmonary problems, since the curved spine will squash the lungs like a pair of bellows.

brocade. If it had looked tatty in the junk shop, he knew it would glimmer in the light of his studio (some time before, when he was still a student, he had painted the windows at the end of the room to imitate stained glass, so that the light fell in coloured oblongs making patches of iridescence). Lizzie found the dress heavy, but didn't complain. She was beginning to hold their art in the same esteem as the painters did themselves. The brocade was even heavier and got drenched when she climbed into the large bathtub filled with tepid water, where she had to lie with her face turned upwards, her long hair loose and floating, as the wretched Ophelia.

True to Millais' expectations and Shakespeare's description, the full skirt, heavy with water, did spread wide and Lizzie, the palm of her left hand curling out of the bathtub, looked perfect. Millais' mother, always thoughtful, had provided an arrangement of candles which were lit beneath the tub in an attempt to keep the water warm: There were preliminary sketches to be made and Lizzie had to keep her pose for long periods at a stretch. Millais always worked swiftly, intensely and for long hours.

Even though Millais did his best to be considerate, it was by far the most demanding subject Lizzie had yet modelled for. When the painting was nearing completion, Millais was thoroughly engrossed in his work and didn't notice that the candles beneath the bathtub had burned out. The water grew cold and so did Lizzie, but she didn't move a muscle or even mention the fact. If he was devoted to his art, then she must be his muse, an equal martyr to the demands of art. By the time the sittings came to an end, Lizzie had caught a chill severe enough to make her sufficiently ill for her to take to her bed. Her parents were alarmed and sent for the doctor. This was very unusual for people in their circumstances, for both doctors and medicines were expensive and usually only employed in cases of extreme danger. Outraged that one of these reprobate painters had so ill-treated his daughter, Mr Siddal stormed up to Gower Street and threatened Millais 'with an action for £50 damages for his carelessness'.[1] Fifty pounds was an enormous sum – about £4,000 by today's standards. After

John Everett Millais, 1865, photographed by
Charles Lutwidge Dodgson (Lewis Carroll).

William Holman Hunt, 1865,
photographed by Eliot and Fry.

William Bell Scott, John Ruskin and Dante Gabriel Rossetti at Tudor House,
Chelsea, 1864, photographed by William Downey.

John Ruskin as a young man,
*c.*1859.

*Euphemia ('Effie') Chalmers
(née Gray), Lady Millais* by
Thomas Richmond, 1851.

The Eve of Saint Agnes, by John Everett Millais, 1863.

The Order of Release, by John Everett Millais, 1853.

The Waterfall (detail), by John Everett Millais, 1853

Elizabeth Siddal, by Dante Gabriel Rossetti, *c.*1860.

Rossetti Being Sketched by Elizabeth Siddal,
by Dante Gabriel Rossetti, 1853.

Clerk Saunders,
by Elizabeth (Lizzie)
Siddal, 1857.

Ophelia, by John
Everett Millais,
1851–52.

Annie Miller,
by Dante Gabriel
Rossetti, *c.*1860.

Elephant Burying Jar,
by Dante Gabriel
Rossetti, 1873.

Beata Beatrix, by Dante Gabriel Rossetti, *c.*1863–70.

some deliberation, a compromise was reached and Millais paid the doctor's fees. But the damage had been done. Lizzie had been ill enough to warrant her going to Hastings, then the most popular health resort in the south of England, to take a cure and convalesce in the bracing sea air.

*

The young Ruskins were not present at the Royal Academy's opening day for the exhibition where Hunt's *The Hireling Shepherd* and Millais' *The Huguenot* and *Ophelia* were both hung well and 'received with whispering respect and even with enthusiasm'.[2] Effie and John were in Venice, enjoying what was the happiest period of their ill-fated marriage. Even so, they couldn't help hearing of the sensation *Ophelia* had caused.

> I came home last night with only *Ophelia* in my mind and wrote to my son nearly as follows [Ruskin's father, John James, wrote to Millais], Nothing can be truer to Shakespeare [sic] than Mr Millais' *Ophelia* and there is a refinement in the whole figure – in the floating and sustaining dress – such as I never saw before expressed on canvas. In her most lovely countenance there is an Innocence disturbed by Insanity and a sort of Enjoyment strangely blended with lineament of woe. There seems depicted, moreover, a growing wonder and fear on Ophelia just awakening to a sense of her situation . . .[3]

With hindsight, this could be read as a chilling prophecy of Lizzie's fate, but, like most prophecies, it went unnoticed at the time. Millais and Hunt had triumphed and the Pre-Raphaelites were, at long last, in the ascendant. Nobody was better satisfied than their public champion, John Ruskin.

7

VENICE REGAINED

On the advice of Rawdon Brown, the young Ruskins had taken rooms in the Casa Wetzlar* on the Grand Canal, which were infinitely more comfortable and spacious than their old quarters. Effie was happy to organize their domestic arrangements – cutting out new curtains, having long consultations with the cook, installing new grates (she wasn't going to shiver over cauldrons of hot coals again), laying down carpets and generally contriving to make their lives as comfortable as possible. She spent long hours playing the piano, reading, keeping accounts (their luxurious lifestyle proved alarmingly expensive and had to be accounted for to Mr Ruskin, who paid for it), and had lessons in what she called Modelling – presumably statuettes of clay. John immersed himself in his work, going out in a gondola, measuring old buildings, climbing steep steps to the tops of the cupolas and getting covered in dust in the process, emerging from crypts and vestibules looking like a long-legged scarecrow, to the delight of the Venetian urchins. He spent whole days at Murano drawing until the light faded, and the rest of the time in his study indefatigably writing up his notes. In the evenings after dinner, he and Effie would stroll over to St Mark's Square, listen to the band and sit in a café with Rawdon Brown and his friend, Edward Cheyney. Sometimes they took a gondola to the Lido, then a desolate stretch of sand and brambles where Effie occasionally swam, to the amazement of the local inhabitants.

---

* Now the Gritti Hotel

On their arrival in Venice, on 1 September 1851, they had both been shocked to hear of the death of Effie's old admirer, Paulizza. The circumstances of his death were mysterious. Effie supposed it was caused by a head wound he had sustained. It wasn't until the end of November that Ruskin could confirm that he was buried, with no commemoration stone, in Murano. The Venetians had an eminently practical attitude to death and dug up the graves every ten years to make way for new ones. The skeletons were 'added to the great mountain of uncovered bones on the island of San' Arianna.'[1]

Both John and Effie were saddened by Paulizza's death. In their different ways they had both been deeply attached to him. 'We shall never see any body like him again for wonderful intellect, great humility and the sweetest disposition . . .' Effie wrote to her mother. 'Such entire want of selfishness I have never seen in man, and the earnest desire he had for the good & happiness of others at the price of his own was only the result of this absence of self.'[2]

To enjoy Venetian society to the hilt, Effie secured the services of Lady Sorrell as her chaperone. Lady Sorrell was of an old French family and the widow of Sir Thomas, who had been British Consul General to the Lomabardo-Venetian Kingdom. Lady Sorrell now lived in Venice with her two daughters. She was immensely well connected and was the ideal chaperone to take Effie out and about into the best Venetian society, even if she was an inveterate chatterbox and, in the eyes of Rawdon Brown, a dreadful bore.

Effie, however, wasn't too particular. She craved the pleasures of high society and respected the conventions of the day sufficiently to know that even as a married woman, or, indeed, particularly as a married woman, she couldn't be seen to gad about and dance with officers without a chaperone approved of by the society she so loved. Under the eye of Lady Sorrell, Effie shopped, flirted, visited such grandees as the Countess Esterházy,* Princess

---

* Countess Esterházy, born Anna Ungnad, Countess Weissenwolff in 1795, had married Count Valentin Philip Esterházy de Galantha of the well-known Hungarian family in 1812. He had died in 1838.

Hohenloe,* the Duchesse d'Angoulême† and the Infanta of Spain, and she, in turn, was visited by them. The choice of Lady Sorrell as chaperone had been a brilliant one on Effie's part. Like Lady Sorrell, Effie was a social snob and a social climber. But she was an innocent one; she wasn't on the make for material reasons. If she didn't hesitate to name-drop in her vivacious letters to her parents, it is also clear that the social scene was her form of fun and that she relished being appreciated as an ornament to society. As her chief biographical editor, Mary Lutyens, wrote of her, 'If Effie seemed flighty it was she loved socializing with fashionable people more than ideas.'[3] The novelist Elizabeth Gaskell had attended Effie's school, Avonbank, although at an earlier date. Her observation of Effie is particularly astute: 'I don't think she has any more serious faults than vanity and cold heartedness . . . she really is close to a charming character.'[4]

John and Effie had discovered a way of life which, if not perfect, suited them both. That their happiness swung on a precarious balance did not escape Effie's notice. She knew perfectly well that her well-being hinged on keeping Ruskin away from his parents. The previous summer, when they had been holidaying with friends in Switzerland before going to Venice, Effie had had a conversation with the archaeologist Charles Newton,‡ who

---

* The Princess Hohenloe whom Effie met was the wife of Prince Egon Hohenloe-Waldenburg-Schillingsfürst, whom she had married in 1849. She was Therese, daughter of Count Thurn-Hofer-Valsassina. She had grown up in Venice and was a remarkable beauty and 'so popular in Venice . . . that during the revolution she went out without wearing the Italian cockade and was never insulted, although an Austrian'. (*Effie in Venice*, Mary Lutyens, p. 195.)

† The Duchesse d'Angoulême, then aged seventy-three, was the daughter of Louis XVI and had been imprisoned in the Temple with her parents. In 1799, she had married her cousin, the eldest son of Charles X, brother of Louis XVI. He died in 1844, the last Dauphin of France. (Author's note: I am indebted to the late Mary Lutyens for having provided the gist of the last three notes in *Effie in Venice* pp. 194–6.)

‡ Sir Charles Newton (1816–94), archaeologist. An engaging character, he was assistant in the Antiquities department of the British Museum from 1840 and

had advised her against the old Ruskins' influence. 'They are so peculiar,' she wrote to her mother, 'that, as Newton said to me when we were travelling together, he could not understand how I got on so well – he thought two days at Denmark Hill with Mrs Ruskin without prospects of release would really kill him and yet he thought her a very good woman but very queer – but he advised me never to let John away again so long with them without me. He said it did us both a great deal of harm and he knew the effects it had on all our acquaintances.'[5] But how long Effie could keep Ruskin apart from his parents was doubtful. Ruskin could no more do without them than a kite without a string.

She knew from her correspondence with her parents that Mr Ruskin had been writing letters to them complaining of her extravagance and fecklessness. Like any young wife, she objected violently to their meddling in her affairs and sending biased speculations of her behaviour back home. But it is worth mentioning that the habit of sharing letters and their contents was then a widespread practice, not such an act of indiscretion as it might appear to us today. Letters were then the only means of communication between people separated by geography; the price of franking a letter was high and so they were freely exchanged, though more discreetly than the London gazettes and newspapers in country districts. It wasn't until February 1852 that Effie learned that the house in Park Street was to be given up. This was understandable. It was expensive and, all the time she and John had been away, Mr Ruskin had paid not only for the rent but also

---

left in 1852 to become Vice Consul at Mitylene. Between 1856 and 1857, he had the good fortune to discover the remains of the Mausoleum at Halicarnassus, one of the Seven Wonders of the World. In 1860, he returned to the British Museum where he supervised the construction of the Mausoleum Room. The friendship between Newton and Ruskin was close and made stronger by family ties. Both of them had been at Oxford together. Then, in 1861, Newton married Ann Mary, the daughter of Joseph Severn. Ann was the sister of the painter Arthur Severn, who married Ruskin's cousin and ward, Joan Agnew. Ann was also a painter of note. She died in 1866.

for the wages of the three servants kept there to maintain the house. What she could not stomach and never forgave John for was that he had completely ignored her feelings and with his father had arranged to take a house in Camberwell, ominously close to Denmark Hill. She did not know, but might not have been surprised, that John had written to his father:

> I do not speak of Effie in this arrangement – as it is a necessary one – and therefore I can give her no choice. She will be unhappy – that is her fault – not mine – the only real regret I have, however, is on her account – as I have pride in seeing her shining as she does in society – and pain in seeing her deprived, in her youth and beauty of that which ten years hence she cannot have – the Alps will not wrinkle – so my pleasure is always in store – but her cheeks will.[6]

The discovery in February, towards the end of their sojourn in Venice, that John and his parents had all three connived to lease the house in Camberwell dismayed Effie. The very idea of going back to London appalled her, but that she should live so far from the centre of town and so close to her dreaded in-laws filled her with despondency. She foresaw, quite rightly, a dull, suburban existence far from her friends, in intolerable proximity to the old Ruskins and, even more importantly, realized that she had lost any hope of saving the marriage on her terms.

Their last weeks in Venice passed as though in a disturbed, nightmarish dream. It was filled with events, balls and carnivals, packing, settling bills, making travel arrangements and above all was, for Effie, overshadowed by a sense of doom. She couldn't help being surprised when John insisted that they went out together to the carnival. The tiny streets and alleyways were lit with flares and lanterns, the lights reflected weirdly in the water of the canals. Everyone wore masks, most of them grotesque yet beautiful after the fashion of Pulcinello, with long beaky noses, swivelling eyes and scarlet lips. John and Effie wore dominoes; long cloaks of black silk with hoods. The crowd seemed to sneer, at least in Effie's imagination, at both her and John. They made lewd gestures and uttered almost incomprehensible remarks which, to her horror, Effie half understood and John appeared not to. She couldn't make out what he was up to. It made her feel sick and faint. She tried not to think at all, but couldn't help it.

Twice, the Ruskins travelled across the Veneto to Verona to go to the balls given in honour of Radetzky,* the invitations highly coveted and much prized by Effie. Normally, she would have been in her element, but although she looked lovely and was much admired, she felt as though she was drugged and everything distracted and bemused her. When they got back to Venice from Verona, they learned the shocking news that two Austrian officers had had a duel over Effie. Of course, given her pride in her discretion, Effie was distraught, even if privately she couldn't help feeling flattered. Ruskin was adamant that they should take no notice. In any case, he couldn't shoot for the life of him.

Effie had been putting the finishing touches to her personal packing back at the Casa Wetzlar. Naturally, the servants had done most of the packing, but Effie was particular about her clothes and liked to fold them properly herself and to pack the ones she would need on the journey back to England in a separate trunk. Her maid was worse than useless and had packed everything upside down. Effie considered herself, with reason, to be eminently practical. Although in the middle of packing, and, it must be assumed, her possessions scattered hither and thither, Effie dashed out in the pouring rain to say goodbye to a distinguished noble Venetian acquaintance, Maria Venier. When she got back to the

---

* Johann Josef Wenzel Radetzky of Radetz was a Czechoslovakian nobleman and Austrian general, immortalized by Johann Strauss's *Radetzky March*. He spent over seventy years in the Austrian army and is best remembered for his victories at the Battle of Custoza (1848) and Novara (1849). After his triumph at Novara, he was made Viceroy of Lombardy-Venetia (1849–57). A firm disciplinarian, he was also a highly cultured gentleman much liked even by the Italians under his rule. The fact that he was evidently physically attractive may have helped to enhance his reputation.

Casa Wetzlar, Effie snatched up a jewel case where she kept a wedding present – a bracelet of considerable value. It felt strangely light: 'I opened it – it was gone! I rang for Mary [the maid]; she knew nothing. All my Jewels were lying together and all my best things gone – my Serpent – my Diamond bird and a heart – John's Diamond studs and several other things. Whoever took them must be most experienced, for my money was left, my other bracelets left and a number of trinkets.'[7] Effie summoned the police who were baffled, although they claimed the whole affair was so puzzling it must have been the work of professionals. They also insisted that both John and Effie should stay in Venice until Effie's possessions had been traced. 'The Police came and have set their agents to work and I hope something may come of it, but the thing is most mysterious for nobody saw anybody come in or go out, and after I left, Mary locked the door and only opened it for John, who however left it open for ten minutes, not more, before I came in.'[8]

8

THE HORROR OF HERNE HILL

The occurrence of theft and duels gave cause, not unjustified, to gossip and scandal which horrified the old Ruskins, who didn't fully understand the circumstances, back in Denmark Hill. Eventually, Effie and John returned home to England, arriving on Tuesday, 13 July 1852. The home that the elder Ruskins had chosen for them at Herne Hill was far worse than either of them could have envisaged. The house, a nasty suburban villa, was built of bright red brick, the interior done up with hideous mottled carpets. It was stuffed with furniture of unparalleled monstrosity. One might expect that a young married couple would bond together about the one thing they did agree on: the beastly house at Herne Hill. Far from it. At first, John refused to move in. Effie, at her wits' end, found herself beguiling him, even if only to pacify her parents-in-law. To make matters worse, the old Ruskins demanded that both John and Effie should dine with them nightly at Denmark Hill. The pretty blue barouche Effie had grown used to back in Park Street was a thing of the past. She had no means of transport and could only go up to town on Wednesdays, when Mr Ruskin allowed her the use of his carriage. But there seemed little point in that when everyone in their right minds knew that Thursdays were the 'at home' days for fashionable ladies to pay morning calls.*

---

* 'Morning calls', a convention whereby women, often with their daughters, pay uninvited visits on each other, were, in fact, paid in the afternoon after luncheon and before tea. The business of domestic life had been got through

One of the main reasons for Effie's discontent was that she had relatively few responsibilities. Since she and John were obliged to dine at Denmark Hill, she couldn't even order and supervise the dinners. In any case, there wasn't anyone to cook them. For the time being, they had no servants apart from John's man, George (with whom Effie was on increasingly good terms), and Mary. It is tempting to speculate that the old Ruskins had conceived of a diabolical plan: to render the villa so hideous that John would hardly ever be in it, leaving Effie alone with no means of transport and no cook. To the modern reader, it may sound as if having two domestics in such a small villa was more than enough, but for a woman in Effie's position in society, the lack of a cook, a gardener and a carriage was a source of extreme embarrassment.

The amount of domestic work that had to be carried out in any respectable household, and the Ruskins were anything but bohemian, was immense: the cleaning, the laying of fires, the running of errands and messages, the waiting in each shop which sold each separate item (butcher's, baker's and candlestick maker's), was enormously time-consuming. The laundry could be sent out, usually to Battersea or Shepherd's Bush, both of which districts housed an inordinate number of laundresses. This added to the household bills and the elder Ruskins were constantly accusing her of unnecessary extravagance. Even so, Effie tried to

---

during the morning, leaving the afternoon free for social intercourse. The etiquette of leaving cards, *cartes de visite*, was strictly observed. For example, turning down a corner of the card meant that the caller had paid the call in person, rather than having the card delivered by a servant. Equally, it was an accepted practice for the mistress of the house to tell her servant she was 'not at home', even though she clearly was. Gentlemen did pay calls but, in practice, this was not so frequent since most of the men were obliged to work whereas their wives mainly stayed at home (if they weren't out calling). Most middle-class Victorian women, certainly in London, had specific 'at home' days, generally on Thursdays, when calling was the preferred day for the hostess to receive the caller. The kind of family which Effie had married into would send someone like George (John Ruskin's valet) to deliver a card if she, Effie, had a headache or was feeling out of sorts.

make the best of it. At least she had a small garden at the back of the house where she enjoyed growing flowers, and, of course, she had a piano. But pounding away on the keyboard hour after hour led to headaches and a general feeling of malaise. John spent most of his time working in his study in his parents' house, so he didn't notice – or he chose not to notice – Effie's discontent. The root of the trouble, even though she hadn't yet admitted it even to herself, was that John no longer needed her. Just as John later said that the problem in his childhood was that he had no one to love, so this was now true of Effie. In a letter she wrote to her mother in February 1853, she made things as plain as she could:

> I have not been able to write to you for some days past, because I have been unwell with a bad cough and cold which has left me in bed several mornings ... The Ruskins are bothering me now because I won't visit at all without John or go to Balls alone. How is one to please them? They will be kind to me but then I must be their Slave in return. I must praise them as three perfect people and be treated as a fool or a child, whichever suits me best, but then I must never complain or else get a torrent of insults in return.

Effie's sense of uselessness and sheer boredom reduced her, not surprisingly, to fits of the sulks. She longed for Venice.

And then, quite unexpectedly, John changed her life. He hadn't forgotten Millais and, on a surprisingly well-calculated whim, he agreed that Millais should paint Effie as the model for *The Order of Release*, a narrative painting of a Jacobin Highlander clasping his wife in a deep embrace after she had succeeded in securing his release from prison. A highly emotive painting, it is probably one of the best portraits of Effie. The only deviation from accuracy is that, for aesthetic reasons concerning the colour scheme of the painting, he changed Effie's hair from auburn to dark chocolate. 'These last days,' Effie wrote to her mother on 20 March 1853, 'I have been sitting to Millais from immediately after breakfast to dinner, thru all the afternoon till dark which gave me not a moment, and now I am rather tired and a stiff neck.'

She might have got a stiff neck but, starved as she was of company at Herne Hill, she found Millais unexpectedly to her liking. During the sittings, they discovered that they had met previously at a dance at Ewell Castle in Surrey, where Effie had been staying with her father's friends, the Gadesdens. He reminded her that he had asked her to dance, that she had declined, and that he had been mortified. Millais was almost a year younger than Effie. It was a long time since she had frequented the society of people of her own age. For his part, Millais found Effie's face fascinating and inexplicably difficult to capture. She was a good model, kept stock-still while managing to keep a lively expression (not the easiest thing in the world), didn't chatter, yet contrived to make him feel at his ease, an equal and at home. Even while modelling for him, Effie remained a natural hostess, in complete control of her tiny, hideous suburban drawing room. Yet she felt ill.

> Mrs R says it is a good thing if I do feel ill that in losing my strength I don't lose my looks, and Mr R who really is without exception the most extraordinary man alive, on my marriage date [the anniversary of Effie's marriage to John Ruskin] . . . kept hunting [sic] disagreeable things at me all dinner time and was in a very bad humour . . . he said he had taken pen in hand to John to expatiate on my perfections of appearance and manner, that in his Life he had never seen anything so perfect as my attitude as I lay on the sofa the night before and that no wonder Millais etc., etc., but it sickens me to write such nonsense as I could spare such writing and excuse it from a fool but from Mr R it sounded, to say the least, I thought, unnatural and almost suspicious.[1]

The sittings continued, Effie feeling unaccountably unwell.

The nature of the relations between artist and model are, by definition, intimate. That is not to suggest that there was any impropriety between Effie and Millais when he was making studies for his painting in her parlour at Herne Hill. In those days, there was scarcely any occasion for long stretches of silence to last between two people who were not either married or had some other formally recognized bond. It was considered the height of bad manners to stare directly at a woman and Millais clearly had to in order to paint Effie; and there is no doubt that Effie relished the fact that she was the source of his inspiration and enjoyed the notion of believing that she was his muse. To a certain extent she was. He wouldn't have been able to paint the picture as he did without her, but he wouldn't have needed a so-called muse if he hadn't already got his own inspiration.

Effie was right to harbour suspicions, even though she hadn't formed them clearly in her mind. Because Ruskin had consented to her posing for Millais, Effie had finally been caught off guard and, however unwittingly, had left herself open to gossip and public speculation, one of the things she most abhorred and always went to great lengths to avoid. *The Order of Release* was exhibited at the Royal Academy and was immediately a wild success. The critics raved, the crowd went wild. The day after the private view on 2 May 1853, Effie wrote to her mother, 'Millais' picture is talked of in a way to make every other Academician frantic. It is hardly possible to approach it for the rows of bonnets.'

The authorities at the Academy saw fit to put a rail around the painting to protect it from possible damage by the mob of admirers, 'a practical measure viewed as an honour previously only granted to David Wilkie's *Chelsea Pensioners* in 1822'.[2] Effie didn't mind being the centre of attention, but she did mind being gossiped about. Although she had previously sat for the painters George Richmond and G. F. Watts, that was for her portrait to be seen by the family and guests, something perfectly in accord with the mores of polite society. But to pose for an artist in a genre painting was quite different and not socially acceptable – it might be construed as though young Mrs Ruskin was nothing better than a professional model, a loose woman. To make matters worse, she had been portrayed embracing a man who, although his face is not visible, was clearly not John Ruskin and, to cap it all, she had *bare feet*. The general public, however much they might appreciate the painting, could hardly be expected to be conversant with how it had been executed. They were not to know that Effie had never even met the man she appeared to be embracing, that Millais had used a lay figure to stand in for the man, the dog and the baby during his sessions painting her at Herne Hill, that she had never taken off her shoes and stockings, and that the bare feet were actually the feet of someone else altogether. As Ruskin's wife, it would have been inadmissible to portray her naked feet, and it is arguable that it is partly these feet, even if they are not Effie's, which make the painting so thoroughly convincing and pleasing. It is generally thought that Millais used the professional model Annie Ryan for the feet, painting only Effie's face and figure at Herne Hill and on one later session at his studio in Bloomsbury.

Nevertheless, the intimacy between artist and model – Millais and Effie, in this case, should not be underestimated. Not unlike two dancers in perfect step, it is a relationship – between the muse who inspires the canvas and the artist – of perfect intimacy which, largely because of the conditions required by the artist, is conducted in silence complied with by the model and painter. It is an intimacy, a perfect understanding of what is required by both parties, satisfactory to both, colluding, for the sake of art, for the painting in question. Effie had never experienced such a degree of intimacy with a man before, tacit though it was, and Millais was overwhelmed not only by her beauty but by her complicity.

Ruskin had been asked to give a series of lectures in Edinburgh. In addition, he had to compile the index for *The Stones of Venice*. It occurred to him to spend the summer in Scotland and he invited Millais and his brother William, a minor landscape painter, together with Holman Hunt, to accompany them.

If there was one thing Ruskin enjoyed it was the company of younger men who looked up to him and could be influenced by him. Hunt couldn't go: he was finishing *The Light of the World* and was preparing to go to the Holy Land. Millais and his brother accepted. Effie was delighted. She immediately began making preparations for their sojourn, knowing the limitations of creature comforts in such a remote district as the Dalreach where they planned to stay. On 20 June 1853, Effie wrote to Rawdon Brown, '[They] will be very busy sketching and walking over the Mountains and I shall occupy myself in trying to make them all as comfortable as I can ... there seems no certainty of any thing to eat but Trout out of the Tummel or the Gary, but it would amuse you to hear the Pre-Raphaelites and John talk. They seem to think that they will have everything just for the asking and laugh at me for preparing a great hamper of sherry and tea and sugar which I expect they will be extremely glad to partake of in case of returning home any day wet through with Scotch mist.'[3]

Nothing went according to plan. Originally, Ruskin had intended that they should travel to Dalnacardoch for a sketching holiday in Scotland, and stay at a riverside inn which Effie's father had recommended, with Hunt, Millais and his brother William as their guests. Ruskin had been working all the while on *The Stones of Venice*. At last, all three of the imposing volumes were finished, and only the hefty, eighty-page index remained to be compiled. This was exactly the kind of task to give Ruskin a modicum of mental respite, for, as always, he had worked with such intensity that he was worn thin, his nerves beginning to fray. He found himself looking forward to the company of the young artists. What he fancied to be their reverence verging on adulation, kneeling, as it were, at his feet while he propounded the principles of the new and noble school of art they had formed, was a stimulant to his jaded fancy.

For some reason, the plan of staying at the inn on the river Garry fell through. Ruskin told Effie that he wouldn't be denied the sojourn in Scotland. After all, he had the lecture to give at the Philosophical Society in Edinburgh later, and they might as well

stay in grand houses belonging to his friends on the way, and take
in as many Turners and old missals as possible. The Trevelyans,*
he knew, would welcome them for a week or so up at Wallington,
near Morpeth in Northumberland. Lady Trevelyan, who adored
Ruskin, kept open house for him and was more than willing to
extend her hospitality to his proposed party.

Far from wishing to thwart him, Effie longed to get away from
Herne Hill and her oppressive parents-in-law. 'You may be sure
that so long a visit as we shall probably make in Scotland makes
me extremely happy,' she wrote to her mother, while only half
listening to her husband's plans. He thought she looked coldly at
him, not that that was unusual, with that queer smile he had
scolded her for in the early days of their marriage: the corner of
her mouth turned up, her eyes narrowed, the effect faintly foxy.
Yet everyone had remarked how well she was looking, her complexion, like her gown, brilliantly pink and white. She hadn't felt
in better spirits since their time in Venice and was almost annoyed
that she couldn't hide her radiance since *The Order of Release* had
been on show at the Academy.

Holman Hunt wrote to Ruskin to say that he wouldn't be able
to join them immediately, although he hoped to later. He hadn't
finished painting what would become *The Light of the World*, and
was still stuck in Surrey painting bats and nettles for the background. Ruskin realigned his arrangements for the holiday. He
liked fussing and exact plans were necessary if the party was to
travel in anything like the style and comfort he insisted on, which
Effie had grown accustomed to, but which was unknown to any of
the struggling young artists. For one thing, apart from the initial
run from London to Northumberland, Ruskin rejected out of hand

---

* Sir Walter Trevelyan (1797–1879), geologist and philanthropist, and his
fascinating wife, Pauline (1816–66), née Jermyn. The Trevelyans were
immensely rich, cultivated and influential. Both the Trevelyans were intimate
with Ruskin and recently Pauline and Effie had become friendly. Pauline was a
patron of the Pre-Raphaelites. Her great inspiration was the creation of the hall
at Wallington, which remains a monument to her vision.

going anywhere by train. Admittedly, the railways were less frequent beyond Hadrian's Wall. Unlike most people, who were
thrilled by this new form of travel and enjoyed the novel experience of seeing the countryside as a panoramic vision whisking past
them, Ruskin loathed the noisy, smoky locomotives. He compared
railway journeys to being tied to the handle of a shrieking, whist-
ling tea kettle banging along at indecent speed. No: they would
'cut railroads' and travel north from Wallington in his luxuriously
appointed carriage, the carriage sent freight as far as Morpeth.
Hunt could join them later. In the event, he never did. Had Hunt
gone north instead of east on a long-dreamed of pilgrimage to the
Holy Land, the restraining influence he exerted on Millais might
have altered the dramatic sequence of events which was to reveal
itself that summer in the Trossachs in Perthshire.

Effie let Ruskin fiddle around with his minute arrangements,
but she busied herself getting her clothes in order for the Highland
tour as well as making practical arrangements for everyone's
comfort. As a Scotswoman, she couldn't help being amused by the
optimistic notions expressed by Ruskin and the Millais brothers.

9

AT GLENFINLAS

The six-mile carriage drive along the undulating valley from the railway at Morpeth to Wallington was along rough roads, bordered by low-lying dry stone walls, and seemed very long. It was a heavenly day in June 1853 and, except for Ruskin, who had a bad cold and consequently felt seedy, they were all in high spirits. Neither of the Millais brothers had been this far north before and they were bowled over by the beauty of the wild, romantic landscape; the undulating moors, the rushing streams the colour of beer on a level with the sheep-nibbled turf; the sweet, clear air. Effie was in her element. The further north she went, the freer she became of the constraints of society which exercised such a fascinating tyranny over her.

Wallington was magnificent. Standing boldly amidst tussocks of rough grass, with the wild Northumberland landscape as a backdrop and its immense Palladian façade, it was a testimony to the aggrandizement of wealthy generations of aristocratic landowners. Their hosts, Sir Walter and Lady Trevelyan, could not have been more welcoming. Sir Walter was tall and craggy and somewhat forbidding. Immensely distinguished, he preoccupied himself with the study of geology and the niceties of Christian theology, the two being inextricably bound up in the great contemporary debate about evolution. He was an active philanthropist, a paragon of a landowner, an absolute teetotaller. His wife, Pauline, was much younger, with hazel eyes, engaging energy and a direct manner. She was tiny; not quite five foot, she scarcely reached up to Sir

Walter's elbow. Extremely intelligent, endowed with rare perception, the immediate effect Pauline had was wonderful. The painter
and poet, William Bell Scott, already known to Millais through
his friendship with Rossetti, and, on this occasion, a fellow guest
at Wallington, later recorded his first sight of Pauline: '. . . as I
approached [Wallington], the door was opened, and there stepped
out a little woman as light as a feather and as quick as a kitten,
habited for gardening in a broad straw hat and gauntlet gloves,
with a basket on her arm, visibly the mistress of the place'.[1] Pauline
was an ardent disciple of Ruskin's. A talented artist herself, she
followed his every command, drawing twigs and scraps of lichen
and feather, foxgloves and fossils.* She even went so far as to
always call him 'Master'. Pauline also had a vision of her own. She
was about to transform Wallington into a monument to contemporary art and science, to cover over the dank inner quadrangle
with a glass dome and decorate the resulting great hall with frescos
and other works of art to be executed by modern painters. Bell
Scott and Ruskin, who unfortunately disliked each other, were
already very much involved in her scheme. Bell Scott's painting
shared a direct affinity with Ford Madox Brown's.† Stout and
ringletted, his head wrapped in a kerchief which made him look
like a Venetian Doge, Bell Scott had an attractive appetite for life,
and was an inveterate and amusing gossip. An impressively well-
informed art historian, it was the combination of his quirky sense
of humour with his passion for art which endeared him to Pauline
as it did to Rossetti. As well as painting and writing poetry (mainly
ballads in the border tradition), he taught art to working men at
Newcastle where he was the Head of the School of Design. His
domestic arrangements were interesting and, curiously, not atypical

---

* Pauline's decorations of several of the pillars at Wallington are still extant, as
are Louisa Mackenzie's, and the magnificent frescos by William Bell Scott and
Ruskin.

† It didn't help matters that Ruskin was as antipathetic to Ford Madox Brown
as he was to William Bell Scott.

of the time. Fond of his wife, he divided his time between her and his mistress, Alice Boyd of Penkill Castle in Scotland.

Recently, down in London, Pauline and Effie had begun to make friends. It was Pauline who had arranged for Effie and Louisa Mackenzie to have a stereoscopic* picture taken of them for her. Effie didn't make female friends easily, but Pauline was keen to become intimate with her, not merely because she was her adored Ruskin's wife. She was certainly pleased to be able to get Effie's enthusiastic, if not wholly characteristic, words about Louisa, 'I shall deem myself happy if she likes me half as much as I am sure I should like her.' But although she was attracted by Effie's beauty and spirited manner, Pauline couldn't help thinking Effie a trifle provincial, a little bumptious at times, even if she herself had made the transition from being a penniless clergyman's daughter to a wealthy landowner's wife apparently without effort.

Both women were childless and both were married to men in the public eye. Pauline was genuinely in love with her husband, Sir Walter, and shared an uncommon intellectual equality with him. Unlike Effie, whose constant bouts of physical malaises were never explained, Pauline, who seldom complained, suffered from severe ill health.† She had the happy knack of making friends easily and Pauline had invited her young protégée, the lovely and intelligent Louisa Mackenzie,‡ to join the house party. Included, as a matter of course, was David Wooster, Sir Walter's secretary and resident curator of Wallington's private museum of geological curiosities. Together, they made up a stimulating and knowledge-

---

* Stereoscopy is a method of creating a 3-D effect by presenting two images separately to each eye of the viewer which persuades the brain to perceive the image as three-dimensional. It was invented by Sir Charles Wheatstone in 1838 and became a popular method of taking people's likenesses amongst the wealthier classes of society.

† After her premature death in 1866, an autopsy revealed that Pauline had been riddled with cancer for many years.

‡ Louisa Stewart-Mackenzie (1827–1903), later the second wife of Lord Ashburton.

able gathering, the differences between Ruskin and Bell Scott temporarily skated over.

During those first few days of glorious summer weather, the Millais brothers went fishing. They weren't used to such grand country-house life, but they both had a passion for fishing. When Millais, aged nine, had been awarded his first prize at the Royal Academy, he had startled the Duke of Sussex, who was giving out the prizes, and wasn't used to such boyish requests, by asking for the right to fish in the Serpentine. This desire was duly granted.* Millais' passion for fishing lasted all his life. In Northumberland, on the banks of the Wansbeck, the curlews calling overhead, Millais cast his rod, caught a trout and felt triumphant in spite of being pestered by clouds of midges. Pauline recorded, 'He had never seen a clear stream nor a wild country before.'[2] While the weather continued fine, Pauline showed him over the estate which Sir Walter had replanted to create vistas looking out from the artificial landscape he had devised. 'Millais was in high glee with everything he saw. Water and distances and plants and lilies in the ponds – took him to the Wildwoods.'[3]

Ruskin's cold got better, but that evening Effie stayed in bed with 'a sick headache'. When it poured with rain on Friday, Sir Walter carried Ruskin off to look at the fossils and other curiosities in his museum. Millais made a sketch of Sir Walter for Pauline and let her watch over his shoulder. She was amazed by the speed at which he drew. Even though Pauline didn't record it in her diary, it is inconceivable that they didn't discuss her cherished project of transforming the quadrangle. Effie lay on the sofa looking very pretty with stephanotis in her hair and Millais began another sketch of her, while Ruskin drew holly and hawthorn from the window.

Pauline was beginning to grow increasingly fond of Effie. There was about her something indefinably vulnerable yet, at the same

---

* Told to the author by Millais' great-grandson, the late Hugh Millais. Also quoted by John Guille Millais in *The Life and Letters of Sir John Everett Millais* vol. 1, p. 14.

time, unapproachable. She was, Pauline noticed, always very well
dressed, and her clothes were surprisingly conventional. She was
certainly a good deal more fashionably turned out than Pauline
herself, who tended to wear any old clothes when in the country.
In the lamplight, the folds of Effie's satin gown resembled draperies
painted by old masters, so stiff that they seemed as if they could
stand by themselves, her small waist pulled in, her sleeves puffed
out as modern taste dictated.

The house party all assembled in the immense saloon decorated
with swirls of elaborate eighteenth-century rococo Italian plaster-
work. Sitting beneath the blue and white cornucopias of plaster
fruit, garlands of flowers and winged sphinxes alighting on curlicues
of foliage, it was like looking at the inverted top tier of a royal
wedding cake. Drawing each other, talking sporadically, they were
bound in that delightful intimacy that arises from working in
harmony together. Friends of the Trevelyans, the Collingwoods,
who lived nearby, had come to lunch. In the afternoon, Ruskin,
Louisa and the Trevelyans drove over to Capheaton, the Swin-
burnes' great house,[*] to see their choice collection of Turners.

Ruskin was duly impressed. Their week at Wallington was
memorable. The Trevelyans instinctively liked the Millais brothers,
appreciating their good looks, natural grace and obvious sincerity
combined with a refreshing sense of fun. An immediate bond was
formed between them by their shared love of painting and the arts
in general. William Millais was a talented landscape artist and,
when not prohibited by the pouring rain, sketched by the river.
He had a fine voice and needed little coaxing to sing to them
in the evenings after dinner. It is possible that Effie, who was an
accomplished musician, accompanied him on the piano. Pauline

---

[*] Capheaton, a substantial country house commanding beautiful views of
the wild Northumberland country, is the Swinburne family seat. It was then
occupied by Sir John Swinburne (1762–1860), grandfather of the poet Algernon
Charles Swinburne (1837–1909), who was a close friend of the Trevelyans as
well as Rossetti and other members of the P. R. B.

made a study of Ruskin demonstrating a drawing technique to Louisa at the small round table with the lamp. Millais saved the drawing he made of Effie.

*

They were all in high spirits when they set off for Scotland, Sir Walter and Louisa Mackenzie sending them on their way almost as far as Otterburn in the dog cart. They pulled up at an inn on the moor. Almost immediately, the coachman got so drunk on whisky that, later, he couldn't control the horses. William Millais took over the reins.

When, in 1882, William Minto came to edit William Bell Scott's autobiography, he omitted the following passage, in which Bell Scott claims that it was evident to everyone at Wallington that Millais and Effie were falling in love:

The only one of the Pre-Raphaelite Brotherhood that he [Ruskin] was personally acquainted with was the favourite of the Academy, Millais, whom he had thus carried off to Scotland to initiate him into the only class of painting he, Ruskin, knew anything about or cared for, landscape. But although the critic was interested only in landscape, the born painter was a man as well as an artist, and more Catholic and universal in his loves. Already apparently before they reached Northumberland, the handsome hero had won the heart of the unhappy Mrs Ruskin, whose attentions from her husband had it seems consisted in his keeping a notebook of the defects in her carriage or speech. More than that the lovers had evidently come to an understanding with each other, founded apparently on loathing the owner of the notebook. Mrs Ruskin used to escape after breakfast, and joined by Millais was not heard of until the late hour of dinner. Lady Trevelyan hinted remonstrance, took alarm in fact, but not caring to speak confidentially to the lady who acted so strangely in her house, got Sir Walter to rouse the apparently oblivious husband. Her quick eye had of course discerned something of a telegraphic nature between the lovers, and he was mystified, having pretty good eyes of his own, but was less given to forming conclusions or speaking of what was passing, he agreed however to take Ruskin into his confidence. But that innocent creature pooh-poohed him. Really he didn't *believe* there was any harm in their *pleasure* themselves. He did not see what harm they could do: they were only children! Years after when I could venture to talk over the affair with Sir Walter, I asked him how he explained this mode of taking the warning. He confessed to having thought over the matter, and was inclined to conclude that John Ruskin wanted to get rid of his wife; had it been any other man he would have so concluded, but then the individual in question did not know much about love-making.*

William Millais took over and drove the rest of the way. They spent that night at Jedburgh, thrilled by the beauty of the winding valley, the river tumbling over the flat stones bordered by bracken, cow parsley and with foxgloves growing out of crevices in the rocks. At the inn they stayed at that night, they had a delicious tea of newly laid eggs and fresh butter with heather honey and, Ruskin declared, the best bread that he had ever eaten.[4]

They travelled by way of Edinburgh where they spent a couple of nights. The Millais brothers, who had never been there before, were particularly enchanted by the place and its unexpected grandeur. Effie, who was plagued with inflamed tonsils, went to the doctor who prescribed chloroform pills and ordered her to rub herself all over with olive oil at night. She asked the doctor to look at Millais' throat and he said Millais was suffering from the same complaint and Effie should dose him with her pills. The next morning, they continued on their journey. The way grew wilder by the minute, the mountains rising sharply against the duck-egg-blue sky.

Millais had been overworking. *The Order of Release* had strained

---

* The manuscript is with Scott/Trevelyan Letters in the Troxell Collection at Princeton. The extract is quoted from Mary Lutyens's *Millais and the Ruskins*.

his reserves. He had grown restive, and Ruskin realized that he needed a holiday. If Ruskin's motives were mixed in asking Millais and his brother William as well as Holman Hunt to join himself and Effie on a protracted visit to Scotland, his concern for Millais' welfare was very genuine. Ruskin could not help it that at the root of nearly all his impulses lay a profound desire to control and reform. A born leader of men, and admiring Millais' painting as he did and having persuaded the public to appreciate him too, Ruskin was now impelled to perfect Millais' technique in the art of landscape painting. Ruskin would have made an exemplary missionary. Back in London, there had been a vague notion that Millais might paint Effie in *The Lady of the Lake*, Sir Walter Scott's popular poem, set on the shores of Loch Katrine in the Trossachs. When they arrived, the idea palled beside the grandeur of the real thing. Ruskin's father was keen to acquire a portrait of his son by Millais and it seemed a magnificent idea for Millais to paint Ruskin against the rocks he loved and knew so much about.

They stopped at Brig O'Turk near Stirling, both the Millais brothers staying in tiny rooms, scrupulously clean, at the New Trossachs Hotel, while the Ruskins stayed at the very slightly grander manse just down the road. The dazzling beauty of the place was obscured by downpours of rain. It rained without stopping, or so it seemed, for days on end. It was impossible to do any painting outdoors. The cramped rooms they were cooped up in aggravated the situation. Ruskin worked on his index and on the speech he would give at Edinburgh later in the year. Effie took to sewing and snipped away at a length of dark red linsey-woolsey she was turning into a skirt to keep her warm against the northern winds, and a frock which she was stitching for her little sister, Sophy. The hotel proved too expensive and so the Ruskins and Millais moved into the cheaper, if cramped quarters offered by the local schoolmaster. William Millais remained at the hotel, possibly because he preferred its comfort; probably because there was no room at the schoolmaster's.

To enliven them during the dingy weather, Ruskin challenged

the party to games of shuttlecock and battledore, which Effie, as well as Millais, took up with alacrity. Ruskin also opened up a new avenue of interest for Millais: architectural design, a pursuit which fascinated the young painter and one which he was wholly new to. In a letter to Charlie Collins, he wrote: 'You will shortly hear of me in another art besides painting. Ruskin has discovered that I can design Architectural ornamentation more perfectly than any living or dead party ... Ruskin believes now that I have almost mistaken my vocation and that I was born to restore Architecture. Please say nothing about this, as we don't wish it to become public that we are working in consort.'[5] Millais was working on designs for church windows; the ones he designed, on old grocery paper in shades of green and brown, were of a large window supported by three pairs of angels, all to be wrought in stone. Each angel was the likeness of Effie in profile. 'Millais has done me a beautiful design of angels,' Ruskin wrote to his father. Old Ruskin replied, 'This is pure sublimity.'

Ruskin may have appeared to be wholly absorbed in compiling the index for *The Stones of Venice*, but even he emerged from his task occasionally, nervous, sometimes surprisingly uncertain of himself, and then, on other occasions, sublimely unaware of the effect his presence had on the younger men or of what they thought. Even the Millais brothers scarcely knew what to think: it was hard to equate the Ruskin they looked up to and revered with the pettifogging despot they now saw bullying his wife over apparently trivial details. When Millais observed him writing down hasty remarks made by Effie in the heat of the moment, presumably to be used against her in some mysterious way, he was horrified.

The limited space they were living in promoted an unforeseen intimacy between them. Millais could barely fit into the little box of a room he slept in. 'This new residence is the funniest thing you ever saw, my bedroom is not much larger than a snuffbox. I can open the window, shut the door and shave all without getting out of bed.'[6] Effie slept in its replica beyond the panelled wall while Ruskin made his own arrangements on the sofa in the small parlour. Millais could not help noticing that the Ruskins didn't share a bed, and that they never exchanged any physical gesture of intimacy. Innocent and virginal though he was, Millais felt a natural repugnance at such coldness and began to wonder whether the Ruskin he admired so much as an intellectual exponent of the history of art was not in some way negligent of, if not downright cruel to his wife.

Given the incessant rain and the proximity of their quarters, it is not surprising that Millais and Effie became increasingly intimate, while Ruskin, whose appetite for work was gargantuan, was embroiled in his Edinburgh lectures and the index for *The Stones of Venice*. Once, going for a walk together, they got caught in a shower of rain, tumbled over in the mud and both sheltered beneath the same cloak. Later, Millais did a charming sketch of the incident, which indicates an unusual degree of familiarity. So, too, does the drawing he did of Effie cutting his hair, and another of her wearing the linsey-woolsey dress she had made, standing over Millais, who is crouching down to paint while William is casting his rod in the background. Effie, who had every reason to be proud of her forethought in having packed provisions for them back in London, couldn't help laughing at Millais when he declared, in the middle of the frugal and impoverished Trossachs, that he was pining for fresh young garden peas* and could he possibly have strawberries? In spite of her mockery, Effie opened an account with the greengrocer at Stirling.

---

* Fresh peas, before freezers were invented, were rightly regarded as a great delicacy by the Victorians. Their association with the rapidly disappearing pastoral life made them a symbol of purity, quite apart from the fact they are delicious to eat. Ruskin's claim about the pleasure of shelling peas is substantiated in Penelope Fitzgerald's posthumously published collection of writings *A House of Air* (Harper Perennial, 2005), p. 470. One of Millais' illustrations for Trollope's *Framley Parsonage* is of Lily Dale sitting in a reverie beside a basket of peas when she is interrupted by the maid, 'Please, ma'am, cook says, can we have the peas to shell.' At Leighton House there is a portrait by Millais of a young girl shelling peas.

Her efforts were much appreciated. Millais wrote to Charlie Collins describing a delicious lunch they ate on the rocks consisting of roast lamb and the desired peas, blackcurrant pudding and champagne to drink. Ruskin asserted that shelling peas was one of the great pleasures of life. Such involvement with ordinary tasks is one of his considerable charms. Many years later, one of Ruskin's admirers, Edward Hicks, would describe the joy Ruskin took in shelling peas 'with the keenest relish . . . the pop which assures one of a successful start, the fresh colour and scent of the juicy row within, and the pleasure of skilfully scooping the bouncing with one's thumb into the vessel by one's side'.

Ruskin didn't seem in the least perturbed about Effie's evident affection for Millais. Indeed, he rather seemed to encourage it in spite of appearing to ignore her with studied deliberation. But he did evince concern for his young protégé, Millais. There was every reason to do so. By any standard, Millais' behaviour was becoming increasingly strange. If he wasn't racing over the hills or spending long hours over his easel, he flung himself face down on the sofa and moped. At night, in the close quarters of their lodgings, he could be heard to weep. A few days before Effie sent to the greengrocer at Stirling for the desired fruit and vegetables, he had suffered a series of accidents, none of them life threatening, but all humiliating. He banged his nose and forehead so hard against a rock while diving into a waterfall that he bled profusely and Ruskin dashed back to their lodgings for whisky to revive him. That very same afternoon, Millais crushed his thumb between some stones he was trying to dam the stream with so that Effie wouldn't have to wet her feet crossing it. Back at their rooms, Effie sat him down, bandaged him up and cut his hair. The pain was so bad that he couldn't sleep, and read Tennyson all night. To make matters worse, he caught a bad cold, which demoralized him. He put the cause of his moodiness down to the imminent departure of Holman Hunt for the Holy Land where he would paint an aged goat in startlingly dazzling colours, stranded on the desolate shores of the Dead Sea, to represent Christ taking the sins of the world upon himself. Later, Hunt was to boil a dead horse at the bottom of his garden in Kensington to study the skeleton, which would enable him to paint a horse that looked as though it was alive. This was taking the accepted rule of making studies of the model in the nude before dressing them several steps further. The stench of boiled horse in Kensington made its respectable residents gag as they walked past the house. Millais had also worked himself up to a state of anxiety about the state of his close friend Walter Deverell's health. It didn't strike any of them as strange that Millais was so openly miserable because his bosom friend was leaving him. Ruskin took it upon himself to write to Holman Hunt, trying to dissuade him from travelling to the East. When Millais learned of this, he wrote to Hunt telling him to take no notice of Ruskin's intervention. It didn't occur to any of them, Millais least of all, that his wretchedness was because he was rapidly falling in love with Effie and the situation was intolerable.

Deverell was dying. Since the demise of both his parents, he had been left destitute in charge of his younger siblings. Then he contracted tuberculosis. His friends did what they could, but nothing could save him from his incurable illness. Millais gratefully accepted Ruskin's offer to send his dying friend some highly prized fine rice through his mother, Mrs Ruskin, and, at a later date, to try to find one of Deverell's younger brothers a post as clerk in Mr Ruskin's sherry business.

Most of Holman Hunt's preparations for leaving England were not so directly concerned with what he would require in the Holy Land as with making arrangements for the sexy slum girl, Annie Miller, to be transformed into an eligible lady, suitable to become his wife, on his return. Quite how this was to be accomplished puzzled and intrigued his friends. Yet, despite their derision, Hunt persisted.

Annie had already revelled in the notoriety of having her portrait painted by Holman Hunt as the model in *The Awakened Conscience*, one of his most inspired paintings, which illustrates the flash of illumination in the conscience of a 'fallen woman'. Annie

Miller was undoubtedly ambitious and had an eye for the main chance. Much to the amusement of his fellow brethren, Hunt put Fred Stephens nominally in charge of her and set Annie up in a local boarding house run by an old termagant of a landlady, Mrs Bramagh. He hired a well-meaning but naive young woman to initiate Annie into the mysteries of gentility. The very notion of such an education exasperated Annie, but she tried not to show it, because she felt that if she bettered herself, her stakes in climbing the social ladder would radically alter her life very much for the better. Annie Miller had an easy-going good nature which made her popular with Hunt's friends. It was relatively simple for her to promise to wash, to wear clean linen, pronounce her aitches and be dutiful and faithful. Holman Hunt had promised to marry her on his return. It wasn't a bad incentive. Holman Hunt, however, was, like most reformers, adamant on his conditions. She could, of course, he said, pose in his absence for certain painters – but only those whom he trusted. He listed James Richardson Holliday, Augustus Egg, Fred Stephens, George Price Boyce and Millais, but not Rossetti. Hunt, quite understandably, didn't trust Rossetti within an inch of a female model and certainly not one with Annie's bawdy charms. Annie's education would cost Hunt at least £200, not to mention subsequent mortification.

Of all this, Millais, up in Scotland, was somewhat hazy. Because he was far away from the London scene, he was separated from his erstwhile brethren, the Pre-Raphaelites, in a way that could never be wholly breached. The existence of the Brotherhood depended on intimate and constant communication. Although Millais frequently wrote to Holman Hunt and to Charlie Collins, his involvement with the Ruskins and, subsequently, with the Establishment in the form of the Royal Academy – the very institution from which the young students had all rebelled – diluted the bonds between them. Conversely, it indicated their approaching maturity, which is not only reflected in their painting but also in their relationships with the women who inspired them.

Millais' portrait of Ruskin in urban cloth, standing astride a rock in front of a cascading waterfall, Glenfinlas, was held up by the constant rain. In despair, Millais had a shelter made for him, much like the one he had had constructed at Ewell in Surrey. It helped, but wasn't entirely waterproof and the light in the torrents of rain was frequently so dark that it was impossible to see. For the rest of his life Millais continued the habit of having shelters made for him when painting out of doors. The other abomination was the predominance of midges which exasperated both the Millais brothers. Millais made a sketch of them both with their faces wrapped up in handkerchiefs, making them look uncommonly as though they were wearing gas masks in a vain attempt to outwit the wretched insects.

Usually, when it poured with rain, they all spent the afternoon in the schoolmaster's barn, playing shuttlecock and battledore. In the evenings, after a supper provided by their landlady, the schoolmaster's wife, they amused themselves by enjoying simple paper games, watching Millais turning out wicked mimicries of old masters, 'such as Vandyck, Poussin, Greuze, or a Turner'.[7] Effie spellbound both the Millais brothers by her retelling of old Scottish legends and the histories of battles and kings with which she was familiar and which they had never heard. Ruskin generally pegged away at the text of the lectures he was due to give in Edinburgh that autumn, which would subsequently form the backbone of *Lectures on Art*. Sometimes, Effie sang Scots ballads to them, but for once, she had no piano to play.

Millais took to calling Effie 'the Countess' and started to give her drawing lessons, finding her a decidedly talented pupil. At some point, quite when or in what particular circumstances it is now impossible to say, Effie told Millais the truth of her unconsummated marriage. Millais was appalled, although he knew almost nothing of women and was far less experienced than any of the other breth- ren. The initial nature of his adoration of Effie had much of the Pre-Raphaelites' obsession with Arthurian legend about it. At first, he had seen himself as her gallant defender, his love for Effie echoing the courtly love demonstrated by the medieval knights of old, not thinking, perhaps, of the results of Lancelot's passion for King Arthur's Queen Guinevere. Now that he knew the truth about Effie's marriage, his ardour was not only inflamed, but the nature of his love became plain. He would be her champion and rescue her from her miserable fate.

Clearly, for the first time since her marriage to Ruskin, Effie was under the spell of another man. While she had enjoyed the attentions of Paulizza, the young Clare Ford (the son of a neighbour in Mayfair who became besotted by her), and those others in Venice, and Count Thun, Effie had remained in control of the situation, a strict observer of propriety. Her feelings for Millais were different. This was not merely an enjoyable flirtation but the real thing. It was all she could do to disguise the depth of her passion.

If Millais' feelings for Effie were inspired by Arthurian legend, Ruskin could not lay claim to having been inspired by the King of Camelot. When the time came for Millais' brother William to leave, Ruskin moved into his room in the overpriced hotel at Brig O'Turk, thus leaving Effie unchaperoned in the schoolmaster's lodgings with Millais. This, considering the conventions of the day, was a scandalous state of affairs. It began to appear that George Gray was not far off the mark in his suspicion that Ruskin was deliberately trying to compromise Effie.

Finally, in October, the time came to end the prolonged sojourn at Glenfinlas. Ruskin was committed to delivering his series of lectures at Edinburgh University. He and Effie set off; Millais, who was feeling wretched, was left behind to continue with the still-unfinished painting. Millais found his solitude unbearable. Two days after the Ruskins' departure, he packed up and followed them to Edinburgh. It was hard to find a convincing explanation. So far, Ruskin had turned a blind eye to Millais' infatuation. In fact, he had, somewhat perversely, encouraged it. Some people, Effie's brother George in particular, were convinced that if Effie could be sufficiently compromised, then Ruskin could be rid of her. It was hard to find an acceptable explanation for Millais' presence in

Edinburgh. When Effie's parents, Mr and Mrs Gray, arrived from Perth to attend the lectures, Mrs Gray could see at once what the situation was. She liked Millais immediately, but knew only too well the nature of the Ruskins' treatment of her daughter and was understandably nervous of how they would use Millais' open admiration of Effie against her.

Ruskin's lectures in Edinburgh were a resounding success. Effie did everything to ensure that the right people obtained tickets and generally acted as hostess for dinners, suppers and light entertainments. It was a role she excelled in and which, given Ruskin's reluctance to appear in public, she seldom had an opportunity to play. No one, except for her mother, could possibly have suspected that there was anything wrong in the Ruskins' marriage, and even Mrs Gray, while recognizing Millais' evident passion for her daughter, did not begin to suspect how deeply the marriage had foundered.

10

CONSEQUENCES

If Mrs Gray didn't recognize the state of her daughter's marriage, Millais clearly did. When he got back to London (Effie having returned for a short respite to Bowerswell with her parents), Millais wrote with remarkable moral courage, given the mores of the day, to Mrs Gray:

> *The worst of it all* is the wretchedness of her position . . . Why he ever had the audacity of marrying with no better intentions is a mystery to me. I must confess that it appears to me that he cares for nothing beyond his Mother and Father, which makes the insolence of his finding fault with his wife (to whom he has acted from the beginning most disgustingly) more apparent . . . If I have meddled more than my place would justify it was from the flagrant nature of the affair – I am only anxious to do the best for your daughter . . . I cannot conceal the truth from you, that she has more to put up with than any living woman . . . She has all the right on her side and believe me the Father would see that also if he knew all.'[1]

In another letter to Mrs Gray, Millais strongly advised that Effie should not go back to Herne Hill unaccompanied by one of her much younger sisters. He didn't trust Ruskin, he feared for Effie and, although a supremely conventional man himself, was prepared to step out of contemporary conventions, even if to put himself beyond the pale of them, for the sake of Effie whom he loved.

Much though she may have valued Millais' championship of her daughter, Mrs Gray was thoroughly alarmed. Neither Effie nor Millais had confided the frustrations of Effie's marriage to her. That would have been a betrayal on Millais' part and, for the time being, Effie could not bring herself to do so. It is worth remembering that in 1853, the Women's Property Act had not yet been debated and was not resolved until 1875 and amended in 1882. This meant that, as Ruskin's wife, Effie was his chattel and all of her property (not that she had much except for those monies which Ruskin's father had settled on her upon their marriage), was his. If he wanted to be rid of her, one of the easiest ways in which to do so was to declare her mad and have her certified. Then Effie and her parents would be unable to contest his decision to have her detained in a lunatic asylum. Ruskin, during their protracted last visit to Venice, had already hinted to Effie's father that she was of unsound mind.

Effie was aware of this. She and her parents were uncommonly frank in their correspondence about almost everything except the fact that Effie's marriage had not been consummated. The mere notion that Ruskin might have her certified was one of Effie's nightmares. Having Effie put into an asylum would have been far less scandalous for Ruskin than a divorce – which was not only extremely time-consuming and expensive, but also had social consequences. On the other hand, had Ruskin succeeded in having Effie confined to a lunatic asylum, he would have been unable either to divorce her or to remarry. But, as was becoming increasingly clear, Ruskin's imagination found no fulfilment either in the nuptial bed or in the marriage market. 'Perhaps for my health,' he wrote to his father, 'it might be better that I should declare at once that I wanted to be a Protestant monk: separate from my wife, and go and live in that hermitage above Sion which I have always rather envied.'[2]

Bearing this in mind, it is understandable that when Millais wrote to Effie's mother suggesting that she would be safer if chaperoned by one of her much younger sisters, Alice, perhaps, or

Sophy, Mrs Gray complied. At the same time, she asked Millais to cease any correspondence with Effie. 'Believe me I will do everything you can desire of me, so keep your mind perfectly at rest,' he replied. 'I should never have written to your daughter had not Ruskin been cognisant to the correspondence, and approving of it, or at least not admitting a care in the matter – If he is such a plotting and scheming fellow, as to take notes secretly to bring against his wife, such a quiet scoundrel ought to be ducked in a mill pond.'[3]

When the Edinburgh lectures ended, Effie went back to Bowerswell with her parents. She stayed for a month, claiming she needed a rest after the strain of acting as hostess for Ruskin in Edinburgh. Remembering Millais' advice, Mrs Gray arranged for her ten-year-old daughter, Sophy, to accompany Effie to Herne Hill on her return from Scotland in December. If, in retrospect, this seems short-sighted on Mrs Gray's part, she was not to tell, then, what disastrous results this would have on little Sophy, an uncommonly sensitive and intelligent child.*

---

* For anyone interested in the subsequent effects of the Ruskins' behaviour towards Sophy Gray, I recommend *The Model Wife* by Suzanne Fagence Cooper (Duckworth, 2010).

11

THE GREAT ESCAPE

The return to Herne Hill in December 1853 was worse than anything even Effie could have foreseen. Hating the house and denied a carriage, Effie found herself virtually a prisoner in the suburbs. Ruskin deliberately avoided her, spending most of his time at his parents' house at Denmark Hill. Effie was grudgingly allowed the use of Mr Ruskin's carriage on Wednesdays to take her into town. She took solace in looking after her little sister, supervising her lessons, twisting her hair in curling papers at night, teaching her the piano. Unwittingly, Sophy provided Effie with precisely what Ruskin had been denied in his childhood, something to love. But even this source of pleasure was spoiled for her. Old Mr and Mrs Ruskin, sensing that Sophy was Effie's Achilles heel, took it into their heads to have the child at Denmark Hill for a considerable time every day. Mrs Ruskin spoiled Sophy with fruit and cake which unfortunately gave the child indigestion. She also required Sophy to give accounts of how Effie spent every minute of her day, and made poisonous insinuations that Effie was mad and would come to no good. Worse still, Ruskin, who was drawn to Sophy, as he was to all pretty, intelligent little girls, hinted to her that if Effie did not mend her ways, he would beat her; that, according to Sophy, 'he is going to begin his harsh treatment . . . as you won't go to Perth and remain there, he is to try what harshness will do to break your spirit . . . He says, you are so wicked that he was warned by all his friends not to have anything to do with you, but that you were so bold and impudent and made such advances to him that you just threw your snares over him in the same way that you had done over Millais, and that you were all the cause of Millais' present unhappiness.'[1] This was indeed extraordinary talk on Ruskin's part, by any standards, to a child of ten. Effie was convinced, and with good reason, that the Ruskins were now deliberately trying to get her into a public scrape so as to be able to get rid of her and have John back at Denmark Hill 'all to themselves'.

Not only was Sophy made to trot between Denmark Hill and Herne Hill, but she was also being sent to Millais' studio in Gower Street, ostensibly for him to draw her portrait, and, at the same time, passing messages between Effie and Millais. Millais did indeed draw Sophy's portrait and it is a stunning sketch of an unexpectedly sharp-faced, determined-looking child, almost frightening in its prophecy of the young woman with a will of iron whom Sophy was to become.

The situation was made more poignant when Millais had delivered a parcel, addressed to both John and Effie, containing a picture he had painted of St Agnes. In Scotland, while Effie had quoted from Scottish ballads and Hyperion legend during the wet and windy nights, Millais had recited poetry. On one occasion, he read Keats's poem *The Eve of St Agnes*:

> *As she had heard old dames full many times declare.*
> *They told her how, upon St Agnes' Eve,*
> *Young virgins might have visions of delight,*
> *And soft adorings from their loves receive*
> *Upon the honey'd middle of the night,*
> *If ceremonies due they did aright;*
> *As supperless to bed they must retire,*
> *And couch supine their beauties lily white;*
> *Nor look behind, nor sideways, but require*
> *Of Heaven upward eyes for all that they desire.*

Of course, Effie had not forgotten Millais' recital of this poem and, being conscious of the meaning of the references within the poem, she knew immediately that Millais was referring without words to her virginal state. St Agnes had been martyred. She had been tied to a stake when Diocletian, that infamous emperor, thrust out his sword and chopped off her head when she, Agnes, was only thirteen. Effie, who had been well educated by the Misses Ainsworth at their school in Stratford-on-Avon, knew that St Agnes was the patron saint of young virgins. Effie also knew that the Eve of St Agnes is commemorated on 21 January and that the snowdrop Millais had painted pinned to her breast was St Agnes's flower and a symbol of virginity.[*]

Ruskin professed to be delighted by the beauty of the painting. Effie interpreted the gift, which was addressed both to herself and her husband, as a private message of love for her from Millais. She was also struck by the resemblance of St Agnes's face to Millais' own 'looking out on the snow with the mouth opened and dying-looking'.[2] It is possible, but unlikely, that the significance of St Agnes did not immediately occur to Ruskin. At all events, when it did dawn on him, he threw consistency to the winds and announced he knew everything that was going on between Effie and Millais. He was as nasty as he knew how and Effie panicked.

To complicate things further, Ruskin was also sitting for Millais for the final touches to his portrait begun at Glenfinlas that summer, which now seemed so far away and long ago. What Ruskin felt during these sessions is difficult to fathom, for he seldom made his feelings known unless it suited him. For Millais, the completion of this masterpiece was an act of torture. The completion of Ruskin's portrait, which took long hours in Gower Street was, Millais wrote to Mrs Gray, 'the most hateful task I ever had to perform'. Through his correspondence with Mrs Gray and

---

[*] St Agnes's Day is 21 January. According to *Aubrey: Miscellany* (p. 136), on St Agnes's night, you take out a row of pins, and pull out every one, one after another. Saying a paternoster, stick a pin in your sleeve, and you will dream of him or her you shall marry. (*Brewer's Dictionary of Phrase and Fable*, Cassell, London, 1895).

the idle observations little Sophy let fall, Millais was perfectly aware of Ruskin's knowledge of the feelings running high between Millais and Effie. Yet Ruskin maintained a cool, unruffled outward appearance, behaving as though nothing had taken place and insisting on treating Millais as the innocent young protégé whom he had originally taken under his wing. Millais, who was the embodiment of convention, was dismayed by Ruskin's proposal for their continuing friendly relations:

> Looking back on myself [Ruskin had written to his father while still in Scotland], I find no change in myself from a boy – I am exactly the same creature – in temper – in likings – in character precisely the same – so is Effie. When we married, I expected to change her – she expected to change me. Neither have succeeded, and both are displeased. When I came down to Scotland with Millais, I expected to do great things for him. I saw he was uneducated, little able to follow out a train of thought – proud and impatient. I thought to make him read Euclid and bring him back a meek and methodical man. I might as well have tried to make a Highland stream read Euclid, or be methodical. He, on the other hand, thought he could make me like Pre-Raphaelitism and Mendelssohn better than Turner and Bellini. But he has given it up now.

It was a good, if partial, summing-up but did nothing to mitigate Millais' discomfort. For his part, it was impossible for him not to be disillusioned about the mentor he so much admired yet had every reason to despise. 'An undeniable giant as an author,' he wrote to Mrs Gray, '[he is] a poor weak creature in everything else, bland, and heartless, and unworthy, with his great talents, of any woman possessing affection, and sensibility.'[3]

Later, he was to say that nothing had ever given him so much difficulty as painting Ruskin's hands. Ruskin was full of admiration. The portrait is arguably the cynosure of all Pre-Raphaelite portraits. The combination of the sharp focus, typical of the Pre-Raphaelite lens, and keen detail in the depiction of rock and waterfall in the landscape combined with the intimacy of Millais' portrayal of Ruskin, is masterly. Certainly, Ruskin appreciated it, with the proviso that Millais had made him squint, although he added that, as he had had to stand on one leg for three hours at a time and staring at the chimney pots of Gower Street through the window of Millais' studio, it was 'no wonder I looked rather uninterested in the world in general'.[4] Old Mr Ruskin was equally impressed. The painting was sent to Denmark Hill where it hung in a prominent position, the latest of the Ruskins' enviable acquisitions.

Millais' unhappiness was further accentuated by the rapid dwindling of his friend Walter Deverell's health. He went to see him as often as he could. The visits were painful. Finding Deverell dying and destitute, confined to bed and neglected by the siblings who had been entrusted to his care, Millais successfully persuaded Holman Hunt to club together with him to buy Deverell's last painting in an attempt to provide him with the necessary invalid nourishment as well as a nurse to care for him. Millais sat by Deverell's bed and read to him, fed him bread and milk and was shocked that Deverell's sister had let the fire go out while she went dancing and that Deverell was 'hanging partly out of his bed, with his hands as cold as ice'.[5] He mentioned Deverell's plight to Ruskin who immediately had chicken and jellies sent round, although Deverell could eat nothing but bread and toast sopped in milk. As it happened, Millais was in the house when Deverell died.

Millais' grief over Deverell's death and his despondency about the emotional morass he had fallen into in his entanglement with Effie, was only compounded by Hunt's eventual departure for the Holy Land on Friday, 13 January 1854. Hunt 'took a cab and made a round of calls on all my friends to say good-bye. The dear old Millais was astonished when I said I was going that night by the mail train.'[6] Millais went back with Hunt to his lodgings and helped him to pack. They went together to the station for Hunt to catch the boat train. Realizing that Hunt hadn't had time to have any supper, Millais 'rushed to the buffet and seized any likely food he could, tossing it after me into the moving carriage. What a leave-taking it was with him in my heart when the train started! Did other men have such a sacred friendship as that we had formed?"[7] For Millais, more disconsolate than ever, this was the last straw.

Matters at Herne Hill had worked up to such a pitch, with Ruskin openly quarrelling with Effie and the atmosphere so poisoned with jealousy, malice and hatred, that Effie became hysterical – which shows in the letters she wrote to her mother. She felt ill and wretched, and developed a nervous tic in her forehead which was so strongly pronounced that she began to refuse invitations to dinner. Even when it seemed as though she was on the verge of a nervous breakdown and that everything she held dear – the image of her marriage – was about to collapse, Effie showed, once again, an extraordinary instinct for survival. She got in touch with the woman whom she admired most in London – Lady Eastlake.

Lady Eastlake, noted by the novelist Thackeray to be famous for her tirades, was indeed a force to be reckoned with. She had grown very fond of Effie during the time the young Ruskins had lived in the small house in Mayfair, which Effie still missed. Now, Effie invited her to tea at Herne Hill and took the plunge of confiding the true state of her marriage to her. Effie could not have chosen a better confidante. Her choice was as brilliant as her earlier decision to go to Venice with Ruskin.

Sweeping all before her with the vast circumference of the silk skirts of her crinoline, Lady Eastlake was the essence of urbanity. She sat stock-still on Effie's sofa, her back upright as always, and listened to Effie's confession with intent concentration. She was shocked by Effie's story, but not for the same reasons that most of her female contemporaries would have been. The daughter and sister of two eminent gynaecologists, Elizabeth Eastlake, though childless herself, was not in the least shocked by Effie's necessary reference to sex. What did shock Lady Eastlake was the lack of it in Effie's marriage, compounded by the lack of love. Here is a prime example of the Victorians' curious attitude towards sex. Subsequent generations have frequently accused the Victorians of hypocrisy, of maintaining double standards. This is simplistic. Like every other generation, they believed in their own sincerity.

On the one hand, certainly in the upper middle-class circles Effie mingled in, the subject of sex was taboo. On the other, a direct result of biblical teaching, was that one of the stipulations of the marriage covenant was to propagate the human race. Deliberate failure to do so was accordingly considered a mortal sin. Thus, Ruskin, whose mother had desired him to be a bishop, was condemned in the eyes of the Church. Most importantly, as Lady Eastlake lost no time in pointing out, the law was on Effie's side. Effie, Lady Eastlake went on, stood every chance of getting an annulment from the husband she had grown to hate and who, according to Effie, now reviled her. Of course, there were obstacles, but these, Lady Eastlake insisted, could be overcome. Effie would have to prove that she was a virgin; would have to submit to the humiliation of gynaecological examinations and, if the annulment went ahead, endure the ensuing publicity which was so evidently abhorrent to Effie. She would also have to prove that she had not consented to a sexless marriage. Lady Eastlake would have a talk with Lord Glenelg,* who had been fond of Effie since her days in Park Street, and ask his advice.

Effie listened to her friend, her mind racing. It was all hateful, but, as Lady Eastlake declared, it was better to end the marriage, which had become thoroughly obnoxious, with the law on her side. Lady Eastlake would see to it that general public opinion would be, too. Distasteful though it would be, Effie must prove that she was a virgin and, by showing Ruskin's ardent letters to

---

* Charles Grant, 2nd Baron Glenelg (1778–1866), was a lively and controversial figure in politics. He left the Tory Party over the Reform Bill issue and joined the Whigs. In 1839, he resigned from Parliament, a renowned Canningite. His resignation only increased the esteem in which he was held within Parliamentary circles.

her before her marriage, prove that before their wedding, there had been no question of their marriage being unconsummated by mutual consent.

A week later, on 7 March 1854, Effie wrote to her father, finally telling him the truth about her marriage:

> I do not think I am John Ruskin's Wife at all – and I entreat you to assist me to get released from the unnatural position in which I stand to Him. To go back to the day of my marriage, the 10th April 1848, I went as you know away to the Highlands. I had never been told the duties of married persons to each other and knew little or nothing about their relations in the closest union on earth. For days John talked about this relation to me but avowed no intention of making me his Wife. He alleged various reasons, Hatred to children, religious motives, a desire to preserve my beauty, and finally this last year told me his true reason (and this to me is as villainous as all the rest), that he had imagined women were quite different to what he saw I was, and that the reason he did not make me his Wife was because he was disgusted with my person the first evening 10th April . . . This last year we spoke about it [the consummation of their marriage] . . . He then said, as I professed quite a dislike to him, that it would be sinful to enter into such a connexion, as if I was not very wicked I was at least insane and the responsibility that I might have children was too great, as I was quite unfit to bring them up. These are some of the facts. You may imagine what I have gone through . . .

Shocked and distressed though Mr and Mrs Gray undoubtedly were by their daughter's revelation, it must have come as a relief. For a long time they had known that Effie's marriage had proved unhappy, that Mr and Mrs Ruskin were unkind to her, and they could not help suspecting, along with their son George, that Ruskin had deliberately tried to compromise Effie, possibly with the intent of either divorcing her or getting her put away in an asylum. Their reaction was staunchly supportive of Effie. Between Mr and Mrs Gray, Lady Eastlake and Effie, a plan for Effie's great escape was hatched.

From now on, Effie was as deliberately unpleasant and distant to Ruskin as she knew how, if only to ensure that he would not suddenly thwart her plans by consummating the marriage they both knew was a sham. Both had begun to hate each other with all the ardour that had previously been lacking in their marriage. Effie told Ruskin that while he and his parents went to Switzerland, she would take Sophy back to Bowerswell and remain there for the interim. Since he was seldom in the house, hardly ever even dining with her because he was with his parents up in Denmark Hill, it was relatively easy for her to make the complicated arrangements for her departure. She was lucky that Crawley, Ruskin's new valet, was sympathetic to her and did not betray her plans. Even so, it is hard to believe that a man of Ruskin's supreme intelligence could have failed to notice what was afoot, especially when, on 10 April, the day of the Ruskins' sixth wedding anniversary, Effie asked him to sign a paper in which she expressed her desire to have the paintings Millais had given her to be declared her own, with Ruskin's approval. She also wished it to be made plain that he should state whether she had any other thing in her possession given to her of which he didn't approve which had been given to her by a third party during their marriage. This was by no means an everyday request. By now, things had become so complicated between the pair that they were playing a game of tacit defiance, dodging each other in a shadowy, dubious light. What he thought she wanted his signature for is open to speculation. Guided by Lady Eastlake, she claimed that 'I (Effie Ruskin) have devised and written this letter to prevent future misunderstandings on this point.'[8] To an extent, this is true. But it is not clear whether Ruskin divined her purpose of leaving him for good, taking her possessions with her. Nevertheless, Ruskin signed the paper, adding a reasonable and objective note to the effect that he agreed to Effie's lawyers' stipulations.

Both the young Ruskins were obsessed by what other people thought of them and were constantly tinkering with their public image. It was important for both of them that they should not be condemned and that the other should be held to blame. In both cases, their view of things was simple and they saw things not in variegated shades but in absolute terms of black and white, never considering that it was possible for two conflicting sides to be true at the same time. Millais, too, set an enormous store by public opinion, was thoroughly conventional, and had an inherent dislike of being seen to border on anything bohemian. Apart from the fact that he and Effie were in love, and in spite of Effie's secret love affair with the dramatic, the perilous position they found themselves in vis-à-vis the mores of society was anathema to both Millais and Effie.

The lengths Effie went to in order to plan her escape were remarkable. Her plotting, cunning and inventiveness were worthy of a great dramatist. She persuaded her parents to take the steamer to London and stay in lodgings at Bury Street, St James's. Her father had wanted to beard old Mr Ruskin, but she dissuaded him, fearing that he might blow the gaffe. On Tuesday morning, 26 April, Ruskin took Effie and Sophy to King's Cross Station, together with Crawley to travel with them as their chaperone, and saw them on to the 9.30 train, the Great Northern, bound for Scotland. If he was puzzled by Effie's vast amounts of luggage, consisting of portmanteaux, trunks, hat boxes and hold-alls consigned to the guard's van, he gave no sign of surprise. Their farewells were constrained. At the last minute, just before the train was ready to depart, he pressed a purse containing Effie's allowance into her hand. That evening, a citation to court in Effie's suit to annul the marriage was served on Ruskin at Denmark Hill.[9]

The train stopped, at ten past ten, at Hitchin. It was a short stop, lasting only two minutes. By pre-arrangement, both Mr and Mrs Gray were waiting at the station. Sophy jumped out and Mrs Gray boarded the train. Effie just had time to give her father a package addressed to Mrs Ruskin containing her house keys, account book, wedding ring and an explanatory letter declaring that she could never return to her husband. The train sped north. It was a long journey for both mother and daughter. Little Sophy and her father went on by boat from the London docks, which was considerably cheaper but considerably less comfortable.

Ruskin may have been oblivious to the fact that Effie had left him for good, but for *tout Londres*, it was an open secret, much gossiped about. Lady Eastlake had persuaded her husband, Sir Charles, to go to John Murray's fashionable bookshop in Albermarle Street, famous not only for its enterprising stock of books but also as a meeting place for eminent men of letters who not only browsed but also broadcast by word of mouth any topical scandal. *Le beau monde*, always in love with tittle-tattle, waited with bated breath to hear the outcome while the gossip spread like wildfire.

Back at Bowerswell, Effie came near to collapse. The relief of having effected her escape was immense; the joy of being liberated from her exile and being back in her childhood home amongst her loving family was overwhelming. Her courage and determination were strengthened beyond measure by constant letters of reassurance from Lady Eastlake, while her father, who, as Writer to the Signet, was acquainted with the intricacies of the law and made every effort to further Effie's case. In spite of all the moral support given by friends and family, Effie became sick and was obliged to spend most of her time in bed or resting in an armchair. The doctor put her illness down to the strain she had been under.

Towards the end of May, Effie travelled by steamer with her father to London Docks. She was badly seasick and arrived at their lodgings in Bury Street exhausted. She was not looking forward to the ordeal of making a deposition to the Ecclesiastical Courts at Bennet's Hill, Upper Thames Street.* She was also obliged to repeat the deposition at St Saviour's, Southwark, since she had been living in Camberwell during her marriage to Ruskin. In her deposition she stated that 'He [Ruskin] used to tell me that he

---

* The Divorce, Probity and Admiralty Court was not created until 1857.

would marry me when I was twenty-five. He had a great dislike to children and he gave that as a reason for abstaining from marrying me ... I was living with him occupying the same bed for near upon a year after I had attained twenty-five years of age but it was the same after that as before.'[10]

Ruskin's solicitors, Rutter and Trotter,* advised him not to appear or to give evidence. He didn't but wrote a statement, which was never used, defending his side of the story. It remained in the solicitors' office for the next seventy years. A copy made by Effie's brother, Sir Albert Gray, is now in the Bodleian Library, Oxford.[11] It is an interesting document and does not differ greatly from Effie's account of their marriage except that in the 'Reasons for the aversion felt by my wife towards me,' he averred that 'though her face was beautiful, her person was not formed to excite passion. On the contrary, there were certain circumstances in her person which completely checked ... she thinks she can effect ... a separation from me, grounded on an accusation of impotence ... I can prove my virility at once, but I do not wish to receive back into my house this woman who has made such a charge against me.'[12] How, exactly, Ruskin proposed to prove his virility in court stretches the imagination as much as it would have stretched that of the jurisprudence. Two things should be borne in mind. First, that no matter how virile Ruskin could have proved himself with another woman, it was, in the eyes of the law, his sexual relations with Effie, and, in this instance, only Effie, that the court could take into account. The second factor is that we have it on Ruskin's authority many years later, namely to Lady Cowper Temple, that he was 'another Rousseau', alluding to his lifelong penchant for masturbation. One of Ruskin's tragedies was that he did not realize the difference between auto-erotic practices and making love to someone else. Perhaps the most benevolent judgement on the sorry

---

* It may be a cliché to observe how comic solicitors' names often are, but in the case of Rutter and Trotter it is irresistible. The name of Ruskin's proctor who represented him at the Ecclesiastical Court was Potts.

business was, of all people, Gladstone's when he remarked: 'Should you ever hear anyone blame Millais, or his wife, or Mr Ruskin, remember that there was no fault: there was misfortune, even tragedy; all three were perfectly blameless.'[13]

For Effie, the worst and most humiliating part of the procedure was her having to be examined by two eminent doctors, Dr Lee and Dr Locock, who was gynaecologist to Queen Victoria. On 30 May 1854, both doctors signed their statement. 'We found that the usual signs of virginity are perfect and that she is naturally and properly formed, and there are no impediments on her part to a proper consummation of the marriage.' At last, on 15 July 1854, after many anxieties on Effie's part, she received the decree of nullity of her marriage to Ruskin on the grounds that she had been proven a virgin, and that 'the said John Ruskin was incapable of consummating the same by reason of incurable impotency', and therefore she had never been truly married to him. This was her 'Order of Release'.

Of course, the scandal, which Effie had dreaded, was the talk of the town. Nothing quite so tantalizing had reached the ears of the small world of London's élite since Byron's escapades with Caroline Lamb or his alleged affair with his half-sister, Augusta. Naturally enough, Millais yearned to be by Effie's side at once. Prudent as always, and with Lady Eastlake's approval, she did not meet Millais again until the following year.

*

They were married at Bowerswell on 3 July 1855, but not in the same room as Effie had been married to Ruskin. This time, her wedding gown was covered by a film of exquisite Venetian lace, a present from Rawdon Brown. Once again her bridesmaids were her sisters Sophy and Alice and their cousin Eliza Jameson, dressed in white, their frocks tied with silken sashes. Most engaged couples, understandably enough, suffer pre-wedding nerves. In this instance, both Effie and Millais were distracted. Unfortunately for him, like his predecessor, he had caught a cold on his wedding day. They were dogged by the worry that, if Ruskin had disdained her body, there might, after all, despite the doctors' reassurance, be something sexually distasteful about her. Millais trembled and wept.* His parents could not attend – the journey was prodigiously long and expensive – but they sent superb floral bouquets which arrived fresh and sweet-smelling. The cake was delicious and the wedding guests brimming with good cheer and sympathy. Effie, now Mrs Millais, left with her new husband by train for their honeymoon in Rothesay, Arran and Brodick. The honeymoon was a success. The following spring, the first of their eight children was born. Profoundly anxious, as always, to appear respectable, Effie, as a notoriously remarried divorcée, behaved as though Ruskin had never existed. If Ruskin could deny her charges of malevolence, she would deny his imputations of her frigidity and lack of wifely obedience. There was a magnificence in the simplicity of her solution. Years later, she did take her revenge when Ruskin fell in love with the young Rose la Touche. Effie answered a letter of enquiry from Mrs la Touche to the effect that this would be the end of Rose. Later still, when her son, John Guille Millais, came to write the biography of his father, there is in those two weighty volumes only the briefest allusion to the fact that Effie had spent what she insisted could have been the best six years of her life married to Ruskin. When Ruskin came to write his own version of his life in what is his best-known masterpiece, *Praeterita*, he omitted Effie altogether. Even if Effie managed to deny him, Ruskin continued to haunt her.

Her loathing of him was a reversal of emotion, for she had once felt affection, some degree of love for him, and had also learned a great deal from him. What she had not realized was that in her revenge, she was excluding herself from the very thing, social acceptability, which she held most dear. When her daughters grew to be young women and were invited to the fashionable

---

* Men wept freely, with no feelings of embarrassment, which does not tally with the prevalent view of the Victorians as being stiff upper-lipped and undemonstrative.

gatherings she still hankered after, Effie was not included.* Millais must have known what a bitter pill this was for her to swallow, but it was not until he was on his deathbed that he arranged through the offices of Queen Victoria's artistic daughter, Princess Louise, for Effie to be invited to a 'Drawing Room at the Palace', where she had first been received as the wife of John Ruskin.

It is an unkind and often repeated verdict that Effie was detrimental to Millais' art. Unkinder still is the glib assumption that if Ruskin had remained married to her, he would have written the equivalent of *Bubbles*, the sentimental but technically brilliant portrait of Millais' grandson blowing a soap bubble. For many years the image of *Bubbles* was used, much to Millais' fury, to advertise Pears soap. Millais never received a penny in royalties.

It is, however, arguable that Ruskin did manage to write his version of *Bubbles* when, in 1866, he wrote *The Ethics of the Dust, Ten Lectures to Little Housewives on the Elements of Crystallization.* What is seldom acknowledged is the extent to which Effie was Millais' muse. She sat for Millais hour after hour, and it was Effie's face which determined Millais' concept of ideal beauty. Her need to make protracted visits to Scotland led to his painting a series of magnificent landscapes of the Highlands. Her ambition urged Millais to become one of the richest and most famous painters of his time. When he died, in 1896, he was President of the Royal Academy he had so long before rebelled against, a baronet and a very rich man. Again and again, Effie's face gazes out from the canvas and informs many of the literary illustrations he accomplished, her eyes half veiled, a testament to her beauty, the muse who inspired two of the most influential men of the nineteenth-century art world.

---

* This ostracizing of women whose relationships with men were in any way tainted was quite usual. Christina Rossetti refused to receive Effie. Even such an enlightened woman as Lady Strachey refused to receive George Eliot, although she would visit George Eliot (a great friend) at her home, North Bank. (Told to the author by Duncan Grant, Lady Strachey's nephew, with thanks to Richard Shone for reminding me.)

12

THE DISSOLUTION OF THE P. R. B.

The P. R. B.

The two Rossettis (brothers they)
And Holman Hunt and John Millais,
With Stephens chivalrous and bland,
And Woolner in a distant land –
In these six men I awestruck see
Embodied the great P. R. B.
D. G. Rossetti offered two
Good pictures to the public view;
Unnumbered ones great John Millais,
And Holman more than I can say.
William Rossetti, calm and solemn,
Cuts his brethren by the column.

CHRISTINA ROSSETTI, 19 September 1853

The P. R. B. is in its decadence:
For Woolner in Australia cooks his chops,
And Hunt is yearning for the land of Cheops;
D. G. Rossetti shuns the vulgar optic;
While William M. Rossetti merely lops
His B's in English disesteemed as Coptic;
Calm Stephens in the twilight smokes his pipe,
But long the dawning of his public day;
And he at last the champion great Millais,

Attaining academic opulence,
Winds up his signature with A. R. A.
So rivers merge in the perpetual sea;
So luscious fruit must fall when over-ripe;
And so the consummated P. R. B.

CHRISTINA ROSSETTI, 10 November 1853

Christina could not have put matters better. As so often, she is witty and somewhat acerbic. But from our vantage point, she becomes misleading: she makes it sound as though the dissolution of the P. R. B. was sudden and decisive. It wasn't. It was a gradual and almost inevitable process. They had banded together as a group of enthusiastic students holding in common pronounced views on art. Now they were maturing, with the exception of Holman Hunt, who clung to his concept of Pre-Raphaelitism throughout his life, refining their earlier attitudes. Part of the reason for disbandment was simply geography. Thomas Woolner had emigrated, for the time being, to join the gold rush in Australia. He, like many other miners, didn't find gold. He returned to England and became a successful sculptor and poet. Holman Hunt had gone to the Holy Land. Collinson's religious leanings became more important to him than painting. Millais' marriage to Effie meant that for a lot of the time he was busy painting up in Scotland and slowly evolving into what he had always been at heart: a thoroughly conventional Englishman who enjoyed hunting, shooting and fishing, a good dinner at the Garrick Club and the company of such friends as Thackeray, 'Blicky' Leech*, Anthony Trollope and Tom Taylor, the playwright and editor of *Punch*. As time went on, he was naturally occupied with his large family. His enormous output of work never faltered, but, looking at his magnificent later

---

* John Leech 1817–64. Prolific illustrator and cartoonist best known for his frequent contributions to *Punch*. He also produced the inimitable *The Comic History of England* in 1843, followed by *The Comic History of Rome* in 1852, in which the ancient Romans are depicted cavorting about in Victorian dress.

landscapes and portraits, and prolific book illustrations, it is hard to believe that once he had been arguably the greatest of the Pre-Raphaelites. Fred Stephens stopped painting altogether and became a discerning art critic. Christina's brother, William Michael, while continuing to earn his living as a tax man, had, by now, become the art critic for *The Spectator*. Her other brother, Gabriel, was as neurotic as he was notorious. He never came to terms with the agony of exhibiting and who, after all, could blame him. Possibly Lizzie Siddal did. Curiously enough, Rossetti, whose name is practically synonymous with Pre-Raphaelitism, was, strictly speaking, not a Pre-Raphaelite at all. The only painting he ever did *en plein air* was the unfinished *Found*. Fundamentally, he was not really interested in being true to nature so much as using aspects of nature to represent what he meant. And generally, what he meant was complicated, profound and intensely literary. The dissolution of the P. R. B didn't mean that the members stopped seeing each other: they maintained a life-long affection for one another. The one exception was the earlier friendship between Millais and Rossetti, which had never recovered from Rossetti's earlier defection to the Free Exhibition.

Back in November 1853, Millais had been elected an Associate Academician of the Royal Academy – the very institution which all the Pre-Raphaelite Brotherhood had attended and revolted from. If this seems a shocking betrayal, his fellow brethren didn't view it as such, but rather as yet another stroke of luck for 'The Child', who had spent most of his life within the academic sanctuary. He was born for it and, in many ways, it was a return to the fold of security which he craved. The occasion, far from being considered a *faux pas*, was an occasion for jollity, which one of the most attractive aspects of the P. R. B. William Michael Rossetti, the indefatigable recorder of his friends' and family's histories, wrote, 'On the day when the result of the election of Associates at the Royal Academy of Arts was to be made known, my brother, self, Wilkie and Charlie Collins all started off to spend a whole day in the country to alleviate our excitement. Hendon was the chosen locality.'[1] Gabriel was wearing a tiepin he had designed in the shape of a wild goose – he had also had a tiepin made for William Michael, resembling a wild duck. Somehow, they stumbled, trying to get out of the way of a wagon and cart horses, and Gabriel's tiepin fell off. They all felt this to be an ominous sign; they were all, in varying degrees, superstitious. They swore and cursed Millais' luck but, at the same time, wished him well. Wilkie Collins insisted that they should retrace their footsteps. There, in the ditch, lay Gabriel's tiepin 'glistening like the Koh-i-noor itself'.[2] All of them went on to the Academy to celebrate Millais' admission. The painter Edwin Landseer greeted them, saying, 'Well, Millais, this time you are in earnest.'[*]

---

[*] 'Earnest' was contemporary slang for homosexual, as in Oscar Wilde's later play, *The Importance of Being Earnest*. Clearly, this did not apply to Millais, despite his deep love for Holman Hunt. Nevertheless, Millais was mistakenly registered as Associate of the Royal Academy as John Earnest Millais instead of John Everett Millais.

13

LIZZIE AND GABRIEL

It was different for the women. They had less choice. Lizzie Siddal couldn't stand Annie Miller. She was jealous and with good reason, for Rossetti continually made advances to Annie and now that Holman Hunt was out of the way in the Holy Land, Rossetti embarked on an intermittent affair with her. But this wasn't the only reason for Lizzie's dislike. As determined, in her own way, as Effie was to maintain her public reputation, Lizzie was anxious not to be cast in the same category as Annie who was loose, wanton and definitely of the lower orders. Lizzie was determined to improve her image, to better herself.

Earlier, there had been an unfortunate episode when Holman Hunt, in one of his clumsier, more boisterous humours, had pretended that he and Lizzie were husband and wife. This, understandably enough, outraged her pretensions to gentility. When, later on, there was a fleeting notion that the Pre-Raphaelites should live together in a commune, Lizzie lost her temper and declared that she would have nothing to do with it if Annie was to be included. It was a sign of Lizzie's deep insecurity, yet she needn't have worried. While Lizzie knew the rungs of the social climbing ladder, Annie had the scantiest of notions of bettering herself, which were in direct proportion to her foul language, lack of soap, hygiene and underwear.

On another occasion, several of the painters decided to spend a few days at Knole, not far from Ewell, where Millais and Hunt had previously spent several months painting. Lizzie and Annie were both invited to join the party. Lizzie refused to go if Annie was going to be there. In the event, Lizzie had the last laugh, however much she was humiliated by Rossetti's brief desertion: the flies were intolerable, it poured with rain, the company bickered, and they returned to London thoroughly disgruntled. This was one of the very few occasions when Rossetti, unlike the rest of the Brotherhood, attempted to paint out of doors. He disliked the discomforts of the country and wasn't prepared to put up with them for the sake of his art.

Lizzie was determined to marry Rossetti who, unfortunately for her, showed no sign of wanting to marry anybody. She had virtually moved into his studio at 14 Chatham Place, in Blackfriars, which he had rented in November 1852. Rossetti's studio in Chatham Place was perfect for him. Overlooking the Thames, it had a balcony, a large drawing room and an even larger studio. The bedroom was poky, but he didn't seem to mind that any more than Lizzie did. They didn't have a kitchen, but that was quite usual in gentlemen's lodgings. It was part of the landlady's duties to prepare suppers. Alternatively, they could send out to the cook shop for ready-cooked meals, fry sausages over the open fire or, more to Lizzie's taste, go out to the newly fashionable restaurants that had opened in the West End.

Most of their acquaintances took them to be lovers. When, earlier, Bell Scott had called on Gabriel unannounced at his previous rooms in Highgate, he had found the couple in irrefutable domestic intimacy: 'I came across them like Adam and Eve in Paradise, only they wasn't naked and he was reading Tennyson.' Naturally, Lizzie felt compromised by Bell Scott's intrusion. It was enough to ruin her reputation, particularly since Gabriel failed to introduce her – he was probably feeling flummoxed by the situation they had been caught out in, and Lizzie fled, humiliated and angry.

Lizzie was beginning to feel old. She was only twenty-five, but in those days, when people married very young, she considered she was already on the shelf. She was also instantly recognizable as the model for Millais' hugely popular *Ophelia*. If Gabriel didn't marry her, it was highly unlikely that anybody else would. It has to be said that Lizzie showed no signs of proving an ideal Victorian wife. She wasn't in the least bit domesticated, she never cooked or did any housework, and whenever Gabriel was ill, she was such a bad nurse that he would go and stay with his mother or friends in the country. Lizzie began to take refuge in increasing amounts of laudanum, a mixture of alcohol and opium, then as readily available, with no prescription required, as aspirin is today. The tension between them became as highly strung as a snare set for a weasel. They loved each other, but not enough to stop tormenting each other. Lizzie had never been robust, was alarmingly thin and now her health failed, her malady mysterious. It seemed that whenever Gabriel had to leave her to fulfil a commission elsewhere, Lizzie would have an attack, or spasm, or not be able to eat until his return. There is little doubt that these episodes were directly linked to her morphine habit. Neither Lizzie nor Gabriel could make each other happy, yet they were inextricably bound together. Gabriel, who needed Lizzie as his muse as much as she needed him, grew increasingly anxious.

> *She never told her love,*
> *But let concealment, like a worm i'the bud,*
> *Feed on her damask cheek.*
> *She pin'd in thought,*
> *And with a green and yellow melancholy*
> *She sat like Patience on a monument,*
> *Smiling at grief.*

Viola in *Twelfth Night*, Act 2, Scene 4, WILLIAM SHAKESPEARE

> *Prithee, why so pale, fond lover,*
> *Prithee, why so pale?*
> *If, when looking well won't move her,*
> *Shall looking ill prevail?*

SIR JOHN SUCKLING

At that time, there was a curiously morbid notion that the invalid was a romantic figure; that melancholy was both alluring and erotic. This was partly a result of the earlier wave of Romantic poets such as John Keats, Percy Bysshe Shelley, Samuel Taylor Coleridge, and partly a veneer to make appealing the alarmingly high rate of ill health particularly noticeable amongst middle-class women, the very category to which Lizzie aspired. This is not to say that women of the lower classes did not suffer equally – they probably suffered more than their better-off sisters – but they could not afford to indulge their infirmities. They disguised their profound fear of the workhouse and anaesthetized their physical distress with gin or, like Lizzie, laudanum.

Such notions as illness being romantic were too far removed from the hideous reality for the poor to entertain. Not so amongst the middle and upper classes. They were arguably fortunate enough to veil their very real illnesses (often, for women, involving unenviable complications arising from their sex: menstruation frequently left them prostrate; childbirth often resulted in death), quite apart from other incurable diseases then rife, such as tuberculosis, cholera and myriad fevers. These women needed to be seen to be attractive even while ailing. So it came about that the image of a woman reclining on a sofa,* pale and languid, was perceived to be attractive.

Lizzie was certainly of this persuasion. When Ruskin's friend, Dr Acland, declared that he could find nothing organically wrong with Lizzie, she became frantic. It would be too simple to say that she was merely a hypochondriac. She may have been to some extent. She certainly did suffer agonies. They were never successfully diagnosed, possibly because she didn't want them to be. She might have wished to preserve what she considered to be a romantic mystery about her, and was probably a victim of how illness, if it was not contagious, was viewed in her day. That she was a well-known model, not received by her lover's family, cannot

---

* It is indicative of the attitude then prevalent that a sofa was often referred to as a 'sick couch'.

have helped but only contributed to her sense of not belonging and her feeling of unease and uncertainty regarding her future.

*

In April 1853, Rossetti's close friend Ford Madox Brown finally married his second wife, Emma Hill, with whom he had been living openly and with whom he had had a child three years earlier. Emma was a working-class girl, uneducated, with no pretensions to gentility; she was a farm girl whose mother, Catherine, had been a friend of Lizzie's mother. Robust and unabashedly sexy, Emma was stunning and inspired much of Brown's greatest work. With her 'pink complexion, regular features and a fine abundance of beautiful yellow hair, the tint of harvest corn',[1] her face is familiar through Brown's best-known paintings: *Work*, *The Last of England*, and the ironically titled *The Pretty Baa-Lambs*. She had very short, sharp, even teeth like a field mouse.

Brown hadn't married Emma earlier because, although he undoubtedly loved her, he didn't consider her a suitable stepmother for his elder daughter Lucy, who remained in the care of a respectable aunt. It's more than likely that Emma and Lizzie had known each other in childhood. They swiftly became intimate: shopping, gossiping and being girls together. Apart from having moved into the world of artistic bohemia, becoming muses and models to painters of note, they shared a dependency on drink and, in Lizzie's case, drugs. Emma hadn't yet become an alcoholic, but she was frequently too tipsy to cope with the demands of daily life. Later, her stepdaughter Lucy* said that Lizzie was as given to drink as Emma, her penchant for alcohol only disguised by her addiction to laudanum.

Rossetti and Lizzie frequently visited the Madox Browns, who then lived in Finchley. More often than not, they ended up

---

* Lucy Madox Brown later married William Michael Rossetti, thus becoming Gabriel's sister-in-law, although it can't be claimed that either of them ever had much in common.

spending the night, sometimes several nights, unexpectedly. This wasn't as unusual as it might sound, for it was then the norm for people to stay overnight, especially in the country, in cases of bad weather. But Finchley wasn't the country and Gabriel and Lizzie's frequent abuse of the Madox Browns' hospitality became a sore point with 'Bruno', as Rossetti nicknamed Ford Madox Brown, who was generosity itself, but was continually strapped for cash. Rossetti was always borrowing money from him and seldom returned it. To make matters worse, Rossetti was growing paranoid about the friendship between the two women, fearing that Emma was a bad influence and wanted to cause trouble between himself and Lizzie. In response, Emma was often hostile towards Rossetti. Moreover, Madox Brown wanted to get on with his painting and the prolonged presence of Lizzie and Rossetti, who had usually only been invited to dinner, got in his way. Nevertheless, their friendship survived. It was impossible to remain angry with Rossetti for long, even knowing that the situation would occur again. His charm and humour were irresistible. Nor were Lizzie or Emma prepared to give up their intimacy. In any case, Madox Brown was not only generous but tolerant by nature.

*

LISTENING

She listened like a cushat dove
That listens to its mate alone;
She listened like a cushat dove
That loves but only one.
Not fair as men would reckon fair
Nor noble as they count the line:
Only as graceful as a bough,
And tendrils of the vine:
Only as noble as sweet Eve
Your ancestress and mine.
And downcast were her dovelike eyes

And downcast was her cheek
Her pulses fluttered like a dove
To hear him speak.

CHRISTINA ROSSETTI

By 1854, Lizzie's health had deteriorated so much that Gabriel sought the advice of three women, all remarkable and all sympathetic to Lizzie's plight. They were the painter and illustrator Anna Mary Howitt;* the artist, feminist and philanthropist Barbara Leigh Smith, later Bodichon;† and her friend, the talented amateur painter, Bessie Rayner Parkes.‡ Anna Mary was keen that Lizzie should be seen by Dr Garth Wilkinson, who diagnosed her as having a curvature of the spine. A painful condition, it can, if severe, be dangerous. Her newfound friends suggested that she should go to Hastings where they found her suitable lodgings. Barbara also reassured Lizzie that she herself would be staying at her house in the country near Hastings, Scalands Gate, with Bessie and Anna Mary so that Lizzie would not be lonely. They urged Gabriel to accompany Lizzie.

Gabriel could not go. His father was dying. By now, old Gabriele Rossetti was blind and suffering all the indignities of a wretched old age. His son Gabriel wasn't much support to him, a fact he later regretted, but he used his father's imminent death as an excuse not to visit Lizzie down at Hastings. Gabriel wasn't as unfeeling as this makes him out to be. He was genuinely absorbed in his work, as all great artists must be; infuriated and frightened by Lizzie's persistent demands, he wanted to be left alone as well as to comfort his family.

---

* Anna Mary Howitt (1824–84) attended Sass's Art School in 1846, where her fellow students included Rossetti, Holman Hunt and Woolner.

† Barbara Leigh Smith, later Bodichon (1827–91).

‡ Bessie Rayner Parkes (1829–1925) was a poet, essayist and prominent feminist and campaigner for women's rights. She married Louis Belloc and was the mother of Hilaire Belloc.

Gabriele died on 26 April 1854. Almost immediately after the funeral, Barbara Leigh Smith wrote to Gabriel from Hastings, asking him to come down to be with Lizzie, who was apparently very unwell. Gabriel went.

Barbara Leigh Smith, the illegitimate daughter of the MP Benjamin Leigh Smith and a milliner, Anne Longden, was an exceptionally prepossessing woman. Despite her abundant golden hair, she wasn't obviously beautiful either by Pre-Raphaelite or conventional mid-Victorian ideals. Barbara was handsome, with strong features which betrayed her independent, energetically humane spirit. Her father was a fierce believer in the equality of the sexes and it may have been for this reason that he never married Barbara's mother, Anne. Anne died when Barbara was seven and, most unusually for those days, her father brought her up on equal terms with her brothers. Barbara shared her father's views on rights for women and, on a walking holiday with her friends in Germany, shortened her skirts, discarded her corsets, wore stout boots and blue-tinted spectacles.

> *Oh! Isn't it jolly*
> *To cast away folly*
> *And cut all one's clothes a peg shorter*
> *(A good many pegs)*
> *And rejoice in one's legs*
> *Like a free-minded Albion's daughter.*

Best remembered for her important contribution to women's suffrage, and as a founder of Girton College, Cambridge, Barbara was fun, original and good company. Like Rossetti, she had been a pupil of Holman Hunt's and played a significant role in the lives of the Pre-Raphaelites. Both Lizzie and Gabriel were fortunate to be amongst her friends.

Barbara had found Lizzie lodgings at 5 High Street, Hastings, though Gabriel didn't consider Lizzie to be any weaker than she usually was. Fortunately, the landlady, Mrs Elphick, was an understanding woman and after a couple of days, she didn't object at all to Gabriel moving into a room next to Lizzie's, or seem to think it unusual that he should go, quite openly, into Lizzie's chamber and spend hours reading aloud to her, and, with the poker, stir up the fire he insisted on. Gabriel's arrival had a marvellous effect on Lizzie's condition. Quite soon, she was well enough to go out walking with him on the sands, breathing in the sea air. She was even strong enough to walk on the Downs, in spite of the strong winds. Twice, they managed to go as far as Scalands to see Barbara, Mary and Bessie, who all made a tremendous pet of Lizzie. Lizzie posed for Barbara, Anna Mary Howitt and Gabriel, who painted her with irises in her hair. The conversation was lively, the food delicious and the atmosphere thoroughly sympathetic. Together, Lizzie and Gabriel spent an idyllic time. In hindsight, it appears to have been one of the happiest times they spent together.

Then Gabriel decided to return to London. He was running out of money and he hadn't been doing any serious work. Lizzie had a sudden relapse. Gabriel stayed on. Lizzie made a remarkably quick recovery, which she generally did when Gabriel remained with her. It seems more than possible that her relapse was brought on by a rational fear that if Gabriel returned to London to paint, he would also dally with Annie Miller.

It has often been debated whether Lizzie and Gabriel were physical lovers before their marriage. Jan Marsh makes a good case in her admirable book, *Dante Gabriel Rossetti: Painter and Poet*, that they were not. However, no matter how plausible Marsh's case, I am not convinced by her argument any more than were Rossetti's friends and relations at the time. While it is true that the word 'lovers' was used to describe an intimacy not necessarily physical, and that the expression 'making love' might be interpreted as nothing more than flirtation, Rossetti's physical lust was as rapacious as that of his imagination. It is difficult to believe that he and Lizzie had not consummated their passion in the small bedroom at Chatham Place, his London lodgings where she often stayed. That she should spend the night unchaperoned in an unmarried man's rooms was something which would have been considered scandalous and would have seriously ruined her reputation. The question of their physical intimacy, then, can never be established for certain. I suspect that they did share possibly unsatisfactory sexual relations which might well partially explain their tortured need of each other. Diana Holman-Hunt, granddaughter of Holman Hunt, claimed that Lizzie had become pregnant and possibly had an abortion, which is why she went to Hastings to convalesce.* Contraception, never infallible, has always been available in one form or another, certainly since the times of the ancient Egyptians. By the mid-nineteenth century, douching, pessaries and an elementary form of condom were widely used as well as a variety of herbal remedies. Jumping up and down, energetic exercise and, for those who could, a fast gallop on horseback, all followed by the hottest of baths and a quantity of gin were also held, with some reason, to terminate a pregnancy should the contraceptive have failed. By this time, English laws against abortion had toughened.† If Lizzie did procure one, she had every reason to keep quiet about it.

*

---

* When the late Diana Holman-Hunt first told me this, I believed her. On reflection, I find her statement as debatable as that of Jan Marsh. Family anecdotes abound. Just because they are repeated doesn't make them necessarily true.

† It wasn't until the thirteenth century that Church teaching, upheld by the law, held abortion acceptable before the quickening (when the foetus stirs within the womb), approximately between sixteen to seventeen weeks after conception. It was believed that with the quickening, the soul entered the foetus and it was therefore one of God's children, after which it could not be aborted. In 1803, the Ellenborough's Act was passed which ruled that an abortion procured after quickening would incur the death penalty. In 1837, the Ellenborough's Act was amended with the result that no distinction was made between before and after quickening, so that that all abortion became illegal, carrying the same penalty. Later still, in 1861, self-abortion carried the penalty of life-imprisonment. Naturally, these prohibitive laws resulted in illegal abortions which had previously been carried out within the law.

'Rossetti says Ruskin is a sneak and loves him, Rossetti, because he is one too and Monroe because he is one too and Hunt he half likes because he is a sneak, but hates Woolner because he is manly and straight forward and me because I am too. He adored Millais because he was the prince of sneaks, but Millais was too much so for he sneaked away his wife and so he is obliged to hate for too much of his favourite quality.'[2]

After the annulment of his marriage in 1854, Ruskin, understandably bored and at a loose end, got in touch with Gabriel and Lizzie. By now, despite Rossetti's disinclination to exhibit his work, he had gained a considerable reputation through private sales, although these transactions hadn't yet made him the wealthy man he was to become. Even so, Rossetti had a wonderful ability to dispose of any money he ever made almost before he had time to bank a cheque. He was constantly in debt, particularly to his old friend and mentor Ford Madox Brown. Ruskin was emerging from his shell, not altogether with the happiest results, and wanted to mingle with the new, fashionable set of young painters, apparently unaware that the Brotherhood had disbanded. One of Ruskin's most endearing characteristics is that, even at his lowest ebb, he found not only therapy but also positive pleasure in involving himself with the needs and advancement of others. Clearly this tallied with his own perception of himself as a successor to Pygmalion, but also and more convincingly, as a philanthropist and, one of the rarest of breeds, a genuine teacher.

Lizzie, with Gabriel's encouragement, had taken up painting. Gabriel let her use his brushes and paints, which weren't cheap. He was pleased that she had found an interest and delighted when she showed talent. Her talent was very real, but not so remarkable as he came to believe. He made a charming pen-and-ink and wash sketch of her drawing him at Chatham Place, which betrays the undeniable intimacy between them. She had, too, begun to write poetry, mainly in the form of border ballads. They are beguiling, but it's unlikely that they would be much read now if it wasn't for the legend that history has made of her life. Whatever the merits of Lizzie's painting and poetry, they not only betray a genuine sensitivity to language and art, but also strengthened her bond with Gabriel, whose ruling passion both these disciplines were.

In 1855, Rossetti showed Lizzie's paintings and illustrations to Ruskin, who was ecstatic. 'About a week ago,' Rossetti wrote to Allingham, 'Ruskin saw and bought on the spot every scrap of designs hitherto produced by Miss Siddal. He declared they were far better than mine, or almost anyone else's, and seemed quite wild with delight at getting them.' Ruskin bought Lizzie's entire work for £30 and was 'going to have them splendidly mounted and bound together in gold, and no doubt this will be a real opening for her, as it is already a great assistance and encouragement'.[3]

For a girl of obscure background, to be taken up by the giant art critic of the day was a stroke of good fortune beyond anything Lizzie had ever dreamed of. She probably never would have thought of painting had it not been for Rossetti's influence, let alone have been brought to Ruskin's attention, and it was a triumph for Lizzie. Moreover, when she and Ruskin eventually met, he took to her at once. He was captivated by her strange, almost unearthly beauty, her frailty, her vulnerability. All the qualities which exhausted Rossetti and drove him frantic appealed to Ruskin.

It was not merely Lizzie and her painting which attracted Ruskin. Like many lonely people, he was drawn towards the pair of lovers whom he assumed to be happier and more blessed than was actually the case. He wanted to be part of them. The only way he could achieve this was by being their patron, directing their way forward to even greater prosperity. He offered Lizzie an income of £150 a year on the understanding that he would have first refusal of all her paintings. It was a staggering sum for a completely unknown young female painter. At the same time, Ruskin came to an agreement with Rossetti that he would buy Rossetti's work, so long as he liked it, for a desirable sum.

Probably the kindest thing Ruskin did for Rossetti was to

persuade him to become a teacher at the Working Men's College. This institution, the earliest of its kind in Europe, was established by philanthropic Christian Socialists in 1857 with the aim of providing an education, both liberal and useful, to workmen who had received scant teaching, if any at all. They could not afford it and had often begun working during childhood. It was also partly a response to the Chartist Movement. If working men could be educated, it was felt that not only would they benefit, but they would also be less likely to be a revolutionary threat. The guiding light of the college was F. D. Maurice, a profoundly influential Christian Socialist, very much ahead of his time in his practical attitude to the needs of the poor. Of course, like all controversial thinkers and reformers, he had his critics. Aubrey de Vere* said that listening to him was like eating pea soup with a fork. Jane Carlyle complained that he gave her 'mental cramp! he keeps one always with his wire-drawings and paradoxes as if one were dancing on the points of one's toes (spiritually speaking) – And then he will help the kettle and never fails to pour it all over the milk pot and sugar bason[sic]!' Even Ruskin, who was a great admirer of Maurice, said that he was 'by nature puzzle-headed and indeed wrong-headed'. Perhaps the most illuminating remark about him is that of his wife, who said, 'Whenever he woke in the night he was always praying.' He figures, together with Carlyle, in Ford Madox Brown's remarkable painting, *Work*.†

---

* Aubrey de Vere (1814–1902) was an Irish poet noted for his mingling of Celtic verse with resonant echoes of Greek lyrics and also for his remarkable contribution to the revival of early Irish literature. In this respect, he had much in common with William Allingham, and later was understandably revered by W. B. Yeats.

† *Work* (1852–65), by Ford Madox Brown, is an epic painting ahead of its time of Irish navvies digging up the road to put in drains. A typical Victorian street scene full of bustling life, it depicts a group of grand ladies, street sellers and beggars all mingling together, while F. D. Maurice and Carlyle, whose book *Past and Present* very much influenced Brown, look on philosophically at the 'progress' in process.

In spite of, or possibly because of, Maurice's complex nature, the Working Men's College was an immediate success and remains so to this day. It was then situated in Rossetti's old haunt in Red Lion Square. The classes were held in the evening; Rossetti taught on Mondays. The teachers worked on a voluntary basis, which did them good, released their energies and made them popular in quarters where previously they had not expected a following. Ruskin was an enthusiastic teacher. He spent hours collecting twigs, catkins when in season, feathers and pebbles for his mature students to draw in painstaking likeness, denying them the use of colour, except for Prussian blue, and analysing their work with minute attention to detail. Rossetti's methods could not have clashed more heavily. It's possible that he kept in mind his own experience as a student of Ford Madox Brown (who could have taught him a great deal, if only Gabriel had been more diligent). Diligence was never one of Gabriel's strong points, and he had grown recalcitrant when Brown required him to make studies of old jam jars, bottles and decanters.

When Gabriel saw that the men's work was almost entirely executed in Prussian blue, he was appalled. Without further ado, he confiscated all the pieces of blue pigment Ruskin had donated to the school from the cupboard where they were kept and threw them away. When Ruskin discovered what Gabriel had done, he couldn't help but burst out laughing. While Ruskin commanded respect, classes with Rossetti were generally considered to be much more fun. Rossetti gave his students licence to use coloured pigments, paint bold brush strokes – as opposed to Ruskin's minute marks made in pencil, and to splash out in scarlet, gamboge, cobalt blue and viridian green. Gabriel's charm was irresistible, his sense of colour and evident devotion to his art so out of the ordinary that his workmen students became devoted to him.

Ruskin, with his engrained habit of wanting to change his protégés, took to calling Lizzie 'Ida' after Tennyson's princess. Shortly after their first meeting, Ruskin invited Lizzie, together with Gabriel, to spend the day at Denmark Hill. Gabriel had been there before. For Lizzie, it was an awe-inspiring experience, but she was determined not to show her nerves or to be daunted by the old Ruskins' pretensions to social superiority. What she hadn't banked on was the tedium of the occasion. She was obliged to submit to being shown watercolour after watercolour of rock and waterfall, fossils in glass cases, globes, precious books and missals. She behaved beautifully. The old couple fell under her spell and deplored the fact that she was so thin and delicate. They did not even criticize her unconventional dress. Lizzie disdained the fashionable crinoline, now generally *de rigeur*, and had adopted, instead, a mode of dress which later became known as 'aesthetic'. To her contemporaries, it might have seemed as though she went about in her night shift. Her day dresses were plain, cut with a high, round neck, belted loosely at the waist, and fell in soft pleats. The sleeves were long. Her favoured colours were sage green, grey and russet. They suited her. She made most of her clothes herself. She disdained frills and furbelows and other fashionable fripperies. Out of doors, she wore a long shawl; being tall, she carried it off well. Occasionally, she wore a locket, but otherwise very little jewellery; she probably didn't have very much. Her abundant hair was gathered loosely at the nape of her neck with a snood. When she was alone with Gabriel at Chatham Place, she often wore it completely loose, not only because he preferred to paint her that way, but also as an expression of her intimacy with him.

Rossetti was obsessed by female hair. When the novelist Elizabeth Gaskell met him on a visit to London, she liked him immediately and found him easy to talk to: 'always excepting the times when ladies with beautiful hair came in when he was like the cat that turned into a lady who jumped out of bed and ran after a mouse. It did not signify what we were talking about or how agreeable I was; if a particular kind of reddish brown, crepe wavy hair came in, he was away in a moment struggling for an introduction to the owner of said head of hair. He is not as mad as a March hare, but hair-mad.'[3] Lizzie's eccentric dress was emphasized by her extreme thinness. Quite when she adopted this style is unclear. It's doubtful that Mrs Tozer, back in the milliner's shop where Lizzie had worked in Cranbourne Alley, would have tolerated such outlandishness. It's more likely that, having met the Pre-Raphaelites through Walter Deverell, she was influenced by the clothes they pictured in their paintings; yet another instance of how life mirrors art as well as vice versa.

The day after Lizzie's visit to Denmark Hill, Ruskin arrived at Chatham Place with a small parcel addressed to Lizzie from his mother. It contained ivory dust. Extremely expensive, ivory dust was considered a sovereign tonic and had to be prepared very much in the manner of calf's-foot jelly, simmered for at least eight hours until it jelled when cooled on ice from the fishmonger's, after which it was reheated with sugar and brandy, sherry and the juice of lemons, which were expensive and were added to make it palatable. Then it had to be strained at least twice through the finest muslin and allowed to cool again in small pots or moulds. Lizzie, who was thoroughly undomesticated, had no idea how to prepare it. Instead, she and Gabriel took the precious packet up to Finchley, where Lizzie persuaded Emma Madox Brown to make it up for her. Mrs Ruskin was unaware of what a palaver the ivory dust would cause; it was a token of her esteem for Lizzie, although it is more likely than not that Ruskin had chivvied her into making such an atypically extravagant gesture. That Mrs Ruskin should make such a gesture, even if under her son's suggestion, is also evidence of Lizzie's ability to charm when she chose to do so.

None of Rossetti's friends could fully comprehend his attitude to Lizzie, his 'darling Guggums'. Ford Madox Brown wrote in his diary on 10 March 1855: 'She is a stunner and no mistake. Rossetti once told me that, when he first saw her, he felt his destiny was defined. Why does he not marry her?' On another occasion, Brown put the question directly to Rossetti who replied, somewhat unconvincingly, that he hadn't the money to buy the licence. With typical generosity, Brown proffered £10. Rossetti promptly spent it on something else.

Ruskin, who for the time being had become inextricably bound up with the vicissitudes of his new protégés, couldn't understand Rossetti's reluctance to marry Lizzie either. It was clear to everyone who knew Lizzie that as well as suffering from recurrent ill health, she was miserable and longed for Gabriel to marry her. What his friends failed to connect was Gabriel's enthusiasm combined with his consequent panic. Gabriel was obsessed by Lizzie. He loved her and was inspired by her. His names of endearment for her were variously The Sid, The Dove, Gug and Guggums. He drew and painted her repeatedly. As Ford Madox Brown noted on 7 October 1854: 'Called on Dante Rossetti saw Miss Siddal looking thinner & more deathlike & more beautiful & more ragged than ever, a real artist, a woman without parallel [sic] for many a long year. Gabriel . . . drawing wonderful & lovely Guggums one after an other each one a fresh charm each one stamped with immortality.' While he affected a nonchalance about what other people might think of him, the very thought of the public made Gabriel sick. He couldn't bring himself to exhibit. Later, the critics' opinion of his published verse was to result in his having a severe nervous breakdown. Rossetti's neurosis, which later developed into severe paranoia, should never be underestimated.

He, as well as Lizzie, suffered agonies. Lizzie's continual ill health, together with the demands this entailed, made him hesitate to commit himself to her. Any commitment was anathema to Gabriel. He preferred to keep Lizzie to himself, away from his family and any society acquaintance he frequented. Like most of the things he treasured most, he wanted his relationship with Lizzie to remain private. Even so, he must have been impressed by the Ruskins' reception of her, for, shortly afterwards, he arranged for Lizzie to be introduced to his mother.

Now that Ruskin was paying her a handsome allowance, Lizzie could afford to buy her own paints. Rossetti arranged for Ford Madox Brown to take her to Roberson's paint shop behind the British Museum and help her choose her paints. He couldn't go himself since he was in debt to them. After buying the paints, she was to go to tea with his mother, taking Brown with her, which was a diplomatic move, since Mrs Rossetti was fond of him. Rossetti joined them soon after their arrival. The tea party was a dismal affair, painful and embarrassing for Lizzie. Everybody began to wish it had never been thought of. Lizzie knew that, with their devout piety, Mrs Rossetti and her two daughters, Maria and Christina, disapproved of her relationship with Rossetti. She sat haughty and affronted, saying nothing. It was a great relief when finally Gabriel rose to take Lizzie back to Chatham Place.

Ruskin was perfectly genuine in his admiration of Lizzie. He particularly admired her painting, *The Witch*. Like Ford Madox Brown, he couldn't understand why Rossetti didn't marry her. Once, he wrote about the matter directly to Rossetti, asking him if it was lack of funds that prevented him. Rossetti didn't reply.

'The plain hard fact,' Ruskin wrote to Lizzie on her protest against continuing to receive his allowance, 'is that I think you have genius; that I don't think there is much genius in the world; and I want to keep what there is, in it, heaven having, I suppose, enough for all its need. Utterly irrespective of Rossetti's feelings or my own, I should simply do what I do, if I could, as I should try to save a beautiful tree from being cut down, or a bit of Gothic cathedral whose strength was failing. If you would be so good as to consider yourself as a piece of wood or Gothic for a few months, I should be grateful to you.'

It's not clear how much Lizzie relished the notion of being a bit of chopped-up wood, but she needed Ruskin's patronage if she was going to succeed in a profession which was almost entirely dominated by men. He was also concerned about her poor health and persuaded her to go to Oxford to see Dr Henry Acland, whom he had known since his days as a student at the university. She went with her sister Clara and they took lodgings in town. The visit was not a success. Mrs Acland, who had gone to a great deal of trouble to entertain Lizzie as befitted a friend of Ruskin's, was offended by her haughty manner and Lizzie wasn't impressed by Dr Acland's diagnosis. He couldn't find anything wrong with her that a few months wintering abroad wouldn't cure. If he suspected what large amounts of laudanum she was taking, he didn't mention it.

From Oxford, Lizzie and Clara went to Clevedon, a pretty seaside town on the Somerset coast which recently had become popular. Nearby was the beautiful, fourteenth-century manor house, Clevedon Court, which had been the girlhood home of Thackeray's close friend, Jane Octavia Brookfield (née Elton). Jane was a cousin of Arthur Hallam, who died tragically young and was immortalized in Tennyson's poem *In Memoriam*, and who had been a constant visitor there. Lizzie and Clara both liked the glamour and grandeur of Clevedon, and when they were joined by Rossetti, he and Lizzie spent one of the happiest times in their often turbulent relationship. They strolled on the sands and Lizzie started sketching.

She would use her sketches for the background of her small landscape painting *Sir Patrick Spens* or *The Ladies' Lament*, showing the ladies in the ballad by Sir Walter Scott clustered on the shore, waiting for the ship which would never come. Gabriel and Lizzie went on donkey rides and were amused when the donkey boy, startled by her unusual red hair and general appearance, asked her if there were any elephants in the exotic lands he supposed she came from. They were happy and enjoyed going out in a boat and admiring the beauty of the unspoiled coastline.

Ruskin was alarmed when, on their return to London, Lizzie spoke about going to Paris. He didn't think it suitable, especially in her semi-invalid condition, and advocated the south of France and, specifically, Switzerland. There could be no question of her travelling alone, ill and unchaperoned. Ruskin was keen for Rossetti to stay in London and get on with his painting during Lizzie's absence. Then Rossetti confounded him by producing a relation, a Mrs Kincaid, respectable and matronly, who seemed pleased to be asked to go as Lizzie's companion. The two women, with a great deal of luggage, took the steamer for Le Havre. Ruskin grumbled. He had managed to land himself with the two most ungrateful protégés in existence. 'Tell Ida she is to go South immediately . . .

Paris will kill her or ruin her, Like Sir Dean Paul's bank.* I cannot have you going to Paris or near Ida at all until you have finished Miss Heaton's drawing.'

After six weeks of gadding about in Paris, Lizzie was obliged to write to Gabriel and beg him to come, bringing her some more money. She had spent all she had been lent. Ruskin was pragmatic. 'They will have more debts than they say; people are always afraid to say all at once.' He insisted she went south before winter set in.

Gabriel arrived on 2 November 1856, having travelled with his friend Alexander Munro, and found Lizzie looking well. Paris evidently suited her. She had bought a good many fashionable clothes, preferring the crinoline to her previous, lank Pre-Raphaelite dresses. There was the National Exhibition to see and all sorts of marvels to admire. Lizzie was having a lovely time. Finally, on 12 November, Gabriel and Munro saw Lizzie and Mrs Kincaid on to the train to Nice.

They stayed at the Hôtel des Princes and at first all went well. Lizzie wrote an amusing letter to Rossetti, describing the infernal procedure of picking up the post and showing one's passport to didactic petits Napoleons:

> On your leaving the boat, your passport is taken from you to the Police Station, and there taken charge of till you leave Nice. If a letter is sent to you containing money, the letter is detained at the Post-Office, and another written to you by the postmaster ordering you to present yourself and passport for his inspection. You have then to go to the Police Station and beg the loan of your passport for half-an-hour, and are again looked upon as a felon of the first order before passport is returned to you. Looking very much like a transport, you make your way to the Post Office and there present yourself before a grating, which makes the man behind it look like an overdone mutton-chop sticking to a gridiron. On asking for a

---

* A bank which failed spectacularly in 1855, when the directors were tried, convicted and imprisoned for embezzling customers' money.

letter containing money Mutton-chop sees at once that you are a murderer, and makes up its mind not to let you off alive; and, treating you as Cain and Alice Gray* in one, demands your passport. After glaring at this and your face (which by this time has become scarlet, and is taken at once as a token of guilt), a book is pushed through the bars of the gridiron, and you are expected to sign your death warrant by writing something which does not answer to the writing on the passport. Meanwhile Mutton-chop has been looking as much like doom as overdone mutton can look, and fizzing in French, not one word of which is understood by Alice Gray. But now come the rewards of merit. Mutton sees at once that no two people living and at large could write so badly as the writing on the passport and that in the book; so takes me for Alice, but gives me the money, and wonders whether I shall be let off from hard labour the next time I am taken, on account of my thinness. When you enter Police Station to return the passport, you are glared at through wooden bars with marked surprise at not returning in company of two cocked-hats, and your fainting look is put down to you having been found out in something. They are forced, however, to content themselves by expecting to have a job in a day or so. This is really what one has to put up with, and it is not at all comic when one is ill. I will write again when boil is better, or tell you about any lodgings if we are able to get any.

She finished by saying they had eaten an English Christmas dinner 'ending with plum-pudding, which was really very good indeed, and an honour to the country. I dined in my room,' she ended ominously, 'where I have dined for the last three days on account of bores. First class, one can get to the end of the world, but one can never be alone or left at rest.' Lizzie's honeymoon with Mrs Kincaid had worn thin and Lizzie wanted to come home.

---

* In 1707, Alice Gray was convicted of assisting in the rape of a ten-year-old girl. Cain, according to the Old Testament, had murdered his brother Abel.

14

THE SECOND GENERATION

THE REVIVAL OF THE P.R.B. AND THE DECLINE OF LIZZIE SIDDAL

Back in London, Gabriel was amusing himself with Annie Miller and a new stunner, an actress who was currently holding London in thrall, Ruth Herbert. He had also met two new interesting young men who had turned up to the Working Men's Club and had been introduced to him by Vernon Lushington.* Their names were William Morris, known as 'Topsy' and Edward Burne-Jones, known as 'Ned'. They were comical enough to look at: Topsy was rotund with frizzy black curls; Ned was thin and lanky. While Morris was solid and emphatic, Ned had a 'certain skittishness or flapdoodlery of demeanour'.[1] But if their appearance was absurd, their intentions were deeply serious.

They came from very different backgrounds. Ned had been brought up in Birmingham, the only child of a penniless picture framer who eked out a frugal existence in one of the back streets

---

* Vernon Lushington (1832–1932) was a determined Positivist, a Deputy Judge General and Second Secretary to the Admiralty. He was closely associated with the Pre-Raphaelites. Influenced by F. D. Maurice, he joined the Working Men's College as a singing teacher and lecturer in art appreciation. He was a close friend of the Stillmans and of Leslie Stephen and his family, with whom he often stayed at Talland House in St Ives, Cornwall, where they spent the summers. Stephen's daughter, Virginia Woolf, later based the character of Mrs Dalloway on Lushington's daughter, Kitty.

of Birmingham. His mother had died in childbirth. Ned got a scholarship to the local grammar school and matriculated with distinction. In 1852, when Ned was eighteen, one of his school friends, Henry Macdonald, took him home to tea. Ned fell in love with the entire Macdonald family. The four Macdonald sisters were spirited, clever and attractive, but it was Georgie, as they called her, who made Ned decidedly her own. She was tiny, with a fastidious mind and indomitable will. She was also extremely pretty, with violet eyes and auburn hair. Georgie was only twelve years old when her brother brought Ned home. Georgie's father, a Methodist minister, had instilled in her the habit of practising Christian principles in daily life. It was a habit which never left her. In 1856, when Georgie was just fifteen, she and Ned became engaged. They knew it would be a long engagement, for neither of them had a penny and it didn't seem likely that Ned would earn much.

Ned Burne-Jones then got a scholarship to Oxford with the intention of joining the Church (Georgie hoped he would become a bishop). Very soon he met William Morris, whom he instantly nicknamed Topsy. Morris had inherited a sizable fortune and entertained clerical ambitions too. They both harboured illusions about High Church observances, but the Oxford Movement was over: they were twenty years too late. If all university students intending to become bishops had succeeded, there would have been a distinct lack of sees in the British Isles. At once, Ned and Topsy recognized they were kindred, if very different spirits. Their favourite reading matter was Tennyson's *Morte d'Arthur*, Ruskin's *The Stones of Venice*, Kenelm Digby's *The Broad Stone of Honour*,* the

---

* *The Broad Stone of Honour: Or, True Sense and Practice of Chivalry* by Kenelm Digby, first published in 1822, was a popular and influential work on chivalry, drawing most of its examples from medieval accounts. Digby was concerned to restore a sense of gallantry and chivalry to modern life. His definition of chivalry was that 'it is only a name for that general spirit or state of mind which disposes men to heroic action and keeps them conversant with all that is beautiful and sublime in the intellectual and moral world'. It is easy to understand how this

works of de la Motte Fouqué, and the vastly popular novel *The Heir of Redclyffe* by Charlotte M. Yonge, as well as the works of Keats and Shakespeare.

Inspired by Ruskin, Morris took Ned on holiday to look at the cathedrals of Normandy. Ned wrote to Georgie daily, illustrating his letters with absurd line drawing of his doings. By now, the Macdonald family had moved from Birmingham to London. Georgie was determined to be an accomplished wife, educating herself as best she could, attending drawing classes at the Schools of London. Instinctively, she adopted a way of dressing which suited her tiny figure, her frocks cut simply, with high necks, full sleeves and gathered at the waist. They were mainly of sage green or dark blue and, like Lizzie in the early days, she made them herself.

Returning by way of Le Havre, Ned and Morris walked on the shore and, intoxicated by the Gothic spires they thought so lovely, abandoned all notion of the Church and vowed to dedicate themselves to art. As far as they were concerned, the man of the moment was Rossetti, who still had all the glamour of a star, and it became their goal to meet him.

It was a meeting of immense consequence. Privately, Rossetti thought his own glamour, like his hair, had worn thin, though nothing would induce him to admit it. The Pre-Raphaelites, as such, had fizzled out. By 1856 Millais was spending most of his time up in Scotland; Hunt, since discovering that Rossetti had been philandering with Annie while he had been in the Middle East painting a goat, had cooled towards him; Collinson, after breaking Christina's heart and their engagement, had become an ardent Roman Catholic and had vanished from the scene.[*]

---

concept would appeal to the Pre-Raphaelites. Charlotte M. Yonge was also influenced by Kenelm Digby. In *The Heir of Redclyffe*, said to be the most popular reading by soldiers in the Crimean War as well as much admired by the Pre-Raphaelites, the local railway station for Guy Morville's ancestral home, Redclyffe, is called Broadstone.

[*]   On seeing Collinson in the street some time after their engagement had been

Woolner had returned from Australia without any gold, but was now living with Francis Palgrave* and finding some success as a sculptor. He had largely abandoned Pre-Raphaelitism in favour of neo-classicism. To be suddenly hailed and hero-worshipped by two much younger men was an unexpected stimulant and had the effect of galvanizing Rossetti to action.

Lizzie's return from her sojourn in France was a disappointment. She was no better than she had been when she had set out. If anything, her health seemed worse. Whatever the nature of Lizzie's malaise, which remained mysterious, it was exacerbated by her addiction to laudanum, which she took in increasingly large doses. There is no evidence that she tried to abstain from it, which, given the widespread use of the drug at that time, is scarcely surprising. If she did try, she certainly didn't succeed. Her excessive abuse of it almost certainly contributed to the depression she fell into on her return to England. The one bright spot was the friendship that sprang up between her and the young Georgie Macdonald.

Everybody liked Georgie. It would be difficult not to, for she was refreshingly young, intelligent, pretty without being a stunner, and so clearly in love with Ned Burne-Jones. Morris swiftly became her devoted champion. Rossetti liked her and was relieved that Lizzie made friends with her, for Lizzie, whose health was rapidly declining, didn't make friends easily and was prone to be jealous of younger women. It was probably Georgie's attachment to Ned that precluded Lizzie's jealousy, although she may have been envious that Georgie was engaged to be married while she was not.

Around that time, Ford Madox Brown had asked Gabriel directly why he didn't marry Lizzie. For people who had known Gabriel for so long, it seemed inexplicable. Lizzie was ill. Lizzie

broken off, Christina, outwardly so self-contained, was so shaken that she fell down in a dead faint on the pavement.

* Francis Palgrave (1824–97) is best known as editor of the anthology *The Golden Treasury of English Songs and Lyrics* (1861).

was aging and losing her looks. Lizzie was miserable. She needed him. Yet those very people who had known Gabriel for so long hadn't really understood him. He didn't want to get married to anyone. As already mentioned, when Brown asked him why not, in a perfectly friendly way, Gabriel replied half jokingly that it was for lack of tin, as he called it, and that he couldn't afford a marriage licence. Brown immediately proffered a hard-earned ten shillings. Rossetti spent it on something else, and Lizzie got to hear of it (probably Emma had told her). Lizzie was mortified and enraged. She got hold of her sister Clara and they fled to Bath.

The sisters took rooms in a lodging house in Orange Grove, a terrace of charming eighteenth-century houses, and spent most of their time taking the waters. Any medicinal value they might have had on Lizzie was negated by her continued use of laudanum. She probably didn't realize quite how debilitating a drug it was. It was legal, widely available, frequently used by people in all walks of life, and regarded as a panacea for any ailment imaginable, even as an acceptable sleeping draught for babies. By December, Lizzie was too ill to do anything but lie in bed feeling wretched. Rossetti went down to see her. As usual, the sight of Gabriel had a remarkable effect and, swiftly, she began to recover. They came back to London at Christmas 1854. Lizzie took rooms in Hampstead, which had the advantage, for her, of being close to the Madox Browns.

*

IN AN ARTIST'S STUDIO

One face looks out from all his canvases,
One selfsame figure sits or walks or leans:
We found her hidden just behind the screens,
That mirror gave her back all her loveliness.
A queen in opal or in ruby dress,
A nameless girl in freshest summer-greens,
A saint, an angel – every canvas means
The same one meaning, neither more nor less.

He feeds upon her face by day and night,
And she with kind true eyes looks back on him,
Fair as the noon and joyful as the light:
Not wan with waiting, not with sorrow dim;
Not as she is, but was when hope shone bright;
Not as she is, but as she fills his dream.

CHRISTINA ROSSETTI, 24 December 1854

During Lizzie's absence in France, Ruskin and Rossetti had both been heavily engaged in involving themselves with a forthcoming exhibition, opening the following May at a small but reputable gallery in Fitzroy Square, one of London's most beautiful squares where, coincidentally, Lady Eastlake lived with her husband, Sir Charles, at Number 7. Between Rossetti and Ruskin, they succeeded in getting several of Lizzie's paintings to be exhibited, which was no small feat when one considers that most female painters, whatever their merits, were almost automatically excluded from that predominately masculine world. While she had been away, Rossetti and Ruskin had also managed to include some of Lizzie's paintings in a small exhibition in Charlotte Street. Hunt inadvertently enraged Rossetti by saying that if he hadn't known they were by Lizzie, he would have thought they were by Walter Deverell. Hunt meant this as a compliment, but Rossetti was incensed and declared that they were infinitely better than anything by Deverell. This was absurd. Lizzie's paintings were clearly sincere attempts, but, like her verse, they were derivative, and obviously inspired by Rossetti. That is not to say that her paintings are no good. They were evidence of her sensitivity to colour and form, just as her ballads were testimony to her feeling for words and rhythm even if the execution lacked authority.

It was a triumph for Lizzie that one of her best-known paintings, *Clerk Saunders*, was included amongst the exhibits.* It was

---

* *Clerk Saunders* is one of Lizzie's finer paintings (1857), now in the Fitzwilliam Museum, Cambridge.

bought by that most endearing American from Boston, Charles Eliot Norton.* *Clerk Saunders*, like many of Lizzie's paintings, is inspired by a border ballad and was first made available in published form in 1802 in the Border Minstrelsy. It is the story of Clerk Saunders and May Margaret who fell in love and were discovered in one another's arms by her seven ferocious brothers, who killed him. An hour before the day of his burial, the ghost of Clerk Saunders stood at May Margaret's window. She wants him to kiss her, but he knows that if he does, she will die. She follows him into the forest and longs to lie buried with him.

> *There's nae room at my head, Marg'ret,*
> *There's nae room at my feet;*
> *My bed it is full lowly now,*
> *Amang the hungry worms I sleep.*

If she plaits a wand of birch and lays it on his breast and sheds a tear upon his grave, then his soul will rest in peace. He bids her to marry another man, but never to love him so well as she did Clerk Saunders.

> *Her lover vanish'd in the air,*
> *And she gaed weeping away.*

Lizzie's painting of Clerk Saunders shows his ghost entering her room with supplicating arms reaching out towards her.

Most people would have thought that this taste of success would have gone to Lizzie's head, to spin her into a Dervish whirl of high spirits. Far from it: she fell into a deep depression and suddenly told Ruskin that she would have no more of his money. Rossetti was baffled; Ruskin was appalled. Neither of them had understood the nature of Lizzie's dependence on laudanum and

---

* Charles Eliot Norton (1827–1908) was an American Bostonian writer, archaeologist and influential art critic, much travelled in Europe. He became a friend of Elizabeth Gaskell, Thackeray's daughters Anny and Minny, and Leslie Stephen and the Pre-Raphaelites. Like Rossetti, Norton also translated *La Vita Nuova*.

how badly it affected her health. It is also possible that Lizzie was drinking as heavily as she was doping herself.

'The only feeling I have about the matter is some shame at having allowed the arrangement between us to end as it did,' Ruskin wrote to Rossetti about Lizzie's refusal to continue to accept his allowance, 'and the chief pleasure I could have about it now would be by her simply accepting it as she would have accepted a glass of water when she was thirsty, and never thinking of it any more.'

While her self-confidence had increased, Lizzie had become simultaneously disillusioned about her relationship with Gabriel. She went with her sister to the spa town of Matlock in Derbyshire, where they spent a fortnight taking the waters and sightseeing. When her sister returned to London, Lizzie decided to go to Sheffield, where she stayed with distant cousins, the Ibbits. They took a great liking to her and, through friends of theirs, Lizzie attended classes at Sheffield Art School where she was taught by Young Mitchell.* Mitchell was a remarkable teacher and very much interested by Ruskin and Rossetti. He bore an uncommon physical resemblance to Rossetti, having intensely dark eyes, a dark complexion and the same high cheekbones.

Mitchell and Lizzie forged a close friendship and Lizzie quite often stayed on after class, talking about the men she knew so intimately and whom Young Mitchell so greatly admired.

Lizzie's time in Sheffield was her one bid for independence. It seemed, certainly for the moment, that she had freed herself from the influence of Rossetti and Ruskin and was at last beginning to be her own mistress. Coincidentally, her health improved while she was at Sheffield.

Rossetti, meanwhile, had embarked with his new young friends on an exciting project at Oxford. For some time, plans to decorate

---

* Young Mitchell (1811–65) was painted by Louis Victor Lavoine in 1833 (Collection Sheffield Galleries & Museums Trust).

the recently built debating hall at the Oxford union had been in the wind and now, through Ruskin's influence, they went ahead. Given the impetus of Ned and Topsy, Rossetti gathered together some other like-minded young artists – Val Prinsep,* Arthur Hughes,† Spencer Stanhope‡ among them – and whisked them all off to Oxford where they would paint frescos inspired by Arthurian legends. Val and Spencer Stanhope could only manage to come down after the others had already arrived. At the station, Val summoned a cab. The union was so recently built that the cabbie took them, in all good faith, to the Oxford Workhouse instead. They all had a glorious and unforgettable time, mingling paint and larks in equal measure, the scheme only marred by their utter lack of knowledge about the technique of painting murals. The university agreed to house and feed them and to pay for their paints. Later, the bursar was astounded by the bill they had run up for soda water. Scholars, used to almost monastic quiet, studying in solitary rooms, had been startled by the constant popping of bottles, to say nothing of the noise and laughter. The bursar might have considered himself lucky that the pops belonged to bottles containing nothing more innocuous than soda water. 'What fun we had! What jokes! What roars of laughter!' Val Prinsep recalled many years later.

At the theatre one evening, the group of painters were bowled

---

* Val Prinsep (1838–1904), the son of Thoby and Sarah (née Pattle) Prinsep, was born in Calcutta and lived with his parents at Little Holland House where he was a pupil of G. F. Watts. In 1884 he married Florence, the daughter of the wealthy shipping magnate and patron of the Pre-Raphaelites, F. R. Leylands.

† Arthur Hughes, R.A. (1832–1915), is best remembered for his paintings of *Ophelia*, *The Eve of St Agnes* and *April Love*. He also illustrated George MacDonald's *At the Back of the North Wind*, *The Princess and the Goblin* and Christina Rossetti's anthology *Sing-Song*.

‡ John Roddam Spencer Stanhope (1829–1908) was a painter of the Pre-Raphaelite school. He was a pupil of G. F. Watts and a prolific artist. He was also the uncle of the painter Evelyn Pickering who married the ceramicist William de Morgan.

over by the beauty of a young girl sitting with her sister in the stalls. The daughter of a local saddler, her name was Jane Burden and she was a stunner. She had a mass of very dark, crinkly hair, her nose was slightly tilted, her dark eyes enormous, and her neck sublimely long. They were wild to meet her and lost no time in doing so. Her voice was low and burry with the soft accent of Oxfordshire. Topsy and Gabriel in particular were smitten by her extraordinary looks and neither of them particularly cared what she said. Having completed his mural of Sir Lancelot's vision of the Sangrael, Gabriel painted her as Guinevere while Ned struggled on with *The Death of Merlin*, which turned out disastrously. While at Oxford, Ned decided to grow a beard which straggled down his chin for the rest of his days. As he was growing it, he wrote to Georgie that it was 'like the outside of the inside of a musical box'.[2]

Morris was having difficulty trying to execute his painting *How Sir Palomydes loved La Belle Iseult with exceeding great love out of measure, and how she loved not him again but rather Sir Tristram*. His difficulties were scarcely surprising; he was almost totally inexperienced and had only attempted his first oil painting a few months previously. Besides which, none of them found it easy painting enormous figures while perched precariously on ladders, their paints being handed up to them on demand by Oxford workmen roped in to help.

Nevertheless, it was scarcely kind to ridicule his attempts, such as *Sudden Indisposition of Sir Tristram in the Garden of King Mark's Palace, recognisable as Collywobbles by the pile of gooseberry skins beside him, remains of unripe gooseberries devoured by him while he was waiting for Yseult*. It may not have been kind, but there was something about Morris, who was nothing if not serious, which was impossible not to laugh at. He ordered the ironmonger to make him suits of armour, ostensibly to help his painting be accurate, and tried on the helmet, which got stuck. His friends would hardly have been human if they had not been reduced to howls of laughter at the sight of him jumping up and down in a frenzy, incarcerated in his visor, as though he had got imprisoned in a cheese grater. Spattered in paint, it seemed to his friends that he used more on himself than on the murals. He had a habit of sticking his thumb into the paint, exclaiming with glee, 'Mine, mine, all mine!' They found him deliciously funny. Fortunately for Morris, he finished his mural in good time and then discovered an enormous pleasure in designing patterns for the borders on the ceiling.

At the same time, they worked immensely hard, starting at eight in the morning (Gabriel making a habit of stripping the sheets from the comatose Ned and Topsy) and carried on till dusk with only a short break for a lunch of bread and cheese eaten in situ. To ensure an even source of light, they whitewashed the windows, which Gabriel then decorated with curlicue cartoons of his favourite wombats. 'All kinds of quaint beasts and birds,' Ned recollected later, peeped out from the leaves and branches they had swiftly painted in on the temporarily obscured windows. Being young and full of high spirits, their work was punctuated by frequent bursts of laughter, jokes and japes being the order of the day.

Gabriel, of course, flirted with Janey Burden while he painted her as Queen Guinevere. If she was bewildered to find herself the centre of attention in a world entirely foreign to her, she appeared to enjoy it as much as she seemed to like Gabriel's attentions. Morris suffered. But given his exceptionally honourable nature, he suffered in silence and did his best not to show it. Even so, everyone knew that Gabriel was as good as engaged to Lizzie and even with his licentious reputation, a holiday fling with Janey Burden was as far as he could go.

In November, the news came from Matlock that Lizzie was seriously ill. During her absence she and Gabriel had corresponded and it seems clear that, reading between the lines, she had grown alarmed by the threat of the new eighteen-year-old stunner they were all so keen on in Oxford. She knew Gabriel only too well and even if he implied that Janey belonged to Topsy, she guessed, and rightly so, that this wouldn't prevent Gabriel from making advances to her. Jealousy apart, Lizzie wasn't crying wolf; she really was in a very bad way.

The years of laudanum addiction were taking their toll. Emaciated, wretchedly weak, unable to eat without being sick, she lay bedridden in the spa, living only for the increasingly frequent doses of the laudanum she was dependent on. Rossetti felt impelled to go to her. It meant abandoning the project in Oxford he found so rejuvenating, as well as Janey, to be with Lizzie. Without Rossetti's stimulation, the others ground to a halt. The frescos were finally finished by William Rivière.* When Coventry Patmore saw them that year, he was transported by their 'voluptuous radiance' and compared their brilliant colouring to a highly illuminated medieval manuscript.[3] Unfortunately, despite, or because of, their exuberance, none of the painters had bothered to research the best method of priming the plaster or how best to mix the tempera they used. If they had asked advice from Ford Madox Brown or G. F. Watts, both experienced mural painters and well known to them, they would have received sound practical advice. It didn't help that, as the building had been only recently built, the plaster hadn't thoroughly dried out. Within a few months, the glorious colours had faded and, for a long time, only their ghosts remained.[†]

Lizzie was so weak that it was out of the question for her to travel to London. There was no telling how long it might take her to recover sufficiently to make the journey. Gabriel, in need of money, had embarked on translating Dante as well as concentrating on his own poetry. He was soon going to be thirty and, having dissipated much of his youth, he was now determined to make his

---

* William Rivière (1806–76) was a drawing master at Cheltenham and later an art teacher at Oxford.

† They were not restored until 1986. Every conceivable effort was made by the Landmark Trust, the West of England Restoration Studios and Cambell Smith & Co., but although the restoration resulted in a vast improvement, it is no longer possible to recover all the short-lived brilliance described by Coventry Patmore.

mark. For the next few months, he travelled up to Matlock whenever he could and did his best to make Lizzie's sorry condition more comfortable. The journey was both expensive and time-consuming. Gabriel became increasingly frustrated, particularly since there didn't seem to be anything he could do to effect a fundamental change.

*

Gabriel had been instrumental in finding rooms for Ned and Topsy in Red Lion Square. They were the same rooms he had briefly shared with Walter Deverell years before, when they had been young, ambitious and rebellious students. The rooms hadn't changed. It was a delightful existence, the two men hard at work; Ned painting, Morris designing furniture and making drawings of armour, the two of them amusing themselves and everyone else. 'Red Lion Mary', an extraordinary character, cooked, cleaned and generally looked after them. Short, squat and cheerful, good tempered and with an intelligence all her own, she entered into the spirit of things, embroidered designs by Morris, read aloud extracts from the newspaper to Ned while he was painting, laughed at their jokes and was quite capable of turning the tables and playing pranks on them. Morris had asked her to set his watch right so he could catch the train to Oxford. Red Lion Mary, who had been put out by his quick temper, got her own back and set his watch an hour early, which meant that he had to seethe with impatience at Paddington until the train came in.

After they returned from painting the murals at Oxford, Ned fell ill. His constitution was never strong, but this time his friends, and Georgie in particular, were seriously concerned. Georgie and her family were now living in Marylebone. It would have broken all the rules of propriety for Georgie to have nursed him, much though she wanted to. Coming from a family of Dissenters, poor, proud, and socially insecure, Georgie was a stickler for observing the conventions she could not afford to ignore. Instead, Val Prinsep, who had become friendly with Ned while painting the murals in Oxford, came to the rescue. Val was strikingly tall, sophisticated, charming and wealthy. Years later, when George du Maurier was writing *Trilby*, he based the character of Taffy on Val. His mother, Sarah Prinsep, was one of the seven beautiful Pattle sisters. Born in Calcutta, of mixed French, English and Bengali descent, they had taken London by storm when they had arrived from India over twenty years earlier. After her husband's retirement from a distinguished career in the administration of India,* Sarah Prinsep set up as a London society hostess. The three most remarkable of the Pattle sisters were Sarah, Virginia (who was the most beautiful and became the Countess Somers), and Julia Margaret Cameron, who became famous as a pioneer photographer. These three were nicknamed 'Beauty', 'Dash' and 'Talent', although it was a fourth sister, Sophia, later Lady Dalrymple, with whom Ned became briefly infatuated. So striking, original and such a law unto itself was the atmosphere the sisters created that it became known as 'Pattledom'.

Sarah turned her lifestyle into an art. Little Holland House, under Sarah's aegis, was a veritable Palace of Art. It made an indelible impression on Ned. The artist G. F. Watts made his home with the Prinseps and most of Sarah's flow of guests came from the *haute bohème* of London society: Tennyson, Richard Monkton Milnes, Thackeray, Carlyle, Dicky Doyle, Frederic Leighton, the opera singer Adelaide Sartoris and her sister, the actress Fanny Kemble among them. For the first time Ned appreciated that an artistic environment could also be luxurious and sophisticated, and was determined that he and Georgie should belong to these privileged circles. South Kensington was then a countrified district with hawthorn and cherry trees growing in the lanes that connected it to Fulham and to Kensington proper.

---

* A specialist in Oriental languages, Thoby Prinsep was very much in favour of the British administration of India being carried out in the native tongue. Lord Macaulay overruled him. It is interesting to speculate how Anglo-Indian relations might have developed differently had Prinsep carried the day.

Little Holland House was a spacious old farmhouse on Lord Holland's estate on the site which is now Melbury Road. The grounds were spacious, with lawns spreading out beneath a large cedar tree. Here, Sarah gave afternoon parties, her guests enjoying champagne and strawberries and cream as well as scintillating conversation. Inside, Sarah had decorated the house in a style which was then most unusual. The walls were painted Venetian red and bottle-green, the furniture was black lacquer with gold inlay and many of the objects and curios had been brought back from India. Watts had painted murals in the great drawing room (technically much superior to those Ned and his friends had painted so recently under Rossetti's direction at Oxford). There was about the place the aura of an enchanted kingdom. 'There, for the first time,' wrote Georgie many years later, 'he [Ned] found himself surrounded without any effort of his own by beauty in ordinary life, and no day passed without waking some admiration or enthusiasm. He had never gone short of love and loving care, but for visible beauty he had been starved all his life.'[4] For the young Ned Burne-Jones, convalescing in luxury, restored by chicken consommé served from a silver saucepan and by beauty and stimulating company, it was the first step in his lifelong ascent up the golden stairs to his idea of heaven: a celestial choir of upper-class stunners.

Initially, Georgie was wary of this glamorous world, but she realized what it meant to Ned, and she wanted to be included in it after their marriage. This didn't prevent her from being nervous when Sarah Prinsep and her sister Virginia, the Countess Somers, paid a call on her at her parents' house in Marylebone, clearly to see if she lived up to their very high standards. It can't have been pleasant to have undergone the inspection of these two remarkably beautiful, eccentric and arrogant women, but Georgie stuck her ground, passed their test and eventually grew fond of them. She made many friends, notably Rosalind Howard, among their circle. Rosalind, who was married to the delightful aristocratic amateur painter, George Howard, was a woman noted for her sense of purpose. She was to become a feminist and to be active in the temperance movement.

*

The summer of 1858 has gone down in history as The Great Stink. Since the dawn of the Industrial Revolution, the population of London had grown rapidly. Sewage, which had previously been disposed of in basement cesspits before being emptied by night soil men into the river Thames, was now directly thrown into the river. Flush lavatories,* which were growing increasingly popular, used much more water than the old-fashioned chamber pots. That year was extraordinarily hot and the river began to dry up, the current becoming stagnant. London became 'a Stygian pool, reeking with ineffable and unbearable horror', according to Lord Palmerston. The stench was so bad that Parliament, right on the river, closed down. There was an outbreak of cholera. Those who could, fled to the country.

The nature of the contagion of cholera was misunderstood, and it was widely held to be spread by miasma or bad air. John Snow† had discovered that germs were carried by water, but his theory was not generally held. There were even some people who seriously believed in homunculi‡, germs which resembled tiny men

---

* The flush lavatory was invented as early as 1596 by John Harington but did not come into general use until the mid nineteenth century. Even in the mid twentieth century, privies were commonplace, as were chamber pots, especially in country districts. They exist to this day in certain remote areas and possibly in more accessible ones.

† John Snow (1813–58) wrote *On the Inhalation of the Vapour of Ether* in 1847 and *On Chloroform and Other Anaesthetics, & their Action & Administration*, which was published posthumously in 1858. He is widely held to have been the first to notice that germs, particularly those of cholera, were largely carried by contaminated water. In 1853, and again in 1857, he administered chloroform to Queen Victoria when she gave birth to Prince Leopold and Princess Beatrice respectively, thus popularizing the use of anaesthetics by the general public.

‡ According to Paracelsus, the homunculus could be reproduced artificially and possessed magical insight and powers.

in top hats, carrying walking sticks, who, though wingless, miraculously managed to fly through the bad air down people's throats and infect them. What hadn't struck any of the doctors, with the exception of the perceptive Miss Nightingale (who, though remarkable, was never a doctor), was that although germs, homunculi or not, were carried by water, they could also be deterred by water with the adjunct of a disinfectant such as carbolic soap derived from coal tar.

It was not surprising, then, that so many of the Pre-Raphaelites became ill. Lizzie was still ailing at Matlock, Ned was convalescing in the comforts and beauty of Little Holland House, while Emma Madox Brown, whose baby, Arthur, had died earlier in the year, was seriously ill in Hampstead. It was a wretched state of affairs for Madox Brown since, as usual, he was broke and could scarcely afford the medicine required for Emma. Georgie came to the rescue. She went to see them and was shocked by their plight. She offered to look after Emma's eldest son, Oliver, an enchanting three-year-old boy, and carried him off to her parents' house in Marylebone, where she much enjoyed his company.

The stink was so bad at Chatham Place, which directly overlooked the river, that Rossetti was obliged to move to alternative lodgings in Bloomsbury – the same rooms he had earlier shared in Red Lion Square with Walter Deverell. The disgusting smell made people want to vomit, but the fear of cholera was very real. Luckily, before the epidemic became rampant, the heatwave was over, the rains fell and the river filled up. The danger had become so great that the Government was forced to take the matter seriously, install a new and remarkable sewage system, and eventually, in 1877, build the Embankment, which made the riverside less picturesque, but helped to make conditions considerably more sanitary.

Where Lizzie was during this time remains a mystery. There is no mention of her in any of Gabriel's letters, in Ford Madox Brown's diary, or in William Michael Rossetti's chronicles of the Pre-Raphaelites up to 1860. It's doubtful that, without Ruskin's allowance, she could have afforded to remain at the spa at Matlock. She may have gone back to her relatives in Sheffield, but it's more likely that she crawled back to her parents in Southwark and stayed there quietly until, in 1860, she became so ill that she summoned Gabriel back into her life. It is also possible that she remained in correspondence with Emma Madox Brown, but if so, none of these letters have survived. If Lizzie had been corresponding with Emma, she would have known of Rossetti's renewed philandering with Annie Miller and of his ardour for Janey Burden. With the advantages of hindsight, it would appear that Madox Brown's eldest daughter Lucy instigated a large bonfire of her stepmother's letters, ashamed of Emma's alcoholism and Lizzie's dependence on drink and drugs, as well as being keen to preserve their whitewashed reputations for posterity.

*

Gabriel had introduced Ned Burne-Jones to Ruskin in 1856. When Red Lion Mary let Ruskin in the first time he came to call, she announced him as 'your father', for the physical resemblance between them was so striking. They took an instant liking to one another and Ruskin was much impressed by Ned's abilities. Ned was ambitious, and it wouldn't be going too far to say that he was on the make. Like Ruskin, he had every faith in his own talent, was understandably anxious to succeed in his career, and, above all, wanted to make enough money in order to marry Georgie. Ruskin persuaded him to become a teacher at the Working Men's College, and although it didn't bring in any money, it enhanced Ned's reputation. Through Ruskin he also took up designing stained-glass windows, a difficult proposition, but one at which he turned out to be exceptionally skilled and, mercifully, it earned him some money. The other thing Ruskin, eternal champion of the Pre-Raphaelites, effected was an introduction to Thomas Plint of Leeds, a rich industrialist who was prepared to invest money in this new generation of painters now rapidly becoming fashionable. Plint, like many of his contemporaries, was a commercial philanthropist who wished to invest in art if only to show that he didn't worship Mammon. He couldn't afford old masters, which were seldom on the market, but he could, and did, buy up what was then considered as being bold and original modern art. Very importantly, to these impoverished painters, he paid in advance and he paid in cash.

In 1859, the Corps of Artist Volunteers was formed. At the time, the English were in a panic, fearing that they were about to be invaded by the French after Napoleon III's appropriation of Nice and the Savoy. Burne-Jones, Morris, Rossetti, Millais, Watts, Frederic Leighton and Ford Madox Brown all joined up. They meant well but turned the corps into a farce. When the order 'Eyes right!' was barked out, Rossetti looked bewildered and asked why. Morris was inherently clumsy and kept turning round in the wrong direction, bumping into his fellow volunteers. Leighton tumbled off his horse.

15

WEDDINGS IN THE WIND

The nature of the somewhat raffish lifestyle of this younger group of Pre-Raphaelites changed when Morris married Janey Burden in the spring of 1859. They were married with the minimum of fuss in Oxford. They honeymooned in Bruges and Paris. It must have been a strange new world for Janey, who had hardly ever been out of Oxford. With Morris's inheritance (his father had wisely invested in the copper mines of Devon), he had no financial problems to delay his marriage. Janey had no hesitations in accepting his proposal. Given his wealth and adoration, together with the fact that she came from a penniless and humble background, her acceptance is scarcely surprising. She was nothing if not pragmatic. Morris, swept away by his own tempestuous emotions, didn't realize that Janey wasn't in love with him. Many years later, Janey felt no shame in telling him so. For her, marriage was indeed a market, and by marrying Morris she was doing very well for herself. Morris moved out of Red Lion Square and set up a temporary residence with Janey in Great Ormond Street until his ideal home, his earthly Paradise, Red House, could be completed. It was designed by the architect Philip Webb according to Morris's instructions, and was in the unspoiled countryside of Kent, near Bexley Heath.

*

Nothing could have been more different from Morris's marriage to Janey than Gabriel's to Lizzie. After a long absence without any explanation, she returned to his orbit, again desperately ill, again at her old lodgings run by Mrs Elphick at Hastings. He rushed down. He was in a horrible state of mixed emotions. Lizzie looked ghastly, emaciated and pale. She appeared to be dying. Gabriel's old fervour for her returned, from a sense of pity compounded by guilt, but it was not exactly romantic love and he knew it. In spite of himself, he retained a sense of chivalry and honour. These may have been rekindled by his recent association with Ned and, in particular, with Morris. No one was more imbued with these notions than William Morris. Gabriel begged Lizzie to marry him. At first this seemed to be nothing but a forlorn hope; she was too ill to get out of bed, let alone traipse down to the church – even in her nightdress – for the wedding she had so longed for.

'Lizzie and I are going to be married at last,' Gabriel was finally able to write to his mother, 'like all the most important things I ever meant to do, this one has been deferred almost beyond possibility.' A few days later, he wrote to William Michael, 'You will be grieved to hear that poor dear Lizzie's health has been in such a broken and failing state for the last few days as to render me more miserable than I can possibly say . . . till yesterday she had not been able to keep anything – even a glass of soda-water on her stomach for five minutes, and this has been the case more or less for a long while . . . if I were to lose her now I do not know what effect it might have on my mind, added to the responsibility of much work commissioned and already paid for, which still has to be done . . . I am sorry to write you such a miserable letter, but really it does me some good to have one person to whom I can write it, as I could not bear to any other than you.'

Eventually, Lizzie was sufficiently recovered to marry Gabriel at St Clement's Church at Hastings on 23 May 1860. No wedding could have been quieter. No member of their families attended and there were no wedding guests. Even the witnesses were comparative strangers whom Gabriel had met briefly during this last stay at Hastings.

*

Few people in the annals of those connected to the Pre-Raphaelites had a kinder heart than Ford Madox Brown. Very fond of Georgie, he gave her lessons in drawing and wood engraving, together with Emma du Maurier. On the side of lovers, of romance, and generally hoping for his friends' happiness, he realized that Ned and Georgie were unlikely to marry until Ned had made enough money; that it was equally unlikely that Ned would make very much money in the immediate future, and that, since neither Ned nor Georgie had ever had any money worth speaking of at all, it wouldn't make much difference to them if they married without any. He invited Georgie to stay with him and Emma in Hampstead. She stayed for a month, learned a lot about life and art, and enjoyed the emancipation from her family. Much later, while writing the *Memorials* of her husband, she recalled, 'Before my visit came to an end Madox Brown had decided that Edward had better be married without further delay, and since his character as counsellor stood high and we had no arguments to oppose to the suggestion, it was suddenly settled.'[1]

Georgie and Ned had been in love since Georgie was twelve. That they became officially engaged in June 1856, when she was fifteen, didn't necessarily mean they could get married in the foreseeable future. As well as Madox Brown's benevolence, the example of William Morris's marriage to Janey might well have spurred them on. When weddings get in the wind, they often go to people's heads and become contagious. Georgie's parents, now living in Manchester, gave their permission for Georgie to marry Ned without delay. They probably knew that if they hadn't done so, both Ned and Georgie would have wanted to hop-scotch to Gretna Green, prevented only by their sense of duty to their families.

Unlike the Rossettis' marriage, Ned and Georgie's wedding was very much a family affair. They were married in Manchester at the Anglican Collegiate church on 9 June 1860 on Dante's day*,

---

* The anniversary of the death of Dante Alighieri's muse, Beatrice.

as they had agreed, four years after they had officially become engaged. Georgie's father gave her away and her mother, her bevvy of sisters and a few friends were present.

The physical resemblance between Burne-Jones and Ruskin is undeniable. So is their attitude to the loss of their virginity. Both of them caught colds on their wedding night. Ned and Georgie had agreed to join Gabriel and Lizzie in Paris for a joint honeymoon. Ned suffered from seasickness long before they reached the shore, so they did not go abroad but spent the night at an inn, pretending to the landlord, not altogether convincingly, that they were an old married couple instead of being two newly-weds.

As a result of their curtailed honeymoon, they came back to London to find their new lodgings in Russell Place, off Fitzroy Square, quite unprepared. They spent the first weeks of their marriage leading a very 'Yonghy-Bonghy-Bo' existence:

> *On the Coast of Coromandel*
> *Where the early pumpkins blow,*
> *In the middle of the woods*
> *Lived the Yonghy-Bonghy-Bo.*
> *Two old chairs, and half a candle,*
> *– One old jug without a handle,-*
> *These were all his worldly goods:*
> *In the middle of the woods*
> *Of the Yonghy-Bonghy-Bo . . .*

EDWARD LEAR, 'The Courtship of the Yonghy-Bonghy-Bo'
Nonsense Songs and Stories (1846)

Georgie received her guests sitting on the table, since they possessed no chairs. Even so, they seemed as happy as larks, their friends delighted by the new arrangement. Their wedding presents included two wonderful cabinets from Philip Webb and William Burges, the latter's cabinet decorated by Edward Poynter. Ned's aunt gave them a piano, much to Georgie's delight, since she both played and sang exceptionally well and, most marvellous of all, G. F. Watts, whom

Ned had got to know at Little Holland House, gave Georgie one of the latest domestic gadgets, very likely on the advice of Sarah Prinsep – a wildly expensive sewing machine.

Lizzie's constitution may not have been as sound as Georgie's, but it didn't stop her from honeymooning in Paris. She and Gabriel stayed at the fabulous Hôtel Meurice overlooking the Tuileries. It was, and still is, extremely expensive and after a few days of opulent living, they had to move out to a much cheaper one.

For years, Gabriel had been working intermittently on an extraordinary work, a watercolour which he mixed with gum-arabic: *How They Met Themselves*. It depicts a pair of lovers meeting their doppelgangers walking through a wood. He had taken it to Paris with him and finished it on their honeymoon. It is a compelling work, haunting in its intensity. Gabriel had always referred to it as his 'bogey-work'. The characters look remarkably like Gabriel and Lizzie in medieval garb. The picture could be interpreted as an image of their relationship: while the couple on the left clasp each other's hands and are bathed in a halo of shining light, their counterparts are more menacing, she, half kneeling, half fainting, her hands reaching out in supplication, while the two men stare blindingly into each other's eyes. The obscurity of the sylvan wood recalls the opening lines of Dante's *Inferno* (in *The Divine Comedy*):

> *Midway upon the journey of our life,*
> *I found myself within a forest dark,*
> *For the straightforward pathway had been lost . . .*

One might consider Gabriel's decision to complete this painting, which had long obsessed him, a strange choice for someone on honeymoon. But then Gabriel was a strange man, his choices frequently peculiar. One of his clients had made an offer for the completed work and, particularly because of the expenses incurred by the honeymoon, he needed the money more than ever.

*

Even though Gabriel and Lizzie enjoyed themselves boating on the Seine, going to exhibitions and dining in crèmeries and opulent restaurants, by the time the honeymoon was over, Lizzie was very ill again. On their return to London, Gabriel found temporary lodgings in Hampstead while his old quarters at Chatham Place were being enlarged and made more comfortable.

It was not until the end of July 1860 that Lizzie was well enough to receive visitors or go out and about with friends. Ned and Georgie were amongst the first. They arranged to meet at London Zoo,* one of Gabriel's favourite haunts, together with the Madox Browns. They met at what Gabriel, who was mad about wombats, called 'The Wombat's Lair' at the Zoo. When they got to the aviary of the owls, Gabriel and an owl had what Georgie could only call a feud. 'The moment their eyes met they seemed to rush at each other, Gabriel rattling his stick between the cage bars furiously and the owl almost barking with rage.'[2]

Later, they all went back to the Rossettis' lodgings at Hampstead. Georgie, who had not known them well during the prolonged period before their marriage, later recalled that she:

> received an impression which never wore away, of romance and tragedy between her and her husband. I see her in the little upstairs bedroom with its lattice window, to which she carried me when we arrived, and the mass of her beautiful deep-red hair as she took off her bonnet: she wore her hair very loosely fastened up, so that it fell in soft, heavy wings. Her complexion looked as if a rose tint lay beneath the white skin, producing a most soft and delicate pink for the darkest flesh-tone. Her eyes were of a kind of golden brown-agate colour is the only word I can think of to describe them – and wonderfully luminous: in all Gabriel's drawings of her and in the type she created in his mind this is to be seen. The eyelids were deep, but without any languor or drowsiness, and had

---

* Originally formed in 1828 as a centre for scientific study, London Zoo eventually opened its doors to the public in 1847.

the peculiarity of seeming scarcely to veil the light in her eyes when she was looking down.[3]

The sensitive description that Georgie wrote of Lizzie is as revealing about Georgie as it is about the Rossettis. Her remark referring to the mixture of romance and tragedy in their relationship is also perceptive. In the two lengthy volumes of Georgie's *Memorials* of her husband, while Georgie sees fit to leave out intimate details about her friends', her own and her husband's lives, in keeping with the mores of her contemporaries, she has an unusual ability to recall visual matters and also to convey her psychological understanding of them. Although very pretty at the time of which she is writing, Georgie was never a muse or a stunner, but an irreproachable wife. It is possible that this was the very reason that enabled her to be so clear-sighted and observant.

16

RED HOUSE

Red House was completed in 1860. A remarkable building by any standards today, it must have seemed extraordinary then. The first time Ned saw it, he called it 'the most beautifullest place on earth'. When William Bell Scott first went there he was astounded. 'If one had been told it was the South Sea Island-style of thing one could have easily believed such to be the case.' Gabriel's comment was that it 'was a most noble work in every way, and more a poem than a house'.

Most architecture, domestic, ecclesiastical or municipal, with the exception of the odd folly, *duomo* and gazebo, is constructed on the basis of a rectangle and, perhaps reassuringly, does not disguise the fact. Red House, although built around two sides of a quadrangle, appeared to be more like a threepenny bit seen through the lens of a kaleidoscope. It included a myriad of gables, rectangular windows, round windows, and slit windows inspired by medieval architecture; and ample porches, tall chimneys, great doors and archways. It was an odd combination of Dutch and medieval architecture. In the south garden there was an unusual well, surmounted by a vast bell-like canopy of red brick.

The name of the house was derived from the fact that it was built entirely of red brick which, though unusual at the time, was by no means unique. When, in 1857, Thackeray had bought 2 Palace Green in Kensington and had found the structure unsound, he had it knocked down and rebuilt in the style of Queen Anne. He called it 'the reddest house in all the town'. It was not the redness of Red House that was so astonishing as its thoroughly original design combined with the concept that one room should lead into another, and the garden should be an integral part of the house: that if the indoors led to the out of doors, so did the outside lead to the inside. The garden itself was designed to encompass botanical chambers, each separate yet each leading to one another and making up a whole. If this, post Gertrude Jekyll, sounds familiar, it should be remembered that not since the days before the Reformation, had such a garden scheme been designed specifically. This harmony led to an affinity, then almost unknown in England, between house and garden, which translated Morris's vision of an 'earthly paradise' into an earthly reality.

Between them, the architect Philip Webb and William Morris, while searching for a suitable site for the house, had hit upon a spot with beautiful white-heart cherry trees and apple orchards which allowed enough space to construct the house without destroying the orchards. Webb and Morris also had the foresight to plan and propagate the garden so that, by the time Red House was completed, the garden seemed as though it had been long established. Roses, red-hot pokers, lilies, sunflowers, rosemary, thyme, sage and marjoram were rampant. Lavender, sweet wivelsfield, santolina and sweet william bordered the beds. Jasmine, honeysuckle and eglantine* were trained to climb the walls. The apples from the orchard became legendary. They were eaten raw, cooked in pies, stored in the loft and used as missiles, pillow fights being considered too soft. On one occasion, Charlie Faulkner, an Oxford friend of Morris and Burne-Jones, barricaded himself in the loft and defended himself from the onslaught of his companions by hurling apples at them. One of them hit Morris hard and gave him a black eye. For Morris, the most generous of hosts, remained the butt of practical jokes. It was impossible to resist teasing him.

---

* Otherwise known as clematis, a relation of the buttercup, belonging to the genus *Ranunculus*. I am deeply indebted to Mark Divall and to my late father, David Garnett, for all botanical knowledge.

They even went so far as to snub him at table, putting him to Coventry, addressing him only through the medium of Janey. He was the fat boy, Topsy. Some of the jokes bordered on cruelty which, although giving them a nasty edge, was precisely what made them so funny.

Unusually for an English house, the reception rooms were on the first floor. On the ground floor were the grand entrance hall, the morning room and the library. The dining room was also on the ground floor, conveniently close to the kitchen. The kitchen itself was large and airy with a window opening on to the garden. Upstairs, as well as the bedrooms, was the studio, the great drawing room and several living rooms. Although undeniably spacious, Red House was not conspicuously grand. It had a certain, almost parochial sturdiness, a family feeling about it; a signal to welcome domestic fun as well as artistic enterprise.

That first summer of 1860 down at Red House remained an idyll in the minds of all those who were there. Ned and Georgie spent the entire summer there and stayed on well into the autumn. Others came and went. Gabriel and Lizzie were noticeably absent: Lizzie was too ill to travel and Gabriel remained by her side in Hampstead, near the Madox Browns. Visitors took the train to Abbey Wood Station and were met by the Red House wagonette, an outlandish vehicle with leather curtains, which gave rise to local mirth as, indeed, did the appearance of the passengers, clad in flowing draperies like medieval knights and damsels.

Their exuberance knew no bounds. Naturally, their excessive energy found its outlet in creative work: Janey and Georgie took to wood engraving and embroidering designs by Morris. Ned and Topsy revelled in paint. They painted everything in sight – the view, the furniture, the women and the walls. They were mad about murals, and tempera became the rage. Arthurian legend, as ever, was the main source of their inspiration. Knights in shining armour gleamed from inglenooks and in niches halfway up the stairs. Ned painted Topsy as a king in robes of blue and gold at a wedding feast and Janey in a wimple as the queen at his side. All the fun and high jinks they had enjoyed while decorating the Oxford union were revived, but here, at Red House, on a more intimate, domestic note.

Unfortunately, the technical disasters they had encountered with tempera at Oxford were repeated at Red House. They hadn't learned their lesson. Red House had only just been constructed. As at Oxford, the walls were new and the plaster hadn't had time to dry. It takes at least six months and a really hot summer to dry new plaster sufficiently to be in a condition to take paint, whether whitewash or distemper, let alone tempera, which is a mixture of coloured pigment mixed with a water-soluble binder stirred up, rather like mayonnaise, into an emulsion with egg yolks. In Kent that summer of 1860, it was exceptionally wet and poured with rain, although not enough to dampen their spirits. The plaster hadn't dried. All too soon, the knights, damsels, kings and queens faded into ghosts to haunt the saturated walls. None of them knew then how soon their works would fade: they were living in a state of glory, occupying a new realm, a kingdom none of them had ever dreamed that they would aspire to rule.

In between the bouts of their intense industry, they spent an extraordinary amount of time getting up to larks and ludicrous activities. It may well have been a sign of the times that, hidebound though they were by sexual manners and mores, by exasperatingly demanding forms of public etiquette, their release was expressed in an explosion of practical jokes.

In the evenings, after dinner – Morris prided himself, with good reason, on his table; his food, his cellar and the fruit from his orchards – they played touchingly funny, simple and childish games such as hide-and-seek, blind man's buff, musical chairs and various other pranks. Perhaps the games were not so innocent as they seemed, but they gave them all an outlet for a considerable amount of fun.

Biographical speculation is a dangerous game to play, considerably more so than the games of blind man's buff that they enjoyed at Red House, particularly during that first summer of

1860. Nevertheless, it cannot go unremarked that neither Topsy, Janey, Ned or Georgie had enjoyed the careless rapture of childhood charades. It is a possibility that they were indulging themselves in a leap from the hop-scotch of childhood into a far more complicated adult dance. Awkward, unpractised and blundering, they believed that they were living in heaven – which, to a certain extent, they were – although unwittingly heading to a form of hell.

One of the most refreshing aspects of Red House, apart from its beauty, was that the women were treated, unusually for those days, on an equal footing with the men. There was no reason why they shouldn't have been: Georgie, as Ford Madox Brown knew, was a gifted designer and illustrator and she was well trained in wood engraving. Lizzie had exhibited her work professionally. Janey was exceptionally sensitive in her interpretations of other people's designs, particularly when executed in embroidery: she was an uncommonly skilful needlewoman. These women were also treated on a par with the men socially. If Georgie and Janey preferred to take themselves off and spend the days embroidering, that was in the nature of things, not at all because they were banished from the men's forum.

Georgie and Janey generally spent their mornings sitting in the southern porch, embroidering designs drawn up by Morris. Janey was an exquisite embroiderer and Morris, who was equally gifted at what Rossetti tauntingly called 'worsted work', quite naturally took full advantage of her skills. It was while they were sitting stitching, side by side, that Georgie noticed in her basket 'a strange garment, fine, small, and shapeless – a little shirt for him or her – and looking at my friend's face I knew that she had been happy when she made it; but it was a sign of change, and the thought of any change made me sigh'.[1]

It would not be fair to describe Morris as a jack-of-all-trades, since he was a perfectionist in every school he practised. Yet it might be acceptable to compare him to the White Knight, who observed the rules of battle while galloping about with beehives, sandwich boxes and mouse traps, all of his own invention, to guard against the bites of sharks. To pursue the analogy a step further, Rossetti, then, must be cast as the Red Knight, a part he played to perfection.

There is always a serpent in paradise. The serpent at Red House was personified by Gabriel's undisguised admiration for Janey. It made Lizzie miserable and put Morris in a rage, which, with great difficulty, he managed to master. Morris was famous for his rages, which were violent and frequently expressed by hurling the nearest object to hand so that paperweights, coffee pots and toast racks went whizzing through the air. It was not his intention to hurt anyone: no one could have been a more fervent pacifist than Morris. It was merely that he needed an outlet. His rages were almost certainly caused by a form of epilepsy.

The uneasy situation brought out the worst in Gabriel. Making advances to Morris's wife and causing his own to be wretched, he couldn't resist mocking Morris in a way which was unpleasant and distressing, and which verged on cruelty. Although Morris had a highly developed sense of honour and chivalry, Gabriel had no notion of gentlemanly behaviour, certainly not as gentlemanly behaviour was defined in nineteenth-century England, as opposed to how it was perceived in the courts of Camelot. The middle classes were only just being invented, the members were financially successful entrepreneurs, manufacturers, scientific thinkers, members of the professional classes and philanthropists.

Morris had a habit of scrawling his motto 'If I can' on his walls. When Gabriel came down from London one summer's afternoon, he seized a brush and scrawled, 'and if I can't?' That evening, there was a row of unprecedented ferocity between Rossetti and his host. Rossetti's jealousy, primarily based on his lust for Janey, was rampant. Janey wasn't the only reason that Rossetti was blue in the face with resentment, like an angry turkey. Before Morris had come along, Gabriel had been the king-pin. Now Morris had taken over. Although he couldn't paint, he seemed to be able to accomplish almost everything else under the sun. Above all, he wrote poetry. If Gabriel was ashamed of his jealousy, he failed to hide it.

Quite how Janey took Gabriel's public adoration is not recorded. None of her own intimate feelings are known. The general impression was that she was aware of Rossetti's passion – how could she not be? She chose to appear to be untouched, uncontaminated. Her friendliness towards Lizzie never failed. Like Effie, she might, with a bit more discipline, have made a good diplomat, although it would have had to be an ambassador to a very different country.

While scouring the city for furniture and fabrics for Red House, Morris found it so difficult to find anything to his taste that he conceived the notion of setting up a commercial company to supply the householder of average income with desirable wallpapers, carpets, lampshades, fabrics and other domestic requirements.

'You may hang your walls with tapestry instead of whitewash or paper,' he declared in what became a mantra for the middle classes aspiring to good taste, 'or you may cover them with mosaic, or have them frescoed by a great painter: all this is not luxury, if it be done for beauty's sake, and not for show: it does not break our golden rule: Have nothing in your houses which you do not know to be useful or believe to be beautiful.'[2]

Morris knew instinctively that objects which are really useful, such as soup ladles, coal scuttles, pen-knives, spoons and teapots, are, because of the intrinsic relationship shared between the utensils and those who handle them, necessarily beautiful in themselves. His fierce and utterly true belief in a sense of practical aesthetics formed the foundation of what is now known as Style and Design. It was the lack of readily available, aesthetically pleasing merchandise that brought about the birth of what they all called 'The Firm', by which they meant Morris, Marshall, Faulkner & Co., Fine Art Workmen in Painting, Carving, Furniture and the Metals, established as early as 1861 – for Morris, impetuous as he was industrious, lost no time putting into practice what he preached.

Georgie might have sighed about impending change, but the birth of 'The Firm' had an immediately beneficial effect on the small society the group had transformed itself into. Part of this transformation was increasingly reflected in the way in which they led their domestic lives. The Firm was to provide them with what they lacked: money. It was all very well to laugh about lack of 'tin', as Gabriel called it, but a constant state of 'tinlessness', particularly when the group shifted into the key of domestic harmony with babies on the way, was an intolerable state of affairs. The Firm made a commercially viable outlet for the manufacture of carpets, candlesticks, stained-glass windows, egg cups, wallpaper, tiles and patterned fabric, to mention but a few of the various items on offer. The Firm was a success. What is more remarkable is how its popularity has continued to the present day. In nearly every middle-class house in England and the Americas, one is almost bound to encounter a version of Morris's willow-patterned fabric, whether translated into upholstery, curtains, paper napkins or oilcloth table coverings. Quite what contributes to such overwhelming success is a mystery, but the exquisitely designed carpets, candlesticks, wallpaper, stained glass and, particularly, rush-seated furniture, settles and Sussex armchairs, represented a collective notion of a vanishing rural, unhistorical notion of an idyll of England. It is this ghost of the past which echoes through the chambers of memory, of buttercups and daisies, church bells and maypoles, even if some only recall such rural rides from within the hard covers of an illustrated book, such as through the eyes of Walter Crane, Randolph Caldecott or Kate Greenaway.

One foggy morning, Val Prinsep took his old friend, Anny Thackeray Ritchie, to the shop in Red Lion Square, and Anny later recalled: 'We came to an empty ground-floor room, and Val Prinsep called "Topsy" very loud, and someone came from above with hair on end and in a nonchalant way began to show one or two of his curious, and to my uninitiated soul, bewildering treasure. I think Morris said the glasses would stand firm when he put them on the table. I bought two tumblers ... I came away ... with a general impression of sympathetic shyness and dim green glass.[3]

Janey was the first of the Pre-Raphaelite women to give birth.

Her daughter, Jenny, was borne at Red House on 17 January 1861. Wisely, Morris had roped in the Madox Browns to be present. Ford Madox Brown's company was of stirling worth and Emma was a good choice as a companion to Janey. Of course, Morris, who had money, hired a nurse as well as maintaining his normal household staff. Tongue in cheek, Rossetti couldn't refrain from mentioning in a letter about the 'little accident which has just befallen Topsy and Mrs T'.

Rossetti should be forgiven for his twisted allusion to the birth of Jenny Morris. Day by day he was tortured by the predicament he found himself in with Lizzie. For by now, Lizzie was heavily pregnant, ill and moping. In accordance with the generally accepted medical view of the day, she took increasingly large doses of laudanum to alleviate her bouts of morning sickness. Even Rossetti, who longed to be a father, had to prepare himself for the worst. The worst was perfectly dreadful. In April, the child, a girl, was born dead, having died, according to the doctors, three weeks previously within Lizzie's womb. All the hopes that Rossetti had clung to for Lizzie's revival and their own mutual happiness were now smashed. Lizzie sank into a decline and Rossetti became desperate. His sense of guilt, compounded by misery, tormented him.

17

LIZZIE'S TRAGEDY

Sonnet LV
STILLBORN LOVE

The hour which might have been yet might not be,
Which man's and woman's heart conceived and bore
Yet whereof life was barren, – on what shore
Bides it the breaking of Time's weary sea?
Bondchild of all consummate joys set free,
It somewhere sighs and serves, and mute before
The house of Love, hears through the echoing door
His hours elect in choral constancy.
But lo! what wedded souls now hand in hand
Together tread at last the immortal strand
With eyes where burning memory lights love home?
Lo! how the little outcast hour has turned
And leaped to them and in their faces yearned:-
'I am your child: O parents, ye have come!'

DANTE GABRIEL ROSSETTI, *Poems*, 1870
(probably written shortly after the death
of Gabriel's and Lizzie's daughter)

By now it was clear that Lizzie couldn't be left alone. She needed company, if only to safeguard her. Rossetti arranged with the ever-obliging Morris to send her down to Red House for a break while he continued to work on various canvases at Chatham Place to pay for the alarmingly high doctor's fees.

Lizzie's visit to the Morrises was a disaster. Nobody realized how much the sight of Jenny, Janey's baby, would torture her; how much the news of Georgie's pregnancy would plunge her into despair. It is quite possible that nobody at Red House knew quite how much laudanum Lizzie was taking. Even if they did suspect, and there was nothing unusual in people doping themselves inordinately, nothing was made explicit. That would have been out of keeping with the order of the day, however bohemian the Pre-Raphaelites might appear to be now in the constrained society of the twenty-first century. Lizzie left Red House precipitously. Perhaps everybody had, by now, become so used to Lizzie's ill health and her unpredictable moods that, although still entranced by her beauty, they no longer noticed her see-saw moods of rapture and despair.

Long after the event, Georgie recalled: 'We found her sitting in a low chair with the childless cradle on the floor beside her, and she looked like Gabriel's *Ophelia* when she cried with a kind of soft wildness as we came in, 'Hush, Ned, you'll wake it!'

Georgie, who was pregnant herself, was deeply moved. Ned became impatient, considering Lizzie to be not only temperamental but overdramatic. She was both, as well as being unhappy and closer to despair than any of them suspected. Rossetti certainly must have known more than he ever cared to reveal later. The day that Ned and Georgie called on Lizzie, Gabriel took them aside before they went into their room and implored them not to accept Lizzie's offering of her dead baby's clothes for their own child. 'Lizzie,' Georgie later recalled him as saying, 'has been talking to me of parting with a certain small wardrobe to you. But don't let her, please. It looks such a bad omen for us.' Ned and Georgie had sufficient tact and diplomacy to leave the Rossettis' apartments without the baby clothes.

*

One of the newcomers to the group was the young poet, Algernon Swinburne, whom they had first met while painting the murals at the Oxford union. Slight, slender and with transparent gooseberry-green eyes, he resembled a parakeet with a shock of orange hair. His talent was precocious, his fizzing energy and appetite for every experience life had to offer boundless. He was immediately attracted by both Lizzie and Gabriel, and they once unwittingly caused a sensation going to the theatre *en masse* together with Ned and Georgie, Janey and Topsy. The boy selling programmes was startled by Swinburne's unusual bright-red hair. When he got to the other end of the row and saw Lizzie looking regal in her flowing garments and mane of red hair, he shrieked out: 'There's another of 'em!'

After the stillbirth of Lizzie's child, Swinburne was one of the few people whom Lizzie allowed herself to be comforted by. Gabriel was attracted by Swinburne and relieved by the cheering effect he had on Lizzie. Swinburne gradually became part of their household, perching on the sofa like a frail foreign bird, amusing Lizzie while Gabriel painted her. On the evening of 10 February 1862, they all three sallied forth, as they so often did, to have dinner at La Sablonière, a restaurant they all liked in the sleazy district around Leicester Square. In the cab on the way there, Gabriel noticed that Lizzie was alternately agitated and drowsy and asked if she wouldn't rather go back home. She insisted on going on. In the event, they enjoyed their dinner very much. Shortly after eight o'clock, Swinburne went on his way to one of his nocturnal assignments and the Rossettis took a cab back to Chatham Place.

When they got home, Lizzie went to bed and Gabriel went out – quite to what assignment he went has never been made clear and has given rise to any amount of speculation. Since it was a Monday evening, it is more than likely that he went off to the Working Men's Club in Red Lion Square once he had seen that Lizzie was comfortably in bed. He may have gone to see one of his lovers, Fanny Cornforth. He got home shortly before midnight. Lizzie was profoundly asleep and snoring loudly. The empty bottle of laudanum lay on the pillow and she had pinned on her nightdress a scrawled message asking Gabriel to 'look after Harry', her younger, disabled brother.* Gabriel tried to wake her but couldn't. Nothing would rouse her. He called for the landlady, for a neighbour, and sent for the doctor. The doctor couldn't revive her. Gabriel sent for three more doctors but it was too late. Lizzie was dead.

Gabriel was in a frenzy, hardly knowing what he did. But he knew enough to take the note Lizzie had written with him when he tore off to Kentish Town to find Ford Madox Brown. Brown burned the note, saying it indicated suicide and that they should keep quiet about it. Suicide was illegal. Nobody who committed suicide could receive a Christian burial but had to be buried outside the church wall in unconsecrated ground.† This would be anathema to both the Rossetti and the Siddal families.

The news of Lizzie's death passed like wildfire among the set of friends who had known her best. When Georgie heard of it, she put her foot down on Ned's going to visit. He had been ill all winter and she judged him too sensitive to bear the sight of her. She went 'directly I heard it and saw her poor body laid in the very bed where I have seen her lie and laugh in the midst of illness,

---

* Long after Gabriel's death, his brother William Michael continued to pay Harry Siddal a regular allowance. Initially, this was denied by his daughter, Helen Rossetti Angeli, although she later admitted it was true and described the appearance of a strange man who appeared at regular intervals in her father's house. The only reason for making such a mystery of carrying out Lizzie's last wishes concerning her younger brother can be the burning of the note she wrote and their understandable desire, given the age they were living in, to cover up any hint of the fact that Lizzie died intentionally of an overdose of laudanum.

† Cremation was only made legal in England in 1885 after much debate and a ruling by Sir James FitzJames Stephen. The first cremation was that of a horse at Woking which caused a public outcry. This was followed, after Stephen's ruling, by the cremation of Lady Charles Dilke which was considered equally outrageous, perhaps because she had been involved with the much publicized scandal, the 'three-in-a-bed' Dilke case during her lifetime. The cremation of the horse at Woking recalls Holman Hunt boiling a dead horse in Kensington. It's interesting to speculate which horse led to the loudest outcry.

but even though I did this I keep thinking it is all a dreadful dream. Brown was with Gabriel and is exactly the man to see to all the sad business arrangements, for of course under such circumstances an inquest has to be held. Of course I did not see Gabriel.'[1]

The inquest was held at Bridewell Hospital on Thursday, 13 February 1862. Gabriel and his close friends were understandably anxious that the coroner should pass a verdict of accidental death, even though no one then, except for Gabriel and Ford Madox Brown, knew of the suicide note which Brown had thrown on the fire. Gabriel, Swinburne, Lizzie's sister Clara, the housekeeper Mrs Birrell and her daughter Eleanor, and the neighbour Gabriel had sent for, were all asked to give evidence. The last four all testified to having known of Lizzie's laudanum habit and had often bought the laudanum for her. Gabriel said there was nothing unusual in her taking as many as a hundred drops in one dose. Swinburne said he hadn't noticed anything out of the ordinary during that last evening except that she seemed tired. The coroner, after some hesitation, passed a verdict of accidental death.

In the interval between the inquest and Lizzie's funeral on Monday, 17 February, she lay in her open coffin at Chatham Place, still looking unbearably beautiful. Gabriel refused to accept that she was dead and would never return. He stayed by her coffin, imploring her to come back. A medical friend of Ford Madox Brown's was sent for to confirm her death. Gabriel remained in despair. On the day of her funeral, a cold and melancholy morning, he impulsively placed beside her cheek his only copy of some poems he had been working on for a considerable time, some of which had been inspired by Lizzie. He also put her copy of the Bible by her still-glowing auburn hair. Lizzie was buried in the Rossetti family grave at Highgate Cemetery close to Gabriele Rossetti, the father-in-law whom she had never met. Gabriel went to stay with his mother and Christina. He took Lizzie's bullfinch in its wicker cage with him, leaving behind a significant chapter of his life.

18

ITALIAN INTERLUDE

Before Georgie gave birth to her son Philip in 1861, they moved to more spacious lodgings – previously occupied by the painter Henry Wallis,* who was known to all the group – in Great Russell Street, opposite the British Museum. Ned, like Wallis, used the well-lit large front room as his studio. The rest of the rooms behind were rather poky.

Ruskin, who had taken up Ned in a big way, invited him and Georgie to go to Italy with him. Georgie had never been abroad before and although she was reluctant to leave Philip, whom she left with her mother in Manchester, she needed little persuasion to travel. She was also, like most Victorians, under the mistaken impression that the freezing cold of Florence in winter and the muggy heat of Rome would restore Ned to health. As Ruskin's guests, they stayed in the best hotels, dined at the finest restaurants and travelled like princes. After the crossing to Boulogne, they went with Ruskin for a walk down to the shore 'where the tide was far out and only a great stretch of wet sand lay before us. Here a mood of melancholy came over him and he left us, striding away by himself towards the sea; his solitary figure looked the very emblem of loneliness as he went, and we never forgot it.'[1]

---

* Henry Wallis (1830–1916) first studied at the Royal Academy and then at Glèyre's studio and at the *Académie des Beaux Arts* in Paris. Best remembered for his painting *The Death of Lord Chatterton*, using George Meredith as the model, he was intimately connected with the Pre-Raphaelites and later ran off with Meredith's wife Mary Ellen.

Italy was an eye-opener for both Georgie and Ned. The richness of Italian art opened up for Ned, as for most artists, a whole new world which he revelled in. He didn't revel so much in the opera. In Padua, Ruskin took them to *Rigoletto*. Georgie enjoyed it so much that Ruskin booked tickets for the following night. Ned had had enough and refused to go. From then on, he showed a decided preference for the new stage form, Vaudeville, and comic songs as opposed to arias. At Milan, Ruskin and the Burne-Joneses parted amicably enough, Georgie and Ned travelling on to Verona, Padua again, and to Venice.

They were staggered by the beauty of Venice, by the paintings, the architecture and the ambience. 'Georgie is growing an eye for a picture,' Ned wrote to Ruskin. 'She darts at a little indistinct thing hung away somewhere, and says timidly "Isn't that a very nice picture?" and it generally ends in being a Bellini or Bonifacio, whom she calls Bonnieface – and O what pictures of his there are here!'[2]

In spite of the glories Venice had to offer and their joint enthusiasm, they both felt it was time to go home. Georgie worried about Ned's susceptibility to 'malarial influence', as he became feverish and ill at night. He longed to be back at work and she was missing their son Philip. Ruskin, who had returned to Venice, begged them to stay on a little longer for he wanted Ned to undertake some copies of certain paintings and sketches of various buildings for him. As Ruskin's guests in Italy, they could only oblige. By the time they left, they had been away for ten weeks. Italy had an immense effect on both of them. Ned's eyes had been opened to the marvel of Italy and what he had seen there is reflected in his paintings. The effect that this visit to the Continent had on Georgie cannot be underestimated. From being a child bride, she had matured into a cultured young woman as well as having understood far more fully how much her husband relied on her integrity.

A few weeks after Lizzie's death, Janey Morris gave birth to her second daughter, Mary, always known as May, at Red House on 25 March 1862. Morris delighted in his daughters, calling them 'The Littles'. He was physically demonstrative in his affection for them and totally engaged when with them and playing with them. Janey's attitude was more languid, but then she was infinitely more languid than her husband in every respect.

19

TUDOR HOUSE

It was obvious to all of them that Gabriel would not be able to go on living at Chatham Place, and in the autumn of 1862, he succeeded in finding, with his friends, Tudor House at 16 Cheyne Walk, overlooking the river in Chelsea. Chelsea was then regarded as being out of the way, old-fashioned and quaint. It still retained much of the charm of the country village it had once been. The Carlyles lived there, as did the impecunious poet and man of letters Leigh Hunt and his large and shiftless family, because they found it sympathetic and, not being fashionable, it was cheap. Jane Carlyle's friend, the novelist Geraldine Jewsbury lived nearby, off the King's Road in Markham Square. Turner, who had died a couple of years previously in 1859, had had lodgings in Cheyne Walk because he was besotted by the light on the river and enjoyed the area precisely because it wasn't fashionable. Tudor House still exists, although in a modified form, its garden mainly built over.

Originally built in the early eighteenth century on the foundations of an earlier building, Tudor House was large and rambling, the rooms well proportioned and spacious. The garden was large and planted with roses, stocks, gillyflowers, snapdragons and an old mulberry tree. Gabriel decorated the inside himself, furnishing the rooms with an abundance of curiosities, bric-à-brac, richly coloured fabrics of velvet, and worked tapestry which he had begun to collect. Everywhere he could, he hung mirrors to reflect the light and the people reflected in the glass. Later, he was to collect blue-and-white china, a passion he shared with the American painter James McNeill Whistler, who was to become a friend and neighbour. They called them 'Long Elizas', a play on the Dutch name for them, *lange lijsen*. It is possible that this craze for collecting Dutch and Nankin blue-and-white china started from the early days when Gabriel and Lizzie used to visit the Browns in Kentish Town. Brown, who had spent many of his early years in Holland, also appreciated the beauty of Dutch tiles and china but, being as poor as a church mouse in those days, he was reduced to buying the much cheaper, very pretty willow pattern plates then in common use. The only letter extant from Lizzie to Georgie in fact makes reference to their passion for china:

MY DEAR LITTLE GEORGIE,

I hope you intend coming over with Ned tomorrow evening like a sweetmeat, it seems so long since I saw you dear. Janey will be here I hope to meet you.

With a willow-pattern dish full of love to you and Ned,

LIZZIE.[1]

Gabriel had always been fascinated by animals, frequently visiting the London Zoo. He had a particular fondness for wombats and now he indulged in acquiring two. These were followed by raccoons, an armadillo, a small zebu about the size of a Shetland pony, a kangaroo and peacocks, which annoyed his neighbours so much by their incessant shrieking that a clause was added ever after to the Cadogan Estate that no tenant might keep peacocks on the property.

He had a marquee erected in the garden and kept the armadillos and raccoons in packing cases from which they constantly escaped, the raccoons stealing into the neighbours' chicken run[*]

---

[*] It is indicative of how rural Chelsea was then that Rossetti's neighbours kept chickens. Carlyle, who lived around the corner at Cheyne Row, was famously tormented by the crowing of his neighbour's cockerel. It distracted him so much, together with the early morning piano practice of his other neighbour's daughters as they diligently pounded away at their scales, that he was obliged

and sucking the newly laid eggs. The actress Ellen Terry said that the only reason Gabriel had bought the zebu was because it had meltingly dark eyes like Janey Morris's. It turned out to be ferocious, tried to bite Gabriel and then, escaping from the rope which tethered it to a tree in the garden, chased Gabriel puffing and panting into the street. Shortly afterwards, the zebu was returned to Cremorne Gardens where Gabriel had bought it.

Indoors, he kept dormice, parrots, owls and woodchucks. None of his menagerie survived long, but lived short, unpredictable lives. The dormice were later found to be dead, not fast asleep, as Gabriel had supposed, in the knife drawer. The peacocks grew bedraggled and failed. The toucan, which Gabriel used to dress up in a cowboy hat, and persuade the llama to ride around the dining room table while he and his friends sat after dinner drinking port, lost its feathers and came to a sticky end. The gaudy parrot, which Gabriel had bought for its propensity to speak, was dumb for months until, late one Sunday morning when Gabriel was tucking into a breakfast of fried eggs, it suddenly squawked, 'You ought to be in church now!' Parrots are notorious survivors and this one was no exception.

Of all his animals, Gabriel displayed most affection for the wombats, seconded by the woodchucks. 'No more engagingly lumpish quadruped than the wombat could be found,' wrote William Michael in his biography of Gabriel, 'and none more obese and comfortable than the woodchuck.'

When the first wombat arrived at Tudor House, Gabriel was staying with Alice Boyd and William Bell Scott at Penkill Castle in Scotland. He wrote a welcoming verse:

> *O, how the family affections combat*
> *Within this heart, and each hour flings a bomb at*

---

to insulate the windows of his writing room. The local dairy kept its cow down in Lot's Road, where there was a small meadow good for grazing. The shepherd herding his sheep down the Fulham Road was a familiar sight.

My burning soil! Neither from owl nor from bat
Can peace be gained until I clasp my wombat.

Sadly, the wombats and woodchucks curled up, gave up the ghost and died. Gabriel was not easily consoled.

I never reared a young wombat
To greet me with his pin-hole eyes
But when he was most sweet and fat
And tail-less he was bound to die!

Shortly after Gabriel had moved into Tudor House, Georgie and Ned went with the Morrises to an evening party where they found Gabriel surrounded by his brother William, the Bell Scotts, Swinburne, the Madox Browns, the sculptor Munro and his wife, the French painter Alphonse Legros with his English wife, and Arthur Hughes, the painter of *April Love*, with his. 'The wide river . . . was lit up that night by a full moon. Gabriel had hung Lizzie's beautiful pen-and-ink and watercolour designs in the long drawing room with its seven windows looking south, where if ever a ghost returned to earth, hers must have come to seek him: but we did not sit in that room, the studio was the centre of the house.'[2]

At this period of his life, Gabriel was fond of entertaining. He was a remarkably good host and those evenings spent in his company were memorable both for the conversation and the surroundings. 'It was a beautiful room by day, when the sun streamed in and lit up the curious collection of Indian cabinets, couches, old Nankin, and the miscellaneous odds and ends with which it was crowded almost to the point of superfluity; and at night, when the heavy Utrecht curtains were drawn and the dining table was extended to its utmost limits, when the huge Flemish brass-wrought candelabra with its two dozen wax lights, that hung suspended from the ceiling midway over the table, was lit up, and the central, old-fashioned epergne was filled with flowers, the room was filled with a pleasant warmth and glow anticipatory of the company expected.'[3]

One of Gabriel's dreams had always been to live in a community with like-minded friends, devoting themselves to art, literature and beauty. Tudor House never became a community, but in the early days of Gabriel's tenancy he shared it with his brother William Michael, Swinburne and the poet and novelist George Meredith.* There can seldom have been so bizzare an assortment of people to make up a household.

Lizzie's power to inspire Rossetti did not die with her. During her life, he had made hundreds of studies of her face, her hands, of her sitting in 'the chair that knew her', standing, often gazing sadly just beyond the sight line of the viewer. Now her spirit haunted Gabriel. For two years after her death, he told a friend, he saw her ghost appear every night. He began to draw her again, partly from memory, partly from the studies that were left. He embarked on an extraordinary tribute to her. He idealized Lizzie as *Beata Beatrix*, one of the most powerful portraits he ever painted. After her death Rossetti, like so many other men of his time, beatified the woman he had loved and who had caused him so much anguish. *Beata Beatrix* is a disturbing picture, almost hypnotic. It captures the moment when Beatrice becomes divine – the moment when she dies. Her hooded eyes are closed, she has an aureole of light around her loosely falling amber hair, her hands are turned upwards as though in supplicating prayer. A russet dove has flown to her bearing a white poppy in its beak. Poppies are symbols of death and it is from poppies that opium and its derivatives, morphine and laudanum, are distilled. Behind her is a

---

* George Meredith (1828–1909) was a novelist and poet and author of such significant works as *The Shaving of Shagpat*, *The Egoist* and *The Ordeal of Richard Feveral*. He was close to both Rossetti brothers, Swinburne, Leslie Stephen, Robert Louis Stevenson, and many other literary luminaries of the Victorian era. He married Mary Ellen Nicholls, the daughter of Thomas Love Peacock and widow of Edward Nicholls, a sea captain who drowned while trying to save the life of a drowning man in the Shannon Estuary. Henry Wallis famously painted Meredith as Chatterton in his masterpiece, *The Death of Lord Chatterton*. Subsequently, Meredith's wife Mary Ellen left him for Henry Wallis.

sundial indicating the passing of time, and in the background are the obscure figures of Dante and Gabriel. It is one of the most haunting images Gabriel ever made of her.

Life at Tudor House was not all an idyll. Ructions were frequent. Swinburne, as ever, played the part of *enfant terrible* to the hilt. He was frequently drunk, but not in the manner of the average English gentleman, who, almost as a matter of honour, was in his cups of an evening. Swinburne passed out, stupefied by drink, so regularly that it became the norm. And when he hadn't passed out, he would have put Ariel out of countenance by his antics. He would bound about the house, prance madly in Gabriel's studio without paying the slightest heed to the notion that he might be distracting Gabriel from work, slide down the banisters often stark naked (one wonders whether he found it more comfortable to slide down facing forward or with his backside approaching the newel), and get up to all sorts of pranks and capers. Maddening though this might be, he was forgiven on account of his lightning wit, his brilliance and his poetry. He often thrilled the company by reading it aloud. It was impossible to be angry for long with someone so entertaining. Swinburne continued to endear himself to Gabriel, who remembered his reciprocated friendship with Lizzie. William Michael was there less often than the others, although his contribution to the rent was disproportionately high. He continued to be stolidly loyal to Gabriel who was then more than usually in need of his brother's moral support.

The real trouble started because, in that household of fun, work and debauchery, George Meredith was a fish out of water. He wasn't nearly so intimate with Gabriel as Swinburne was, and the real reason he was living at Tudor House was that its location was convenient. His own house was in Surrey and he needed a pied-à-terre in London. His wife, Mary Ellen, daughter of the novelist Thomas Love Peacock, had recently left him for Henry Wallis, who had used Meredith as the model in his seminal painting, *The Death of Lord Chatterton.* Unlike Rossetti, Meredith was athletic, went on walking tours with other literary men, and read poetry in the open air. He was a different breed of man altogether. Rossetti flung a jug of milk in his face after Meredith called him a fool; Swinburne threw a poached egg at him over breakfast. Unsurprisingly, Meredith left in a huff. He complained loudly of Rossetti's decadence; that he slept till noon and then stuffed himself with eggs and gristly ham from the corner shop, that he never took exercise but locked himself up in his studio till dusk, then snored on the sofa until ten or eleven when he would go out to some chophouse for dinner. If guests were expected, the dinners were rowdy and went on till all hours. He complained of Swinburne's excessive drinking and deplorable behaviour. He complained of a host of other things too.

What Meredith left out, and what sets him apart from the latter-day set of Pre-Raphaelites, is his moralizing and the fact that he failed to mention that, during the decadent evenings, some of the best poetry written by Swinburne, Morris and Rossetti was declaimed aloud by the authors; that the hours Rossetti confined himself to his studio resulted in some of the most remarkable canvases of the era; that, above all, there was a sense of camaraderie emphasizing the importance of friendship, which was not easy to find in Victorian London except in bohemian circles.

It was round about this time that Gabriel and his friends became involved in spirit-rapping, mediums and the world beyond. People's attitude to their beliefs in spiritual matters is so frequently bizarre and diametrically opposed to their other views that to draw any conclusions would be madness. While the Rossetti women were confirmed Anglicans, the brothers and their father were determined agnostics. They rejected God and any notion of formal religion, but not Christian values. From a logical point of view, this makes it all the more surprising that Gabriel and William Michael should have had any truck with spiritualism. Yet such beliefs have little to do with logic any more than they have to do with Christianity. Although they may share the same matter – manifestations of people who have 'passed over to the other side', whether apparitions of the Virgin Mary in the foothills of the

Pyrenees or eerie limbs levitating to suburban parlour ceilings –
there is a difference. Bernadette's visions of the Virgin at Lourdes
were claimed to be gifts from God. They were seen during those
years when Spiritualism was at its height and were later authenti-
cated by the Vatican. Knockings on the table, furniture spinning
on the carpet, sightings of butterflies, goldfish and levitating bodies
at Spiritualist séances were not necessarily invested with such
claims, although it was understood that these were messages from
the dead. Both required faith. Unlike the sightings of the Virgin,
most of the mediums were later exposed as frauds. The issue was
foggy, open to interpretation. Lizzie was dead. The possibility of
Gabriel getting in touch with her spirit floating somewhere in the
haziness of the afterlife was infinitely enticing. Spiritualism was
very much in the air.

Emanating from America, Spiritualism crossed the Atlantic in
the guise of Daniel Home, a medium as repellent as he was compelling. The immediate question was whether he was a charlatan
or the real thing. It wasn't possible to determine without going to
one of his séances. People flocked to them. He was expensive and
frequented the drawing rooms of High Society. The grander the
people on his cards – the Marchioness of Hastings, Lady Walde-
grave, Lady Grey de Ruthyn – the more he was clamoured for.
Tables rocked. Spoons, aspidistras, limbs and top hats sailed
around the ceilings. Home levitated in the sooty air. When Home
went to Italy, Elizabeth Barrett Browning was hooked. Her husband was sceptical and they quarrelled. The trouble about Home,
alluring though he was, was that he was unsavoury, continually
involved in scandal, accused of fraud, of embezzling money from
rich widows, and of shocking liaisons with the sons of aristocrats.

Mrs Guppy was less distasteful, altogether more extraordinary.
As a child, she had been possessed of strange qualities and the
ability to levitate. Now her girth was vast. In a darkened room,
she could levitate from her chair and soar towards the ceiling. Her
imagination was splendid, her taste beyond expectations. When a
client demanded the sound of the sea, the carpet was inundated

with gallons of sea water, live lobsters, star fish and eels sliding towards the mahogany armchairs. On another occasion, roast ducks whizzed about on dinner plates. Butterflies flew. Strangest of all, Mrs Guppy herself was summoned by a fellow medium holding a séance in Lamb's Conduit Street. Mrs Guppy sailed in, flying through the fog from her house at Highbury to High Holborn, arriving in a deep trance, dishevelled in her nightgown, clutching her account book, one shoe on. She was a marvel.

There is no record of Gabriel frequenting the séances of Home or Mrs Guppy, although, like most of the world, he knew about Mrs Guppy's goings on, which were the talk of the town. He did, however, attend a séance given by the Davenport Brothers from America, who apparently managed to be tied in knots with thick ropes, be bundled into a cupboard together with a variety of musical instruments and emit messages from the world beyond to a vast, hypnotized audience. The Davenports were later exposed as frauds. It was all very fascinating.

Gabriel held less high-powered séances at Tudor House. Lizzie, who had haunted him, as he told William Bell Scott, ever since her death, was also in attendance. She was, he said, invisible, her presence to be recalled through the means of a medium, her voice translated through rappings on the table. Bell Scott wasn't convinced and called such goings-on merely childish. He thought Fanny Cornforth was at the bottom of it, cracking her fingers like walnuts when intimate questions were asked of Lizzie's spirit. Others thought it possible that the staid William Michael was having a wizened joke at his brother's expense.

Like most of such endeavours, the spirit-rapping sessions at Tudor House veiled the misery of the occupants. From then on, Gabriel's delusions took hold of his fancy. The very walls were infested with spies. His paranoia increased.

Several years previously, before Lizzie's death, Gabriel had been sauntering with friends in Cremorne Gardens, an enticing, licentious place of disrepute famous for the prostitutes who made themselves available; for female tightrope dancers clad in pink tights, tutus and sequined bodices; for a nightly display of the most glorious fireworks whose falling roman candles fell dazzlingly into the river; for the sight of hot-air balloons, most gorgeously decorated with ribbons and plumes, carrying people aloft in baskets; for ribaldry not seen since the days of the Restoration and later, the Regency.

Arm in arm with his closest male friends, Gabriel's attention was caught by a new kind of stunner. Unlike Lizzie, who was wraithlike thin, the young woman who was cracking nuts between her teeth and spitting out the shells at him, was buxom, golden haired and voluptuous. Her real name was Sarah Cox; her fancy name Fanny Cornforth. Semi-literate, uneducated, dishonest, possessed of an unusual degree of fun, common sense, and a practicality combined with a rare understanding of other people's foibles, she captured Gabriel's imagination. During the times when Lizzie had chosen to absent herself – ill, doped and miserable – from Gabriel, he had found sexual solace and comfort with Fanny. Now, at Tudor House, he invited her to move in as his housekeeper, which naturally meant being his mistress as well. Gabriel swiftly nicknamed her the Elephant. He once astounded Browning by declaring that he wished he had an elephant. When the poet asked whatever for, Rossetti laughingly replied that of course it was to clean the windows with its trunk.

Fanny was anathema to Swinburne, who had been as much in love with Lizzie as it was possible for him, a declared lover of his own sex, to be. Fanny's presence at Tudor House revolted him, for Fanny was everything that Lizzie had never been. Once Gabriel had installed her, Swinburne openly called her 'the bitch'. This wasn't calculated to endear him to Gabriel. Swinburne was so nasty to Fanny that finally, rather to his regret, Gabriel wrote him a note and told him to clear out.

The fact that this attempt at living communally as brother artists failed so soon didn't mean that the cord of the very real friendship between Rossetti and Swinburne was broken. It was merely another chapter in their continued relationship. Meredith faded from the scene, finding more congenial company among his own sort. William Michael was impervious to such scenes and carried on writing his column for *The Spectator* as though nothing had happened.

20

MR AND MRS BURNE-JONES

In the spring of 1865, Georgie was pregnant for the second time. She and Ned went to join the Morrises for a holiday at Little Hampton, taking Pip, as they called their firstborn son Philip. There was an outbreak of scarlet fever and Pip caught it. He didn't have it badly and, considering the rate of infant mortality and lack of adequate medical treatment of the time, they treated the matter lightly. Pip recovered. Shortly after their return to London, Georgie contracted it. She had it very badly, was delirious, and her baby was born prematurely. Ned named him Christopher. He died before Georgie had recovered. Morris and Janey were down at Red House, Morris suffering from rheumatic fever, and unable to give Ned the support he would have wanted to. Other friends rallied round. The ceramicist William de Morgan and the artist Edward Poynter (soon to be Georgie's brother-in-law) came to relieve Ned. Ruskin ordered straw to be put down in the street below to muffle the sound of horses' hoofs and carriage wheels going over the cobbles.

When Georgie was well enough, they went down to Hastings for her to convalesce. Morris wrote urging them to stay at Red House but, as Ned wrote to William Allingham, 'For these two months I have done no work, but lived most anxiously from day to day. The whole period has been so horrible and dismal that I try to forget it and will write no more about it.'[1]

It was out of the question for them to remain in their rooms in Great Russell Street. Ned would not allow it. At that time, Ned

and Georgie were very deeply in love. Her illness and the death of
her baby had been a traumatic experience for Georgie and she
could not bear to be there any longer. She and Pip went to spend
Christmas with her parents who had now moved to Wolverhamp-
ton while Ned, with the help of his old school friend, Crom Price,*
made the necessary removals to the quiet backwater of Kensington
Square. Their house was on the north side and was an improvement on Great Russell Street; it was more solid and permanent.
For the first time they had a garden planted with fruit trees and
there was just room to play a game of bowls. Ned and Crom Price
had brought the painted furniture from Bloomsbury. Morris gave
them a Persian prayer carpet. Ruskin gave them four engravings
of Dürer: *The Knight, Melancholy, St Hubert,* and *Adam and Eve.* Ned
bought chairs cut price from The Firm's workshops, which Morris
had set up. 'But when we turned to look around us something was
gone, something had been left behind and it was our first youth.'[2]

Georgie never recovered her girlish spirits and in photographs
of her at that time there is a sadness in her expression and a
sudden aging of the young girl-bride into a graver woman. She
was determined to be cheerful. When she had determined on
something, Georgie generally succeeded.

Even so, she found the continual demands of a young child a
strain:

> The difference in our life made by the presence of a child was
> very great, for I had been used to be much with Edward –
> reading aloud to him while he worked, and in many ways
> sharing the life of the studio – and I remember the feeling of
> exile with which I now heard through its closed door the well-
> known voices of friends together with Edward's familiar laugh,
> while I sat with my little son on knee and dropped selfish tears

---

* Cormell Price (1832–1910) had been at King Edward School, Birmingham
with Burne-Jones. They remained lifelong friends. After a few years spent
tutoring in Russia, he became senior teacher at Haileybury College before going
on to be the eminently successful headmaster of Westward Ho!, where George's
nephew, Rudyard Kipling, was once a pupil.

upon him as 'the separator of companions and the terminator of delights'.[3]

Practical as ever, Georgie hired a nursemaid to help her care for Pip and, despite the doleful note of her later recollections, the good times did continue in Kensington Square. Ned's charm was very great and acted like a magnet to his friends to whom he demonstrated not only an unusual degree of intimacy but also a rare loyalty. Their circle of acquaintance was increasing. They saw more of the 'Paris Gang', those friends of Val Prinsep who had studied with him at Glyère's *atelier*. The Howards became close to both of them. George Howard often spent his mornings with Ned in the studio at Kensington Square.

Georgie and Rosalind developed a close friendship, Georgie becoming decidedly under Rosalind's influence. Rosalind, beautiful, discerning and intelligent, was a daughter of Lord Stanley of Alderley. Increasingly, Rosalind became involved with the rights of women, and was a remarkable and tireless campaigner. She was also an ardent teetotaller and when George eventually became Earl of Carlisle and inherited Castle Howard, one of the first things she is said to have done was to tip the contents of its legendary cellar into the lake. This appalled most people in their right minds except for Georgie who, having been brought up as a devout Methodist, never touched a drop of alcohol in her life. Rosalind could surely, argued one wag, have had the claret sent down to Boodles.* Georgie owed a great deal to Rosalind's support and encouragement for her later involvement in the public arena of politics and the pronounced feminist she was to become. As the years passed, and time and events increased her melancholy, Georgie became involved in both women's rights and socialism, much influenced by Rosalind and Morris respectively.

*

---

* Boodles is a Gentleman's Club in St James's, London, renowned for its cellar.

The Burne-Joneses became fond of a young Jewish painter, Simeon Solomon.* Ned much admired his work and Georgie felt protective towards him. Swinburne and Rossetti were both friendly with him. 'He twisted ideas, had a genius for paradox, and when he was in a humorous vein, speaking with assumed seriousness, he convulsed his friends with laughter by his strange, weird imagination.'

It was evident to them all that Solomon was a homosexual (the word wasn't coined until the 1880s). With Burne-Jones and Swinburne he exchanged pornographic caricatures. Swinburne, with his penchant for flagellation and drunkenness, encouraged Solomon in his outrageous behaviour. They both got up to wild escapades, frequently naked, generally drunk. Their erotic drawings made Ned scream with delight. Often, they would all go out to watch a show or one of the tableaux so beloved by Rossetti at the Alhambra or the Empire in Leicester Square. There was about Solomon a cloak of isolation and gloom, apparent in his paintings, the result of his not belonging, of his Jewishness, of his homosexuality.

Later, Solomon came to a tragic end. He was out cruising in search of casual sex one evening in February 1873 and was arrested in a public lavatory for gross indecency, caught while in the act of buggery. He and his fellow offender, a stranger, one George Roberts, were flung into prison for twelve days. Roberts was sentenced to eighteen months of hard labour, while Solomon was fined £100. The difference in their sentences can only be considered an example of Victorian class distinction in its nastiest form. Solomon, although a Jew, was a gentleman. Poor Roberts was a bit of rough trade. The real tragedy lay in his friends' subsequent treatment of Solomon. Almost to a man, they cast him off, rejected and denied him. They were probably apprehensive lest their connection might result in a brush with the law for themselves. The one exception was the continued support shown

---

* Simeon Solomon (1840–1905).

to Solomon by both Georgie and Ned Burne-Jones. Yet even their commendable loyalty had its grotesque, if ludicrous aspect.

Although Solomon had got off without a prison sentence, his career, as he had known it, was at an end. Too much attention had been drawn to the incident to allow any gallery to exhibit his work again. He became a pavement artist, living from hand to mouth and ended up in St Giles's Workhouse in the seedy district of Seven Dials. On one occasion he was admitted to hospital, destitute, clad in rags and with no shoes. Ned gave him money from time to time, an act of kindness which Solomon repaid by turning up at the Burne-Joneses' house at dead of night, undoubtedly drunk, with a professional burglar whom he had met in the workhouse. They broke in and were in the middle of stealing the silver when the racket they made woke Solomon's sleeping benefactors. Georgie sent Ned off for a policeman, who arrested them. When it transpired, to Ned's horror, that the burglar was none other than his old friend Solomon, he then had to bribe the policeman to let him go. Solomon lingered on, a sorry reminder of his own downfall and his friends' betrayal, until 1905 when he died at St Giles's Workhouse.

The same summer, 1865, that Ned and Georgie had moved into Kensington Square and attended Rossetti's unforgettable party at Tudor House, the Madox Browns moved from Kentish Town to Fitzroy Square, inhabiting Number 37, that enormous house which Thackeray described so vividly as the house Colonel Newcome lived in, in his novel *The Newcomes*.

Before moving in, the Browns gave a farewell party at the old house, so familiar to their friends. The Morrises were there, Swinburne in evening dress, Whistler, Legros, Christina Rossetti and Gabriel, who was 'in a magnificent mood – no other word describes it when he passed through a room bringing pleasure to great and small by his beautiful urbanity, a prince among men'.[4] Like most gatherings convened under the benevolent aegis of Ford Madox Brown, this soirée became legendary for its bonhomie and fun.

It was also the first time that most of the party encountered Charles Augustus Howell,* that loose cannon in Pre-Raphaelite circles. Howell was a con man, an impostor, an adventurer, a thief and a liar. He was also charming, unscrupulous and his tall stories could be wildly funny. He claimed to be descended from the Portuguese aristocracy. Certainly, he had been born in Lisbon, the son of an English father and a Portuguese mother. He invariably wore a length of red ribbon in his buttonhole, which he claimed to be of 'The Order of Christ', which he said was an inherited family order. Good-looking, dark-haired, straight-nosed, with a magnificent physique and swarthy skin, and 'with his open manner, his winning address, with his exhaustless gift of amusing talk, not innocent of high colouring and actual blague – Howell was unsurpassable.'[5]

Ruskin trusted him and, for a while, he became Ruskin's secretary. Rossetti didn't trust him and knew all his bad points, but occasionally gave him work in the way of an agent. Rossetti couldn't, for the life of him, help enjoying Howell's company. Whistler positively revelled in it and later declared Howell to be a 'wonderful man . . . genius . . . splendidly flamboyant'.[6]

Howell was a man of mystery and no one quite knew what to believe about him. He certainly added to the fun. He is more reminiscent of Trelawny† than almost anybody else in the nineteenth century. There is one important difference: Trelawny confined his exaggerations to paper and took no material advantage of his friends. Perhaps the weirdest thing about Howell is that, because he had reinvented himself so often, he didn't seem to be entirely real,

---

* Charles Augustus Howell (1840–90) was an art dealer of a somewhat shifty nature.

† Edward Trelawny (1792–1881) was best known as a friend of Byron and Shelley. He was the author of *The Adventures of a Younger Son* (1831), a delightful but not altogether convincing account of his early life. Strangely enough, he physically resembled Howell as can be seen in his portrait by Ruskin's friend, Arthur Severn. He was also the model, with his daughter Louisa, in 1874, for Millais' painting *The North-West Passage*.

but was more like a character in some Restoration play, a Guignol who could be pulled out of an adjacent wing when it suited the plot. As usual, Rossetti made a potentially alarming situation absurd when he dashed off, in a limerick, such pertinent lines as:

> *A Portuguese person called Howell,*
> *Who lays on his lies with a trowel.*

Fanny Cornforth capped this unintentionally by her inability to aspirate her H's, Howell thus becoming 'The Owl', a case of serendipity which delighted Rossetti. She also delighted him by referring to him as 'Rizetti'. In his turn, he called her 'The Elephant', probably on account of her buxom proportions, an endearment which led to a series of charming, half-teasing admonishments illustrated with the most curious elephants ever seen.

It was at the Ford Madox Browns' farewell party to Kentish Town that it became apparent to everyone that the flirtation between Rossetti and Janey had developed into something more real, more tangible and more dangerous. Nobody commented on it overtly at the time, but they all felt it and were afraid of its potential threat.

Bearing the developing relationship between Janey and Rossetti in mind, it may not have been a coincidence entirely that it was at this point that Morris decided to give up Red House. His friends were devastated. Red House had been the pivotal demonstration of all they stood by: their agreed aesthetic values, the stage of their interactions and development as artists, to say nothing of the sheer exuberance and fun they all enjoyed together. Morris was emphatic. He said he was worn out by the incessant commuting to Red Lion Square to see to the business of the The Firm, and that he needed to be on the premises full time. Heartbreaking though it was, the 'Earthly Paradise' had finally eroded. Yet it remained a vision perceived, as Georgie recalled, in their 'dreams for years afterwards as one does a house known in childhood'.[7]

The Morrises moved into Queen's Square, a beautiful oasis in the busy bustling district of Bloomsbury, very close to their old quarters in Red Lion Square, and Morris took the business with him.

The Burne-Joneses decorated their new house in Kensington Square with furniture, wallpaper, glasses and candlesticks almost entirely from the Morris workshops. Georgie even made a gown of the same chintz that covered the wall hangings, which had the effect of making her look like part of the room. When they gave a party and invited the usual crowd of friends, including the 'Paris Gang', Ford Madox Brown noted, 'The house, being newly decorated in the Firm's taste, looked charming, the women looked lovely and the singing was unrivalled.' Morris, who was going to spend the night on the sitting-room sofa, had a narrow escape: the ceiling fell down in the middle of the night and would surely have crushed him. Fortunately, Morris had changed his mind and gone back with Val Prinsep to Little Holland House instead.

In 1866, Georgie gave birth to a baby girl, Margaret. Ned doted on her immediately and for ever. He was absorbed by her progress and made notes of all the little things she did and said. That summer they went to the seaside at Lymington in Hampshire. It was delightful. One day, Ned took the ferry to Freshwater, on the Isle of Wight, and called on Tennyson. Another time, Morris came down with Philip Webb. They had a grand time and buried Morris in the sand, leaving only his tufted head sticking out; a strange species of marine life. The following summer they spent at Oxford, returning to London to discover that the house in Kensington Square had been sold and the new owner wasn't going to renew their lease: they had to be out by Christmas and were forced to look elsewhere.

21

A GREEK TRAGEDY

In the 1860s there was a wealthy and highly cultured Greek community in London. Ex-patriots from the politically turbulent Hellenic and Ottoman states, they made their fortunes as bankers and by importing goods to England or, as the novelist Violet Hunt* put it somewhat unkindly, were purveyors of currants from Smyrna. The community was close knit and although members were to be seen at Mrs Prinsep's soirées at Little Holland House, they kept themselves to themselves in the main, intermarried. The relations between them were complex.

The patriarch of the family, old Constantine Ionides, had been a patron of G. F. Watts for years. His son, Alecco, had lived in Paris studying art at Glyère's studio in company with a group of talented Englishmen including Val Prinsep, Tom Armstrong, George du Maurier, Edward Poynter and the American artist, Whistler. It was an experience which was a turning point for them all. Years later, it was described by du Maurier in his memorable novel, *Trilby*.† On Alecco's return to England, he invited his painter

---

* No relation to Holman Hunt, Violet Hunt (1866–1942) was a novelist, feminist and supporter of women's suffrage. For several years, she was the mistress of Ford Madox Ford. In 1926, she published an autobiography, remarkable for its unreliability, *The Flurried Years*.

† *Trilby* by George du Maurier (1894) was an immensely popular novel with captivating illustrations by the author. Set in Paris in the 1850s, it is the story of Trilby O'Farrell, an artist's model, with whom all the artists fall in love. She comes under the influence of the diabolical Svengali, a Jewish musician and

friends from Paris to one of his parents' weekly garden parties at their opulent home at Tulse Hill some time during the summer of 1861. None of the painters present, who included du Maurier, Armstrong, Whistler and Rossetti, together with Swinburne, all arriving in a four-wheeler from London, ever forgot their first sight of the two ravishing sisters, Christina and Marie Spartali. They were all *à genoux* before them and immediately longed to paint them. Swinburne wept in rapture.* Whistler succeeded in persuading Christina to pose for him for *La Princesse du Pays de la Porcelaine*. Later, Marie was painted by Ford Madox Brown, Rossetti and Burne-Jones as well as posing for Mrs Prinsep's sister, the pioneer photographer Julia Margaret Cameron.

To the small band of painters, it seemed as though the Greek girls came from a more emancipated, less restricted environment than the socially hidebound one they were used to meeting in mid-Victorian drawing rooms. The sight of them eating figs and dates, lingering over them far more sensually than their English sisters would ever have dreamed, their décolletage fractionally lower, was alluring. But the exotic and relatively free and easy atmosphere was deceptive. As du Maurier put it: 'The women will sometimes take one's hand in talking to one, or put their arm round the back of one's chair at dinner, and with all this ease and *tutoiements*, or perhaps because of it, they are I do believe the most thoroughly well-bred and perfect gentlefolks in all of England.'[1]

Marie and her sister were expected, along with their cousins, the other two well-known Greek beauties, Aglaia Ionides and Mary Cassavetti, to make advantageous marriages within the Greek community. The girls were all heiresses as well as beauties, and it

---

hypnotist, but reverts to her true self on her death bed. It is a remarkable evocation of bohemian life in Paris and of Glyère's art school when du Maurier, Whistler, Prinsep and co. were all there.

* Swinburne later told Anny Thackeray how he wept from rapture at his first sight of Marie Spartali. He also burst into tears on saying goodbye to Anny after their first meeting at Fryston, the house of Monkton Milnes. It has to be admitted that he was easily moved to tears.

was part of the Greek tradition to keep the money in the family. Later, Aglaia made a suitable match, becoming Aglaia Coronio. She was noted for her beautiful embroidery and bookbinding, and was a lifelong friend of William Morris. Christina Spartali married a minor member of European royalty, was exceedingly unhappy, addicted to chloral, and sadly died of an overdose when she was thirty-eight. After an affair with Lord Ranelagh, which horrified her parents, Marie Spartali, referred to as 'Mrs Morris for beginners', was a student of Ford Madox Brown and became a painter of distinction. She startled everyone when she married the American painter, diplomat and journalist, W. J. Stillman. Mary Cassavetti married Dr Zambaco, a specialist in venereal diseases and doctor to the Greek community in Paris. It was an unhappy marriage and few people were surprised when Mary Zambaco returned to London with her two children. She went to live with her mother, Euphrosyne Cassavetti, born an Ionides and considered imperious and outrageous, even by Greek standards, in a huge and luxurious house in Gloucester Gardens, Kensington.

The effect these Greek beauties had on Pre-Raphaelite and aesthetic circles in London was profound. Unlike Lizzie, Janey and Annie Miller (Georgie remained all her life in a category of her own), they were exceptionally well educated, confident and rich. Dazzlingly beautiful, they were the antithesis of the Pygmalion syndrome. Not surprisingly, they aroused conflicting emotions: their sultry beauty and talent the cause of passion, anguish and many broken hearts.

There isn't any record of Georgie ever having been to the extravagant Sunday parties that the Ionides gave in Tulse Hill. The Greeks had left Tulse Hill and moved into Number 1 Holland Park. The district of Kensington around Holland Park was rapidly becoming fashionable for successful artists and those connected to the arts who, unlike Rossetti and Whistler down by the river in Chelsea, were part of the Establishment.

What originally had been a pastoral idyll of leafy lanes where hawthorn and dog roses grew, leading between the market gardens in Fulham to Chelsea and Kensington, was now a vast building site with workmen erecting huge and grandiose houses intended for the rich. Where there had been elms and rookeries there were now scaffolding and wheelbarrows. The population of Kensington was growing more quickly than anywhere else in London. The railway which led through the Holland Estate was reopened and Addison Road station* was opened in 1864. Holman Hunt, by now recovered from his painful relationship with Annie Miller, was already living in a large house, Tor Villa, on Camden Hill with his young wife, Fanny Waugh. A few years earlier, Thackeray had bought, knocked down and rebuilt an enormous house in a nineteenth-century interpretation of the style of Queen Anne at Number 2 Palace Green. In 1868, George and Rosalind Howard commissioned Philip Webb to design them a house at Number 1 Palace Green. Again, it was built of red brick in the Victorian version of what they called 'Queen Anne style' with white-painted sash windows, bay windows, gargoyles and gables which would surely have puzzled anyone who had actually been alive in the reign of Queen Anne. Val Prinsep's father-in-law, Frederick Leyland, a wealthy shipping magnate, paid for the site on the Holland Estate and would pay for the building of Val's own house with a large studio close to Little Holland House. Philip Webb, who had designed Red House for Morris, and had been commissioned by the Howards to design their house at Palace Green, was chosen as the architect. Charlie Collins, who had spent the summer painting with Millais and Holman Hunt down at Ewell all those years before, had now married Charles Dickens's daughter Katie and they lived nearby, although in considerably more modest circumstances. Next door to Val Prinsep, the painter Frederic Leighton was having a house built for him, designed by George Aitchison. Millais and Effie took a large house at Kensington Gore.

From being a country suburb of London, Kensington was

---

*   Addison Road Station is now Olympia underground station.

transformed into an intensely respectable urban residential district occupied by rich artists and writers, bankers, industrialists and the well-off rising middle classes – a far cry from Bohemia.

*

If Mary Zambaco had been English, she would have found herself in an ambivalent situation. Once she had left her husband in Paris in 1866 and had brought her children back to live with her mother, Euphrosyne, at Fairfield Lodge, 6 Addison Road in Holland Park, she would have led a demure existence in the background, atoning for her unacceptable behaviour. However, the Greeks didn't see it like their English contemporaries. Zambaco refused to divorce Mary, which meant that she couldn't remarry, but she brought her vast inheritance with her as well as her children (sadly, the son, Frank, was mentally unstable).

During the five years that she had lived in Paris, Mary's beauty had blossomed and she had grown into a remarkably sophisticated and cultured woman. She was also a talented sculptress and medallist; years later, she studied under Rodin. Several of her medallions are now in the British Museum, including a particularly lovely one of Marie Spartali, which has a madonna lily and the legend 'Sine Macula' – without imperfection – engraved on it. She also took lessons with the painter Alphonse Legros, later a professor of etching at the Slade School of Fine Art.

Having established himself at Number 1 Holland Park in surroundings of marvellous splendour, Constantine Ionides now gave frequent soirées, memorable for their lavishness as well as their charm. He invited not only his friends and extended family, but also the artists who used to be entertained at Tulse Hill. Burne-Jones became a regular guest. It must have been at one of these evening parties that Mary's mother, the overbearing Euphrosyne Cassavetti, generally known as 'the Duchess', took it into her head to commission Burne-Jones to paint a double portrait of Mary and her close friend and cousin, Marie Spartali. She left the subject matter up to Ned and he chose an encounter between Cupid and

Psyche. He began the preliminary studies for the painting while he
and Georgie were still living at Kensington Square.

Faced with both these ravishing girls, Ned was, not surprisingly, overwhelmed. If Marie Spartali was the more beautiful,
Mary Zambaco was the more flagrantly sexy. Once, one of Mary's
younger cousins was amazed when, after he had fallen fully
clothed into a swimming pool, she took him to her dressing room
to get dry and then began, without any sense of impropriety, to
undress in front of him. 'Her glorious red hair and almost phospho-
rescent white skin still shone out of the gloom of that dressing
room.'[2]

Marie had had an affair with Lord Ranelagh, the notorious
rake who had also had a dalliance with, amongst many others,
Annie Miller. Later, Marie conceived a passion for Gabriel. Her
father, Michael Spartali, favoured this alliance which would
undoubtedly have changed the course of the annals of the Pre-
Raphaelites. As William Michael Rossetti recorded in his diary
more than fifteen years later:

> It seems tolerably clear that when G first met her as Miss
> Spartali [in 1864], she was very graciously disposed towards
> him and would have accepted an offer from him had he made
> it, which assured G in most express terms that he was himself
> [Michael Spartali, Marie's father], in favour of such a match,
> and would from the first have promoted it.'[3]

After much persuasion, Marie's parents agreed to let her have
lessons in painting, for which she showed considerable talent. She
became a pupil of Ford Madox Brown. She never knew, in all the
years she studied under him, that he had fallen deeply in love with
her. Marie would never have dreamed of having an affair with a
married man. It was not for nothing that Mary Zambaco depicted
her with a madonna lily or chose that particular inscription, 'Sine
Macula'. Mary Zambaco herself was of a different cast.

*

Edward Burne-Jones and
William Morris, 1874,
photographed by
Frederick Hollyer.

Jane Morris, 1865,
photographed by
John R. Parsons.

Proserpine,
by Dante Gabriel
Rossetti, 1882.

Adoration of the Magi, altarpiece, to designs by William Morris and Edward Burne-Jones, 1861–62.

Interior of Kelmscott Manor by William Morris, *c.*1880.

Marie Stillman (née Spartali), 1868, photographed by Julia Margaret Cameron.

The M's at Ems, by Dante Gabriel Rossetti, 1869.

Georgiana Burne-Jones, *c.*1890, photographed by Frederick Hollyer.

The Beguiling of Merlin, by Edward Burne-Jones, 1872–77.

Cupid Delivering Psyche, by Edward Burne-Jones, 1867.

Phyllis and Demophoon, by Edward Burne-Jones, 1870.

Celestial Cupid, her famed son, advanced,
Holds his dear Psyche, sweet entranced
After her wandering labours long,
Till free consent the gods among
Make her his eternal bride;
And from her fair unspotted side
Two blissful twins are to be born,
Youth and Joy; so Jove hath sworn.

Milton, *Comus*

The subject of Cupid and Psyche had long intrigued Ned. Morris had conceived a vision of what he and Ned referred to as *The Big Story Book*, which was to be a collection of classical stories retold in verse by Morris and illustrated by Burne-Jones. Ned had already done seventy illustrations for *The Story of Cupid and Psyche*. Morris had engraved them on the block. Unfortunately, the project came to nothing. It wasn't until the mid-1930s that the American Loyd Haberly made wood cuts from Burne-Jones's original, which were now used to illustrate Robert Bridge's *Eros and Psyche*, printed by the Gregygnog Press.

Cupid and Psyche is a remarkable painting portraying the moment when Psyche is rescued by Cupid, who loves her, after having succumbed to her curiosity and opened the box given her by Proserpine, which Psyche believes contains Venus's secret cosmetics. It doesn't. It contains an infernal Stygian sleep which sends her into a nearly fatal coma until Cupid, in the guise of Marie Spartali, kisses her. Marie, as Cupid, envelops Mary in a deep embrace, her red robes making a wonderful mesh which ensnares Psyche, whose own green garment has fallen loose, exposing her alabaster breast. The opened blue box, now ignored by the lovers, is still puffing out the smoke of Stygian sleep. The sexual ambivalence is both lovely and disturbing and must have been more so to Burne-Jones's contemporaries.

Despite the charm, beauty and intelligence of Marie Spartali, it was the overt sexuality and sophistication of Mary Zambaco that ensnared Burne-Jones. He became enthralled, completely under her spell. It wasn't long before he had fallen deeply in love with her and had engaged on a climactic affair which would affect his entire subsequent life.

Relations between Ned and Georgie hadn't been going well. They never recovered the easy-going interchange and felicity of the early days of their marriage. Having known each other since childhood, they naturally had an especially strong sense of affinity but had matured in very different ways. Georgie remained all her life locked into the confines of the Methodist morals she had been brought up in. Ned had gradually, without fuss or ostentation, relinquished his faith in God, and while continuing to hold certain principles, he had replaced his lost faith with a profound belief in aesthetics. He had also developed a delight in sexual deviations which he couldn't share with Georgie. It wasn't possible for him to confide in her about the correspondence he enjoyed with Swinburne and Simeon Solomon, with all its references to flagellation and sodomy. When he went off with Rossetti and 'the boys' for a night out, to eat at a chophouse or one of the Italian restaurants off Leicester Square, he couldn't tell her how they would all go on to enjoy the fleshly delights of Cremorne Gardens, Piccadilly or the riskier Vaudeville theatres. Nor could he tell her how, later, he took pleasure in the abandoned performances of Kate Vaughn, who performed the erotic and beautifully swirly skirt dance at the Adelphi and Gaiety theatres. Naturally, Georgie knew of his nights out, but she didn't know the details and she didn't want to.

What Georgie didn't want to know, she turned a blind eye to. If Mary Zambaco's skin resembled alabaster, Georgie's determination was that of stone. But when, tidying up her husband's clothes, she discovered a love letter from Mary crumpled in his jacket pocket, even Georgie could no longer deny the truth. It wasn't merely their sexual relations which horrified her (she and Ned had taken to sleeping apart since the birth of Margaret), but the nature of his betrayal; of his desire for precisely the kind of sexual excitement she couldn't, or wouldn't provide. The discovery of Ned's affair with Mary Zambaco had a profound effect on Georgie. She shrivelled. In consequence, the fun, the light and the laughter of her marriage to Ned was extinguished, and outward observances were upheld with a propriety bordering on the fanatic.

Forced to move from Kensington Square, Georgie's choice of the location of their new house was surprising. In those days, Fulham was considered as unknown territory, not really in London proper. Georgie decided on The Grange, a substantial eighteenth-century house with a large garden in the North End Road in the unfashionable, still pleasantly rural district of Fulham.* It has been mooted that Georgie's choice of such a relatively inaccessible place was because, having discovered the unwelcome evidence of Ned's affair with Mary Zambaco, she wanted a definite geographical line between her household and what she now saw as the temptations of Kensington. Difficult to find, the directions were famously said to be: 'Go down the Cromwell Road till your cab horse drops dead, and then ask someone.'[4]

This didn't deter Ned's multitude of friends from seeking him out. The rent was more than Ned and Georgie were used to. They decided to share it with Ned's old school friend, Wilfred Heeley and his wife, for, after all, The Grange had originally been two houses, later knocked into one. The garden was spacious and lovely, planted with roses, rosemary and lilac, apples and pears and a mulberry tree. It was the stage for many convivial gatherings.

Still reeling from the discovery of Ned's infidelity, Georgie steeled herself to decorate the house, faithful, as always, to the school of William Morris. Dimly veiled in hues of green, willows, sedge and mud, The Grange could be considered as a showpiece for William Morris & Co. For the first time, Ned had a splendid, large studio specially built for him. It was lit by skylights and had

---

*   The author can remember when, aged sixteen, she was taken by her future husband, Burgo Partridge, to meet Clare Shepherd, author of *Lobsters at Little Hampton*. Clare told her how she remembered sheep browsing on Parson's Green, at the turn of the twentieth century.

a gallery on the first floor where he would show his paintings, and then, up three steps to the heart of the studio, was his own very private working space where 'only my most dear friends will penetrate'.

*

Mary Zambaco penetrated more frequently than Georgie liked. But Georgie refused to interfere. Her stoicism was frightening. Ned was one bewitched. Loving narrative, he also stated: 'I mean by a picture a beautiful, romantic dream of something that never was, never will be – on a light better than any light that ever shone – in a land no one can define or remember, only desire – and the forms divinely beautiful – and then I wake up, with the waking of Brynhild.'

Ned painted Mary as Dante's Beatrice, as the Image in his Pygmalion series, as herself. He made study after study of her beautiful face and for many years could not bear to part with the images he had made of her. She modelled for the *Chant d'Amour*, reading a volume illustrated by his own painting. He painted her in *Desideratum* from Spenser's *Faerie Queene*; as Nimbue in *The Beguiling of Merlin*; as Circe. He was obsessed by her. When Mary's cousin, Marie Spartali, eventually married the American painter, diplomat and journalist, Willy Stillman, Mary's mother, 'the Duchess', commissioned Ned to paint Mary naked as Venus Epithalamia for her wedding present to Marie. 'The Duchess' liked the portrait of her naked daughter so much that she paid Burne-Jones to paint a copy which she then hung in her grand drawing room on public view at all her soirées. Most famously, Ned painted Mary as Phyllis and used her head to model for Demophoön in the canvas that was to cause so much trouble. *Phyllis and Demophoön* is a wonderful painting. Phyllis, Queen of Thrace, had tried to kill herself when her lover, Demophoön, appeared to have abandoned her. The gods took pity on her and turned her into an almond tree. On his return from the wars, Demophoön miraculously recognized Phyllis in her new guise, embraced the tree which metamorphosed back into the shape of Phyllis, and they were passionately reconciled. The fact that Ned used Mary's head for Demophoön as well as for Phyllis lends the painting a curiously hermaphrodite quality, despite the unequivocal depiction of Demophoön's genitalia.

Earlier, Burne-Jones had been invited to become a member of the Old Water-Colour Society. When, after some deliberation, he finally accepted, neither parties were happy entirely. Ned's use of medium was part of the trouble. He frequently mixed oil and watercolour, sometimes with glue or gum arabic, a form of experimentation he had learned from Rossetti. Purists at the Old Water-Colour Society disapproved, and possibly they had a point. After all, if a watercolour isn't a watercolour, but a bastard of mixed mediums, it can hardly be classed as a watercolour. Ned's view, understandably enough, was that the bigwigs at the society should have thought of this before asking him to be a member. But what they all knew, and what nobody spoke of openly, was that the society's main objection to *Phyllis and Demophoön* was that it was all too recognizably a double portrait of Mary Zambaco; that gossip was now rife about the love affair between Ned and Mary and, even more shockingly, Demophoön was portrayed stark naked, his genitals fully exposed, his thigh erotically draped with Phyllis's scarf which appears to have been blown between his legs by the wind. The finished painting, when framed, bore the epigraph *Dic mihi quid feci? Nisi non sapienter amavi* (Tell me what I have done, except to love unwisely).

Mrs Grundy demanded to be appeased. As is usual in such cases, it was an unpleasant business for everyone concerned. The club first asked Ned to veil Demophoön's genitals. Quite rightly, Ned declined. Then the President of the Society, a perfectly harmless man, Fred Taylor, suggested that Ned could possibly chalk over Demophoön's genitals and scrub out the chalk later. Ned was outraged. He resigned from the club and Fred Taylor showed a remarkable moral stance by resigning as the club's president, too, understandably ashamed of the beastly position he had allowed himself to be cornered into.

Mary wanted to run off with Ned. She tried to persuade him to leave Georgie and his children and lead a sybaritic life on the islands of Greece. They could live a gloriously romantic existence, living off her millions, Hymettus honey, wine, love, figs and goats' cheese. Away from the philistine world of London, Ned would be able to paint canvases worthy of the genius she insisted he possessed. Ned was very much tempted. He was on the verge of eloping with her and only backed down at the last moment. Later, Morris, as much for Georgie's sake as for Ned's, intervened and suggested that he and Ned went off to Italy while matters simmered down.

'Poor old Ned's affairs have come to a smash altogether,' Rossetti wrote to Ford Madox Brown in a state of voyeuristic ecstasy:

> [Ned] and Topsy after the most dreadful to-do started for Rome suddenly, leaving the Greek damsel beating up the quarters of all his friends for him, and howling like Cassandra. Georgie has stayed behind. I hear today, however, that Top and Ned got no further than Dover, Ned now so dreadfully ill that they will probably have to return to London. Of course the dodge will be not to let a single hint of their movements become known to anybody, or the Greek (whom I believe he is really bent on cutting) will catch him again. She provided herself with laudanum for two at least, and insisted on their winding up matters in Lord Holland's Lane. Ned didn't see it, when she tried to drown herself in the water in front of Browning's house &c. – bobbies collaring Ned who was rolling with her on the stones to prevent it, and God knows what else.'[5]

Rosalind Howard wrote in her diary that when Ned backed down, 'Mme Z. . . . produced a poison bottle and said she would drink it and at once a struggle ensued – J. tried to take it from her – the police came up – at the same moment appeared Lucas Ionides – her former friend and he explained matters to the police and walked off with Mme Z. Jones walked away and then fainted – a regular drama   I suspect Ionides followed her to see what she was after and from anger and jealousy repeated the story.'[6]

Both Ned and Georgie were shattered by the episode. Ned went back to The Grange, his tail very much between his legs, and collapsed. When people turned up to see him, Georgie turned them away, pretending, not very convincingly, that Ned was still away. Nobody knew what to do. Georgie's pride prevented any of her friends from approaching her until Rosalind Howard gamely took the bit between her teeth and turned up at The Grange, insisting that Georgie should accept the loan of fifty pounds. Georgie refused the loan, although she could have done with it, but did confide in Rosalind. She also told Rosalind that she and Ned had stopped sleeping together since the birth of Margaret, which Rosalind thought a mistake, although she realized that Georgie didn't want any more children. It would have been a marvellous act of friendship if Rosalind, that fierce defender of women's rights, had enlightened Georgie about the forms of contraception then available.

After putting up a tremendous show of bravery which must have cut Ned to the quick, Georgie took herself and the children off to lodgings in Oxford for a month. In a letter which does not ring true entirely, she wrote to Rosalind:

> Indeed, my dear, I am no heroine at all – and I know when I come short almost as well as anyone else does – I have simply acted all along from very simple little reasons, which God and my husband know better than anyone – I don't know what God thinks of them. Dearest Rosalind, be hard on no one in this matter, and exalt no one – may we all come well through it at last. I know one thing, and that is that there is love enough between Edward and me to last out a long life if it is given us . . .'[7]

Georgie also found solace from George Eliot's understanding and sympathy. She had only recently met George Eliot, going to the novelist's 'At Homes' at North Bank, partly worshipping at her shrine the things George Eliot stood for: Literature, Freethinking and Feminism, albeit in an interpretation all her own. George Eliot had the tact to address her anxieties about Georgie through the medium of Rosalind.

By now, the rift in the Burne-Joneses' marriage was the talk of the town. Georgie and the children returned to The Grange in March 1870. Typically, Georgie plastered over the cracks in her marriage with coatings so deftly applied that the flaws which lasted were invisible to anyone except their closest friends. For, try as she might, even with the blessing of her Dissenting Christianity, Georgie could not forgive Ned. As a result, she never recovered her first innocence or the happy-go-lucky, carefree existence of the early days of their marriage.

22

AFTERMATH

It was a boon when, sometime later, in 1872, the Morrises moved from Queen's Square to Chiswick. Morris developed a habit of breakfasting every Sunday with the Burne-Joneses. It was almost like the old days. The Sunday breakfasts were enjoyable. Morris, whose girth continued to expand to amazing proportions, helped himself to vast amounts of eggs, sausages, bacon, cold pheasant, kedgeree, toast and marmalade. The two men sat about laughing over the antics of Ally Sloper, a character in a cartoon strip, a lazy sod who spent most of his time vainly trying to avoid his landlord, bank manager and various other unwelcome creditors. Then, Ally Sloper consigned to the children's amusement, Ned and Topsy would retire to the studio and discuss forthcoming joint work with all the ardour of the old days.

But there was a difference. Morris, whose wife was conducting an increasingly flagrant affair with Rossetti, which Morris chose to ignore, was beginning to fall in love with Georgie, who had always been close to his heart. Morris and Georgie were both built of the same material. Fiercely moral, clinging to their old scruples, inspired by such early reading matter as *The Broad Stone of Honour*, *Sintram*, and *The Heir of Redclyffe*, neither of them had given up their earlier belief in such values. Morris may have put the tiny Georgie on a pedestal, but it is beyond the imagination to physically make love to anyone on such an inconvenient setting without the stout Mr Morris and the diminutive Mrs Burne-Jones toppling, not exactly head over heels in love, but, rather, smashing the pedestal.

Chivalry dictated that love should be maintained between male friends, honoured between the opposite sexes. This was not to say that Morris considered, as, possibly, Georgie did, either of their errant spouses to be wicked. His battle was to accept his wife's behaviour without condemnation. In the event, he succeeded, even though Janey, much later, told him straight out that she had never loved him. Even though Ned became openly critical about Georgie's dress, her manner and her political views, he never said so directly to Georgie. He had loved her since her childhood. Small wonder, then, that Georgie felt betrayed. Her remark to Rosalind, that there was 'love enough to last out a long life', was all the more heartbreaking. The difference between the affairs between Ned and Mary Zambaco, and Janey and Rossetti, and between Morris's feelings for Georgie, was that Morris and Georgie shared a deep understanding and sympathy. It is more than likely that Morris would have been deeply shocked had Georgie reciprocated his desire. For Georgie, it was out of the question. Morris, too, increasingly indulged in a Platonic intimacy with the sympathetic Aglaia Coronio.

Ruskin, in some typically well-meaning and misguided bid to bring his errant protégé Ned to his senses, arranged for Howell, of all people, to take lodgings close to The Grange. For a time, Howell acted as an interim agent for Ned. Then Howell got it into his head that it was high time Georgie and Mary met face to face. Quite what Howell wished to achieve remains a mystery. Georgie must have glimpsed Mary coming in and out of Ned's studio over the protracted time that he was painting various portraits of her. It is just possible that, with Georgie's steely determination, she had managed to avoid having to greet Mary on her own domain. Howell arranged for Mary to turn up at The Grange when Ned and Georgie were, quite naturally, present in their own home. Georgie, in her most icy manner, refused to acknowledge Mary. How Mary responded to this reception is not recorded. Ned walked in to the drawing room and discovered Georgie and Mary recoiling from each other. He staggered, hit his head on the marble fireplace, and fell into a dead faint. Georgie and Ned refused to receive Howell into their house ever again. It was also the end of relations between Ruskin and Howell, but not the end of the story for Howell and Rossetti.

*

> *Who'll dig the grave?*
> *I, said the Owl,*
> *With my pick and shovel,*
> *I'll dig the grave.*

The summer of 1869 was traumatic for everyone concerned. When Gabriel, in abandoned despair after Lizzie's death, had spontaneously thrust his unpublished poems into her coffin, he had meant this gesture with all his heart. Now he regretted his impetuosity. Since Lizzie's death, Gabriel had been working assiduously on his poetry as much as at his painting. The trouble was that, having buried his poems in Lizzie's coffin, he could no longer remember them. He knew, and he was right, that some of them were certainly worth recalling; that some of them were very good indeed. He was also under the mistaken impression that all of them had been inspired by Lizzie. Gabriel wanted his poetry back. He was also deeply troubled by his eyesight, which he imagined to be failing. His old friend, William Bell Scott, who much admired Gabriel's poetry, exhorted him to concentrate on it. Janey, too, encouraged him to rewrite his old verse.

It was Howell who suggested it. With his combination of insolence and charm he asked Gabriel why, if he was serious about the recovery of his poetry, he didn't dig up Lizzie's coffin, open it and extract the volume of verse. By his sheer audacity, Howell called Gabriel's bluff. There was a man, Howell knew, a friend of William Michael's, someone in the Home Office, who could sign the necessary papers and there was no reason for Gabriel's mother, who owned the family burial ground in Highgate Cemetery to know anything about it. Having initiated the scheme, Howell became eager for it to be carried out. It appealed to his sense of the macabre.

The man in the Home Office turned out to be Henry A. Bruce who was not only the Home Secretary, but also a friend of Gabriel's. Bruce signed the order giving permission for Lizzie's body to be exhumed and the volume of verse to be removed from the coffin. The business was to be carried out in the utmost secrecy in the presence of Howell, two gravediggers and Henry Virtue Tebbs, a solicitor. To avoid publicity, the exhumation had to be carried out at dead of night.

On the evening of 5 October, Rossetti went to Howell's house in Fulham and sat with his wife, Kitty, while the others went to Highgate. They carried a lantern and lit a bonfire in the graveyard. By the light of the flames leaping up and down, the gravediggers started to dig. Any passer-by would be forgiven for starting in terror at the ghastly sight, his hair standing on end, his screams stifled in his throat, before he ran, heading for the nearest asylum. When Howell returned home to his wife Kitty, who had been attending to Rossetti, he reported that Lizzie, mummified by laudanum, remained intact in all her beauty and that her glorious abundant red-gold hair had grown to her feet, enshrouding her still lovely figure.

It was kind of Howell, even if his description is implausible. The book of poems had to be sent to be disinfected. It smelt vile and had been riddled through by worms, the writing almost illegible after so long in the tomb. Gabriel couldn't keep a secret to save his life. A few days later, he told his brother William Michael what had happened. He also told most of his closest friends: Ford Madox Brown, Swinburne and his own assistant, Henry Treffry Dunn. Of course, the truth 'oozed'* out, as Gabriel put it only too graphically, although it is doubtful that Gabriel's mother ever knew of it. The ever obliging William Michael made a clean copy of the poems for Gabriel, however distasteful the task. Gabriel set about rewriting them.

---

* Gabriel may well have been influenced by his reading of Elizabeth Gaskell's novel *Wives and Daughters*, in which a dramatic chapter is entitled *Secret Thoughts Ooze Out*. The phrase, of course, was in common colloquial use.

23

JANEY

At the height of Ned's affair with Mary Zambaco, Rossetti's long, complicated and ultimately unhappy affair with Janey became evident. Even if they did not talk about it overtly, all of their friends knew that the origins of their attraction had started long ago when they had been decorating the inside of the Oxford debating union. They had all been aware of and occasionally embarrassed by Rossetti's undisguised hostility to Morris and his desire for Janey at Red House, and had often been made uncomfortable by Lizzie's transparent distress. Rossetti's feelings for Janey became perceived, on the surface at least, as part of the order of the day. Exactly when the transition was made from fantasy to a *fait accompli*, none of their friends ever knew precisely.

After a visit to Queen Square, Henry James, who was fascinated by Janey, wrote to his sister Alice:

Je n'en reviens pas – she haunts me still. A figure cut out of a missal – out of one of Rossetti's or Hunt's pictures – to say this gives but a faint idea of her, because when such an image puts on flesh and blood, it is an apparition of fearful and wonderful intensity. It's hard to say whether she's a grand synthesis of all the pre-Raphaelite pictures ever made – or they a 'keen analysis' of her – whether she's an original or a copy. In either case she is a wonder. Imagine a tall lean woman in a long dress of some dead purple stuff, guiltless of hoops (or of anything else, I should say), with a mass of crisp black hair heaped into great wavy projections on each of her temples, a thin pale face, a pair of strange sad, deep, dark Swinburnian eyes, with great thick black oblique brows, joined in the middle and tucking themselves away under her hair, a mouth like the '*Oriana*' in our illustrated Tennyson, a long neck, without any collar, and in lieu thereof some dozen strings of outlandish beads – in fine complete. On the wall was a large nearly full-length portrait of her by Rossetti, so strange and unreal that if you hadn't seen her you'd pronounce it a distempered vision, but in fact an extremely good likeness.

In July 1865, Rossetti had arranged for Janey to be photographed in his garden in Cheyne Walk by a professional photographer, John Parsons. The result is of Janey looking suggestively voluptuous, wearing a flowing silk dress, her mane of crinkly dark hair worn in a loose bundle, in various poses: standing, sitting, reclining on a sofa in the garden. She looks sultry, exotic and beautiful. They are the epitome of Janey as she is remembered and the key to the portraits Rossetti later painted of her.

She first began to pose formally for Rossetti after she and Morris had moved to Queen Square. Of course, he had sketched and painted her since they had met back in 1857, but apart from the time he had painted her as Guinevere for the Debating Union in Oxford, he hadn't asked her to model specifically for him. Morris seemed all in favour of the arrangement and at first went along with her to Cheyne Walk for the sittings, and quite often they would both spend the night there.

Gradually, it became an accepted habit for Janey to go to Cheyne Walk on her own. During this time, Rossetti painted her as Mariana, *La Pia de' Tolomei*, and Réverie. In all these paintings, she comes across as languid and sultry; a tragic creature exuding sex. Naturally, their intimacy grew as the sittings progressed. This is fundamental to the nature of the relationship between artist and model. It is not necessarily expressed sexually, although the intimacy necessarily has a degree of sexuality woven into it. It is for the model to allow herself to be read, very much as a camera will reveal the workings of an actor's face on film if the actor is in a close conspiracy with the lens. Given Rossetti's nature, their intimacy was very highly charged with sex. Janey's feelings are harder to determine. She was not given to expressing herself directly but passively allowed things to wash over her. Her complicity with Rossetti was tacit, deep, not defined by words.

In addition to Janey's unchaperoned visits to Gabriel's studio, his manner towards her in public was becoming increasingly unguarded. Given their tightly knit circle of friends, they were bound to meet in one another's homes. When William Bell Scott and his wife, Laetitia, gave a dinner party in his house at 92 Cheyne Walk, Gabriel made a spectacle of himself by his overt attentions to Janey, 'sitting sideways to her, that sort of thing'. On another occasion, he ignored the rest of the party and fed her strawberries one by one, pretending oblivion to Morris's discomfort. Concurrently with his disregard for public opinion, Gabriel, like a strutting peacock, couldn't resist poking fun at Morris. He was unkind, unchivalrous and wickedly diverting.

24

BAD EMS

The small town of Bad Ems is situated in a deep gorge between wooded hills. The town leans against rocks, one of the most picturesque rocks in the world. There are promenades and gardens and everything is delightful.

FYODOR DOSTOEVSKY to his wife, 1874

A secluded and mountainous part of Stiria, there was, in old time, a valley of the most surprising and luxuriant fertility. It was surrounded, on all sides, by steep and rocky mountains, rising into peaks, which were always covered with snow, and from which a number of torrents descended in constant cataracts. One of these fell westward, over the face of a crag so high, that, when the sun had set to everything else, and all below was darkness, his beams still shone full upon this waterfall, so that it looked like a shower of gold.

JOHN RUSKIN, *The King of the Golden River*,
written for Euphemia Chalmers Gray, 1841

Bad Ems, in the Rhineland-Palatinate of central Germany, is situated in the narrow valley of the River Lahn between Cologne and Frankfurt, a few miles as the crow flies over the mountains from Koblenz. Famous for its medicinal springs, it has been frequented for their health-giving properties since Roman times. By the middle of the nineteenth century, it had reached its zenith as a fashionable spa popular not only with Germans but also with

Russians, French, Middle Europeans and, in particular, with the English. The town was a medley of different styles of architecture, reflecting the international nature of its clientele. On the Right Bank of the Lahn were imposing Baroque hotels, the Casino and the Kurhaus, which reflected their extravagant façades into the bubbling river. On the Left Bank, the same was true of a line of elegant white stucco villas, one of the most beautiful being the Schloss Balmoral which was completed towards the end of 1868.

Promenades, shaded by linden trees, ran on either side of the river interspersed with ornamental gardens complete with flower sellers, beer gardens, band stands, medicinal drinking fountains and cafés, where the visiting invalid population could sip the healing waters and gossip with fellow sufferers, while their chaperones could indulge in plum brandy, coffee, delicious sticky cakes and gaze at the swans on the water. It was possible, at very little cost, to hire a boat and either be rowed along the river or, if one was lucky, be propelled by a strong companion to a shady dell on the shore out of town. In the immediate hinterland were moist, luscious valleys with cultivated vineyards and meadows full of wild flowers, the tranquillity interrupted only by birdsong and the mellow sound of cowbells. The evening shadows fell early since the valley was bounded on either side by snow-capped mountain ranges, with dense forests climbing upwards until the tree line was reached. To the north lay Westerwald; to the south, Tanus. Bad Ems and its immediate neighbourhood, including the lead and silver mines to the west of the town, which accounted for the health-giving properties of the mineral waters, gave the place an uncanny resemblance to a fairy tale from the collection of the Brothers Grimm.

None of this appealed to William Morris. He was in a bad mood, fretting and blustering, partly to conceal his very real anxiety, partly because, as a result of his anxiety, he had blundered over the travel arrangements. In London, Janey's health had taken a serious turn for the worse and her doctors ordered her to take a cure at Bad Ems, noted mainly for the waters' therapeutic powers in curing chronic pulmonary complaints, disordered nerves, bronchial diseases and phthisis, sterility and vaginal problems. Morris had messed up the hotel bookings. It didn't help that Morris only spoke the German of Luther's Bible, which the local inhabitants failed to understand, partly perhaps because of his accent. It made him feel a fool and it made the Germans laugh. There was nowhere for them to stay until finally they moved into rooms at the Fortuna, a dowdy auberge where they were the only guests. It was not an auspicious beginning to their visit, which they expected to last for at least two months.

Janey's days were taken up by her treatments. She was seen by the doctors, massaged, drank the nasty, tepid waters and spent time bobbing up and down with other female patients in the baths, the water alkaline and surprisingly bubbly. Clothed in voluminous bathing dresses, the invalid ladies ploughed their way monotonously up and down the length of the baths. Looking like porpoises rigged out for an aquatic dance, they were buoyed up by wooden trays which held glasses of medicinal water and wooden bowls of forest fruit, sour cream and cracked wheat, clamped in place with metal rings. Spoons, carved from goats' horn, were attached by metal chains. Bathing was followed by a steam bath and then a vaginal douche from a jet-propelled fountain with the endearing name of the *Bubenquelle*.

While Janey was immersed in such treatments, Morris applied himself to the finishing verses of *The Earthly Paradise*. The charms of Bad Ems, and they were various, were lost upon him. He was prejudiced against it by the fashionable folk who frequented it – mainly, it might seem, people who had nothing ostensibly wrong with them but who used the resort in lieu of a holiday stamping ground. Amongst the invalids, some genuine, some *malades imaginaires*, were rakes with monocles, fat ladies, bald dukes, females with false fronts to their fringes and large bustles to their behinds, sallow-faced minor royals eking out their grace-and-favour pensions, to say nothing of their retinues of shrill-voiced ladies' maids, foppish footmen and domineering factotums.

Had the Morrises been luckier, they might have met Ivan Turgenev, Pauline Viardot or Fyodor Dostoevesky, who were all *habitués* of Bad Ems. Had they come the following summer, they would have encountered the King of Prussia, Wilhelm I, in frenzied debate with the French ambassador, Count Benedetti, while Otto von Bismarck hovered in the background, over the vexed question of the successor to the Spanish throne – a prince of the Hohenzollern dynasty was being mooted, much to the alarm of the French government. The ensuing disagreement, which was to lead to the totally unnecessary and disastrous Franco-Prussian War of 1870–1, might have seized the attention of the political animal in Morris and kept him on his toes, but he was a year too early for such distractions, disliked the monotony, and consequently brooded. Morris didn't lack a sense of humour, but it was very different from the kind of humour someone such as Thackeray had possessed. Thackeray and Dickens would have discovered an exquisite pleasure in observing the niceties of human folly in such an absurd microcosm of high society. But then, Morris wasn't a novelist and didn't regard the human race from that particular point of view. Instead, he thanked his lucky stars that he had brought the manuscript of *The Earthly Paradise* with him and spent the long hours while Janey was being hosed and pummelled combing over the final verses, and embarking on *The Death of Paris*,[*] which he had shirked until then.

Very much a fish out of water, Morris managed to escape from the torpor of the spa he so disliked in order to roam around the countryside. Although he found it claustrophobic, the narrow valley boxed in by the mountains, he gradually grew fond of it. He familiarized himself with the dense beech woods, the great gorges

---

[*] *The Death of Paris* is a crucial part of *The Earthy Paradise*, in which Paris, the son of Priam, was wounded by one of the poisoned arrows of Hercules. He went in search of Ida, who led him to Oenone, with whom he had once been in love, for she, who knew many secret things, alone could heal him. This time she failed and so Paris died.

and the riverbank. Finding a congenial grassy spot, he could read
for hours on end, appropriately Goethe in translation: *Wilhelm
Meister* and *Eclectic Affinities*. Not that he neglected Janey. He was
concerned that she was slow to show any improvement. She
disliked the food, finding it indigestible, heavy and greasy, and
couldn't eat it. She was in constant pain, her back giving her so
much agony that on bad days she was confined to bed. They both
found the heat of the day intolerable. The one thing they enjoyed
was the local beer which they drank ice cold. Morris was anxious
that Janey should be out of doors as much as possible instead of
staying mewed up in their drab hotel. He took her out on the river
in 'a machine like a butter-boat with a knife and fork for oars'.[1]
On his walks he had discovered a shady spot on the riverbank
where she could lie on cushions and enjoy the peace of the evening.

The fact that Rossetti and Janey kept up a voluminous correspondence all the while, betraying their very real love and
intimacy, didn't help to alleviate the tension of the Morris' stay at
Bad Ems. Morris read the letters Rossetti sent to his wife. It wasn't
just because Janey was no more discreet than Gabriel about their
liaison and left them lying about. Included in the letters were a
great many messages from Gabriel to Morris, asking him to do
favours, run errands, and giving him unsolicited and patronizing
advice.

Gabriel couldn't resist illustrating the letters with wickedly
funny cartoons, mostly at Morris's expense. One of the most
delightful is of Janey in the bath, her nakedness only hidden by
the tub itself, sipping medicinal water and being hosed by a
powerful douche while Morris, seated beside the bath, is declaim-
ing to a resigned Janey from one of the seven volumes of *The
Earthly Paradise*. To complement the volumes, she has seven glasses
of the beastly water to drink. The cartoon can only have confirmed
what Morris and everyone already knew; that his great friend and
former mentor was in love with his wife. Infuriating though it
might be, the cartoon was irresistible. Morris was incapable of not
laughing at a good joke, particularly against himself.

More seriously, Gabriel wrote Janey a letter which Morris might well have found more disturbing:

> All that concerns you is the all absorbing question with me, as dear Top will not mind my telling you at this anxious time. The more he loves you, the more he knows that you are too lovely and noble not to be loved: and, dear Janey, there are too few things that seem worth expressing as life goes on, for one friend to deny another the poor expression of what is most in his heart. But he is before me in granting this, and there is no need for me to say it. I can never tell you how much I am with you at all times. Absence from your sight is what I have long been used to; and no absence can ever make me so far from you again as your presence did for years. For this long inconceivable change, you know now what my thanks must be.'[2]

By September 1869, Janey was pronounced well enough to travel back to England. Unfortunately, the journey was uncomfortable and the crossing to Dover rough with agitated seas, which left Janey quite done up by the time they reached London. Whatever the benefits to Janey's health, the stay in Bad Ems had emphasized to Morris the serious nature of the reciprocation of the feelings between Gabriel and Janey. It was the beginning of a definitive change in the pattern of their marriage.

25

CRACKING UP

Rossetti was working hard, rewriting his poems. By the time he had finished them and had read them to William Michael, he was exhausted, in a highly nervous state, and was suffering from insomnia. In August 1869, his old friend the poet and artist William Bell Scott invited him to stay at Penkill Castle, Ayrshire, the home of Scott's friend and mistress, Alice Boyd. The sixteenth-century round tower, its crenulations like a pie crust, has nineteenth-century additions.

Alice Boyd, who had already met Rossetti in London, wasn't prepared for his overwrought state. The visit was tense, neither Bell Scott nor Alice Boyd were able to keep up with Rossetti's unpredictable behaviour, however much they tried. One afternoon, Alice drove Rossetti and Scott out in the pony and trap for a little excursion to a local beauty spot, the Devil's Punch Bowl. They got out to look at the view and to go as far as the edge of the cliff, overlooking a deep ravine. 'Never shall I forget the expression of Gabriel's face when he bent over the precipice peering into the unfathomed water dark as ink, in which sundry waifs flew round and round like souls lost in hell'.[1] Alice Boyd and Bell Scott were both convinced that Gabriel was going to hurl himself unto death. Scott took a step towards Gabriel, but he couldn't have saved him for the ground was 'as slippery as glass by the wet green lichen'.[2] Suddenly Gabriel put his hand into Scott's and allowed himself to be led away. They sat down, trembling. None of the three of them said a word of what had passed.

On another occasion, Scott and Gabriel were out for a walk, climbing the hill towards Barr, where the River Stincher meets the Water of Greg. They noticed a chaffinch lying in their path. It remained quite still. Gabriel lifted it up. He suddenly seemed in an overwrought state. Bell Scott suggested the chaffinch was tame and had escaped from its cage. Gabriel insisted that it was Lizzie's spirit which had come to warn him of doom. Bell Scott couldn't think what to say and they walked in silence back to the castle, leaving the chaffinch forgotten. Alice met them saying that the strangest thing had happened: the visitor's bell, which needed a good strong tug, had been rung, and apparently by no one. On finding out that the bell had been rung at the same time that Scott and Gabriel had come across the chaffinch, Gabriel gave Scott a penetrating and significant look. Yet Gabriel did not mention the chaffinch to Alice.

Rossetti's spirits seemed to improve and eventually he set off for London. Bell Scott wasn't entirely happy about Gabriel's state of mind, and his own wasn't much cheered when he and Alice were convinced they heard Gabriel's voice intoning his poems at the hour he usually read to them. It's just possible, that if Gabriel had known about it, the uncanny voice would have given him the last laugh.

Bell Scott was right about Gabriel, although it didn't need uncommon perception to realize that he was in a bad way. Back in London, Gabriel was becoming more of a recluse and his moods swung up and down like a pendulum. Worried about the reception of his forthcoming collection of poems, he chafed at the bit, unable to sleep, gnawing the sheets in a state of intolerable anxiety. He was also bedevilled by a terror of losing his eyesight, as his father had done.

Sometime after their return from Bad Ems, Morris and Janey reached an understanding which cannot have been easy for Morris. Janey refused to give up her relationship with Rossetti but would ostensibly remain Morris's wife, continue to live with him and to care for Jenny and May. As silent as Morris was talkative, Janey was an essentially passive, likeable yet elusive character and was hard to fathom. Despite her lack of any formal education, she was intelligent, had become exceptionally well read, and had what her contemporaries referred to as 'presence'. What she seems to have lacked was a sense of humour – something intrinsic to both Morris and Rossetti. Her relations with Morris never developed into that tender intimacy which results from years of close union. After she left Rossetti, she dismissed him as being mad and therefore not worth caring for. It is difficult to be convinced that although, like most people, she enjoyed admiration and adulation, she was ever truly intimate with anybody.

*

By March 1870, Gabriel was still overwrought. His old friend, the painter and feminist Barbara Leigh Smith, who was now married to the French doctor, Eugène Bodichon, suggested that he went to recoup at her house in the country, Scalands Gate, near Robertsbridge in Sussex. She had already offered Scalands to the American painter and diplomat, W. J. Stillman, who was known to Gabriel through his friendship with William Michael. Barbara agreed that Gabriel and Willy Stillman should share Scalands between them, although there remained an unfortunate confusion in the minds of both men as to which of them was nominally the host.

Recently built to Barbara's design, Scalands Gate was a modest yet sizable three-storeyed cottage on the Glottenham Estate, which belonged to her brother and was close to where she had been brought up. With its dormer windows, brick and flint façade, the proportions in keeping with local tradition, it was very much in harmony with the pleasantly wooded sleepy Sussex countryside. The dining parlour, complete with inglenooks, boasted a large chimney piece autographed by her many illustrious guests. As time went by, she added a studio and extended it considerably. Even so, Gabriel found it uncomfortable and chilly, which was perhaps not surprising considering that he and Willy Stillman arrived when there was still snow on the ground. Gabriel and Stillman liked each other and, at first, got along amicably.

'Good, quiet Stillman is the best of accommodating companions,' Gabriel wrote to Barbara, '(surely his name must indicate the hereditary character of race), and walks with me, talks with me, avoids me with the truest tact in the world. His dark grave face on the snowy roads would make any perceptive person turn round and feel an interest of curiosity about him. He has fallen to work a little on painting, but has some preoccupations of a kind which are apt to interfere with art . . .'

Stillman's 'preoccupation' was his turbulent engagement to Marie Spartali, which was viewed with horror by her father. Rossetti, who was deeply fond of Marie, proved a good friend and confidant. 'She is a noble girl,' he wrote to Charles Eliot Norton, 'in beauty, sweetness, and in artistic gifts; and the sky should seem very warm and calm above, and the road in front bright and clear, and all ill things left behind for ever, to him who starts anew on his life-journey, foot to foot and hand in hand with her'.

In spite of the very real affection between Gabriel and Stillman, their lifestyles proved incompatible. Before becoming a diplomat in the Near East, Stillman had spent much of his time in the Adirondacks painting landscapes. With his friends, who included Ralph Waldo Emerson, Henry Wadsworth Longfellow, the Swiss geologist Louis Agassiz, and James Russell Lowell, Stillman founded the Adirondack Club, which set up summer camps in the forest communing with nature and hunting, fishing and foraging for their food. Stillman was a fresh-air fiend, enjoyed taking himself off for long walks, leading a relatively Spartan life, and keeping regular hours. Rossetti was a nocturnal creature, disliked what he considered the discomforts of country living, was self-indulgent and, at that time, suffering more than usual from insomnia. 'I have been here for a few days in company with Stillman, William's American friend, having come for the purpose of recruiting and "working off" my book with the conscientious decency of Mr Dennis the hangman,* he wrote to Allingham. 'Barbara Bodichon does not indulge in bell-pulls, hardly in servants to summon thereby – so I have brought my own [his manservant, not a bell-pull]. What she does affect is any amount of through draft – a library bearing the stern stamp of "Bodichon" and a kettle-holder with the uncompromising initials B.B.'

Stillman, whose first wife, the neurotic New England beauty, Laura Mack, had shot herself in Greece, had already taken to chloral for his own chronic insomnia. From the best of intentions, he introduced Gabriel to it, not realizing how unable Gabriel was to pace himself or treat anything in moderation. 'I gave him twenty grains dissolved in water to be taken in three doses but, as he forgot the first two nights, he took the whole on the third, and complained to me the next day that it made him sleep stupidly for a few hours, and then made him so wakeful that he was worse without it.' 'My brother was one of the men least fitted to try any such experiment with impunity,' William Michael wrote later in his memoirs. Well intentioned though it was, Stillman's introduction eventually proved disastrous.

Apart from keeping idiosyncratic hours, Gabriel complicated their living arrangements by inviting first the Madox Browns to Scalands and then William and Janey Morris. The understanding between Stillman and Gabriel was that they were primarily at Scalands for work, rest and recuperation. Gabriel's visitors disturbed Stillman, who, moreover, was in financial straits and became embarrassed by his inability to contribute to their entertainment. The Morrises were initially invited to dinner but Janey stayed on for several weeks after Morris had returned to Queen's Square. Stillman may well also have been embarrassed by Janey's

---

* Edward Dennis, d. 1786, the last hangman at Tyburn and the first at Newgate, was tried and sentenced to death for actively taking part in the riots at Holborn. Later he was reprieved and died at his home in Newgate.

incongruous presence and intimacy with Gabriel, which neither of them troubled to hide.

As spring advanced, Janey and Gabriel enjoyed their first prolonged country idyll together. He painted her, was inspired to write sonnets about her, and they basked in one another's company. Back in London, Morris was unhappy, missed her company, wrote that the children did too, but behaved with exemplary restraint, sending wine and other creature comforts. It was the first time that Gabriel and Janey had flouted convention so publicly. While Morris steeled himself to assimilate the situation, he couldn't but be aware that, in spite of his friends' inclination to adopt the lifestyle of *La Vie de Bohème*,* they were scandalized by his wife's behaviour.

Down at Scalands, the weather was lovely and Gabriel and Janey basked in the spring sunshine. Gabriel made a portrait of her reading, which he always claimed was her best likeness.

Sonnet XIX
SILENT NOON

Your hands lie open in the long fresh grass,
The finger-points look through like rosy blooms:
Your eyes smile peace. The pasture gleams and glooms
'Neath billowing skies that scatter and amass.
All round our nest, far as the eye can pass,
Are golden kingcup-fields with silver edge
Where the cow-parsley skirts the hawthorn-hedge.
'Tis visible silence, still as the hour-glass.
Deep in the sun-searched growths the dragon-fly
Hangs like a blue thread loosened from the sky:-
So this wing'd hour is dropt to us from above.

---

* *Scènes de la Vie de Bohème* by Henry Murger, published 1851, a collection of stories set in the Latin Quarter of Paris, was the basis for a highly popular play by Théodore Barrière in collaboration with Murger and, in 1896, was the inspiration for Puccini's perennially popular opera, *La Bohème*.

Oh! Clasp we to our hearts, for deathless dower,
This close-companioned inarticulate hour
When twofold silence was the song of love.

DANTE GABRIEL ROSSETTI, *Poems*, 1871

'[I] will keep you informed of all the more stirring adventurous accidents,' Gabriel wrote to Barbara Bodichon, 'by flood and field (which should not be lacking to such a Don Quixote as Stillman and such a Sancho as myself).' He failed to inform her that, if not by flood or field, he had behaved worse than Goldilocks. He drank her wine, smashed her crockery and was an altogether impossible tenant, even though he later apologized and replaced the contents of her cellar. By the end of the month, Janey was back in Queen's Square and Gabriel at Tudor House in Chelsea, continuing to worry about the reception of his forthcoming book. Barbara needed Scalands for her own use.

*

On 25 April 1871, Gabriel's volume of verse, *Poems*, was published by Ellis, who was also Morris's publisher. It was not unusual in the then relatively small literary world for books to be reviewed by friends of the author. In Gabriel's case, he had made sure that Swinburne reviewed it for *The Fortnightly*, John Weston Marston for *The Athenaeum*, and Morris, albeit reluctantly, for *The Academy*. It can't have been easy for Morris to criticize favourably and publicly love poems, many clearly inspired by his own wife. 'I have done my review, just this moment,' he wrote to Aglaia Cronio. 'Ugh!' But in the main, with the exception of a review by John Skelton in *Blackwood's Magazine*, Rossetti's *Poems* were received favourably in the first reviews to appear.

26

KELMSCOTT

The raised way led us into a little field bounded by a backwater of the river on one side; on the right hand we could see a cluster of small houses and barns, new and old, and before us a grey stone barn and a wall partly overgrown with ivy, over which a few grey gables showed. The village road ended in the shadow of the aforesaid backwater. We crossed the road, and again almost against my will my hand raised the latch of a door in the wall, and we stood presently on a stone path which led up to the old house to which fate . . . had so strangely brought me in this new world of men. My companion gave a sigh of pleased surprise and enjoyment; nor did I wonder, for the garden between the wall and the house was redolent of June flowers, and the roses were rolling over one another with that delicious superabundance of small well-tended gardens which at first sight takes away all thought from the beholder save that of beauty. The blackbirds were singing their loudest, the doves were cooing on the roof-ridge, the rooks in the high elm-trees beyond were garrulous among the young leaves, and the swifts wheeled whining about the gables. And the house itself was a fit guardian for all the beauty of this heart of summer.

WILLIAM MORRIS, *News from Nowhere*

Morris's attitude to Janey's affair with Gabriel was as remarkable as everything else about him. He had a strong moral view that love must run its course, that it was a mortal sin to interfere with something so precious. On their return from Bad Ems, he behaved as nobly as any of his adored heroes of legend. He scoured the country for a house he could share with Rossetti and discovered an enchanting 'many gabled house', Kelmscott Manor, situated in a small, remote hamlet in the Cotswolds. Built of pale grey stone, its roofs beautifully tiled with local stone slates, Kelmscott Manor still stands in its profuse garden and orchards, the upper reaches of the river Thames running past the narrow pathway that borders its banks, overhung by willows, those trees so beloved by Morris. Adjacent to the house was a good-sized barn, some farm buildings and a dovecot. It was the epitome of everything aesthetic he stood for.

He decorated the house completely in accord with his unerring taste: cool, calm interiors hung with wallpapers he had designed himself; likewise the furniture and bed hangings. Blue-and-white Dutch tiles surrounded the fireplaces. Everything exquisite, Morris managed to maintain a refreshing simplicity in the decoration. The downstairs drawing room was painted white, then an unusual choice of colour, which set off the rustic-inspired yet elegant furniture. Morris's use of white may well have influenced the painter Charles Furse,* whose own use of white in the interior of his house at Yockley had a profound effect on subsequent interior design. It is arguable that Morris, better known for his intricately patterned wallpapers, was the source of inspiration for the prevalence of white in modern-day interiors. It is hard to imagine just how startling bare white walls were to those used to the sombre tones of Victorian taste. Most of the rooms led into each other directly without passage or corridor, rather as they do in French houses. None of the doors or windows or fireplaces were quite where one expected them to be. The unexpected dimensions lent Kelmscott a particular appeal which entranced Morris.

Leading up to the attics was a staircase with strangely spaced

---

* Charles Furse (1868–1903) was an English painter who married Katherine Addington Symonds.

treads which the children, Jenny and May, liked to clatter up and down in rhythmic leaps. The attics in themselves were beautiful spaces with timbered beams, which soared upwards from a low wainscot in an intricate pattern of intersecting Vs, making up the ceiling. None of the walls, the beams or the gabled windows were at right angles, the light and shadow falling in unexpected places. Apples from the orchards were laid out in wooden trays which, with the lavender that Janey harvested and hung on hooks from the whitewashed ceilings, made the high rooms smell sweet. Everything was lovely; everything beautiful. Kelmscott was Morris's ultimate testimony to aesthetic harmony.

Shortly after the decorations were completed, with the exception of some soft furnishings, mirrors and crockery, which Janey intended to choose with Rossetti, Morris took himself off to Iceland for several months, leaving Janey and the children installed with Rossetti at Kelmscott. Morris travelled with Erikíkr Magnússon, the scholar who had been teaching him Icelandic and with whom he proposed to translate the Icelandic sagas, and with his old friend, Charlie Faulkner.

It was not an easy decision for him to leave Janey with Rossetti in the new house in which he had invested so much emotional effort. 'Copulation,' he wrote to Charlie, 'is worse than beastly unless it takes place as the result of natural desire and kindliness on both sides . . . I should hope that in most cases friendship would go along with desire, and would outlive it, and the couple would remain together, but always be free people.' It was of vital importance to Morris that he treat Janey as a free being in her own right and did not trample on her love for Rossetti. Anything else would have been ignoble. 'A determination to do nothing shabby . . . appears to me to be the socialist religion, and if that is not morality I do not know what is.' Rossetti had been his mentor ever since the early days when they had met at the Working Men's Club. Later, he had been his rival in pursuit of Janey when he, Morris, had become involved with Rossetti's scheme for the murals for the Oxford debating society.

Morris needed to be alone, to be away from Rossetti and Janey, even if it meant being away from Kelmscott and Jenny and May. He had become fascinated by the beauty of the Icelandic sagas. Iceland, with its volcanoes, frozen tundra, glaucous grasses, lack of trees, its strange perpetual light with no zenith to the summer day, its great wastes of ice and snow, as well as its people, who at that time were uncontaminated by any trace of the Industrial Revolution, held vast appeal for him.

*

'It is a most lovely old house, purely Elizabethan in character,' Gabriel wrote to his Uncle Henry from Kelmscott. '. . . The garden, and meadows leading to the river brink are truly delicious – indeed, the place is perfect; and the riverside walks are charming in their way, though I must say the flatness of the country renders it monotonous and uninspiring to me. However, it is of the very essence of all that is peaceful and retired – the solitude almost absolute.'[1] In fact, they made up a household of eight, including the girls' nurse, two servants Rossetti had brought down from Tudor House (he wouldn't allow Fanny anywhere near Kelmscott) and the Comelys, who lived in a cottage in the grounds. Mrs Comely was the housekeeper and her husband the gardener and general handyman.

Rossetti was fond of the little girls, Jenny and May, now aged eleven and ten. Jenny, in particular, returned his affection. An exceptionally intelligent child, she responded to his quirky humour and impressed him by spending hours voraciously reading Sir Walter Scott's novels. At that time, May was less demonstrative and possibly confused by her mother's undisguised intimacy with a man who was not her father, although when Gabriel suggested he should adopt her, she was delighted and furious with her mother for not consenting; an example of the effects of his charm. Previously, he had won their hearts by sending them a pair of dormice, adding in a letter, 'If you love them very much I dare say they will get much bigger and fatter and remind you of Papa and me.'

Rossetti kept a punt on the river and enjoyed taking Jancy out on boating trips in the cool of the evening. It was an unusually hot summer and he found 'walking even at the close of day is no pleasure, and one is tempted to keep indoors altogether'. Although he was notoriously averse to the discomforts of country life and a confirmed town mouse, this is an exaggeration, even though he continued to keep to his unsociable hours, getting up late and going to bed in the early hours of the morning. In another letter, he describes going for six-mile walks with Janey. Unlike Rossetti, Janey was a country mouse and had been brought up not so very far away. Her mother's family came from the next village.

For his studio, Rossetti took over the Tapestry Room, a small, three-cornered chamber opening off Morris's bedroom. Here, he painted Janey as obsessively as ever he had Lizzie. Perhaps the best-known portrait he did during that idyllic summer is *Water Willow*, an exquisite likeness of Janey clasping fronds of water willow branches which grew along the riverbank.* It is one of the few paintings he executed using a landscape background. The setting is recognizably Kelmscott, the manor and the village church clearly visible, as also part of the boat house and the punt by the water's edge. Janey, gazing pensively, not directly at the artist, is blended in perfect harmony with the surrounding countryside. As usual, her voluptuous lips are closed.

The observant but waspish Jeanette Marshall noted in her diary some time later that Janey's beauty was marred when she spoke:

> Mrs Morris and her 2nd daughter May were there [at a ball given by Aglaia Coronio in 1883], and the former looked very well, I thought, though very sloppy, in a cream crêpe, sparingly trimmed with old gold satin, & made high to the throat. Her hair was fuzzy, and she had a white Indian shawl over

---

* *Water Willow*: Oil on canvas, 22 x 26.7cm. Signed and dated by DGR Kelmscott, 1871. Now in the Samuel Bancroft Collection, Delaware Art Museum, USA.

her shoulders. When her face is quiet, it is fine & fascinating, but when she speaks she is spoilt. The daughter in a brown-red bedgown with no tucker, was a guy, everyone voted. She is excessively ugly.[2]

The summer wore on. At Kelmscott, it seemed as though that long and lovely hot summer would go on for ever; that Gabriel and Janey had managed to elude the demands of daily life; that they could continue to bask in the earthly paradise which Morris had been so kind as to create for them.

THE RIVER'S RECORD

Between Holmscote and Hurstcote
The river-reaches wind,
The whispering trees accept the breeze,
The ripple's cool and kind:
With love low-whispered 'twixt the shores,
With rippling laughters gay,
With white arms bared to ply the oars,
On last year's first of May . . .

. . . Between Holmscote and Hurstcote
A troth was given and riven,
From heart's trust grew one life to two,
Two lost lives cry to Heaven:
With banks spread calm to meet the sky,
With meadows newly mowed,
The harvest paths of glad July,
The sweet school-children's road.

DANTE GABRIEL ROSSETTI, Kelmscott, July 1871

Inevitably, the idyll came to an end. In September 1871 Morris returned from Iceland laden with gifts: embroidered peasant costumes for the girls; jewels and trinkets; a lovely, ribboned peasant dress for Janey; and most marvellous of all, a small Icelandic pony who was swiftly christened Mouse. Mouse became a familiar sight in the country lanes near Kelmscott, pulling a light wicker carriage, driven by the increasingly corpulent Morris.

Either Gabriel was possessed of uncommon tact or he had no tact at all when he remained at Kelmscott for the reunion of Morris and Janey. In the event, Morris spent only a few days there before returning to London. By October, they were all back in town; the Morrises at Queen's Square; Gabriel at Tudor House.

The distance between Bloomsbury and Chelsea was of no consequence to theers. That summer, they had become so accustomed to the almost unheard of (in such circles as they inhabited) intimacy, that when they got back to London, they neglected to keep up that vital card for Victorians, respectability. Even their neighbour, William Bell Scott, a sound and good friend of Rossetti, who himself kept a mistress – the heiress Alice Boyd at Penkill Castle in Scotland – was shocked. Morris had sent out invitations for a dinner party at Queen's Square. 'I asked Gabriel the evening before,' Bell Scott wrote, 'if he was to be there, and on his answering no, I said, "Why, then?".' Gabriel's lackadaisical reply was that he had a prior engagement which only too evidently turned out to be Janey spending the night with Gabriel at Tudor House. 'At Top's, there were Jones, Poynter, Brown, Huffer [sic], Ellis and Green. Of course, no Janey. Is it not too daring, and altogether too inexplicable?'

Bell Scott was conducting a *menage à trois* with his wife, Laetitia, and Miss Alice Boyd of Penkill Castle. Unlike Rossetti, Bell Scott took every measure to ensure that neither of the women whom he loved were exposed to gossip or scandal. It wasn't the fact that Janey spent the night with Rossetti at Tudor House which shocked Bell Scott so much as the fact that Rossetti let it be known, thus compromising her reputation and imputing that Morris was cuckolded. If this sounds, to modern ears, like an example of 'Victorian double standards', it should be remembered that Miss Boyd and Mrs Bell Scott were undoubtedly appreciative of Bell Scott's equally Victorian courtesy.

Sunday [30 January 1870 from Tudor House,
16 Cheyne Walk, Chelsea]

Dearest Janey,

You were so sweet as to ask me to let you know how I got on,
so I write to say I am all right again this morning after the
mustard last night. [Janey may have applied mustard papers
to Gabriel's chest or got out a tin can filled with boiling water,
salt and mustard for his chilblains, which, given the exceedingly
cold winter weather and the lack of central heating, would not
have been surprising except for the degree of physical intimacy
involved.] The sight of you going down the dark steps to the
cab all alone has plagued me ever since, – you looked so lonely.
I hope you got home safe and well. Now everything will be
dark for me till I can see you again. It puts me into a rage to
think that I should have been so knocked up all yesterday as
to be such dreadfully dull company. Why should it happen just
when you were here? I shall look you up on Wednesday
evening. Will you see if those spectacles of mine have got into
Top's room, as I am quite sure I must have left them at your
house . . . For the last 2 years I have felt distinctly the clearing
away of the chilling numbness that surrounds me in the utter
want of you: but since then other obstacles have kept steadily
on the increase, and it comes too late.

Your most affectionate Gabriel

Friday [4 February 1870, 16 Cheyne Walk, Chelsea]

Funny, sweet Janey . . .

. . . No one else seems alive at all to me now, and places that
are empty of you are empty of all life. And it is so seldom that
the dead hours breathe a little and yield your dear voice to
me again. I seem to hear it while I write, and to see your eyes
speaking as clearly as your voice; and so I would write to you
for ever if it were not too bad to keep reminding me of my
troubles, when you have so many of your own.

You are the noblest and dearest thing that the world has had to show me; and if no lesser loss than the loss of you could have brought me so much bitterness, I would still rather have had this to endure than have missed the fullness of wonder and worship which nothing else could have made known to me . . .

Your most affectionate Gabriel

[18 February 1870]

Dearest kindest Janey,

How good you are to write to me so nicely when you are suffering torments in your dear throat . . . I never cease to long to be near you and doing whatever might be to distract and amuse you. To be with you and wait on you and read to you is absolutely the only happiness I can find or conceive in this world, dearest Janey; and when this cannot be, I can hardly now exert myself to move hand or foot for anything. If I ever do wish still to work, it is that I may not sink into utter unworthiness of you and deserve nothing but your contempt.

I shall come up on Saturday evening and see how you are. But if I should be prevented then (or rather to speak plainly if I should resolve that it would be much pleasanter to come when no visitors were at your house) I will then come on Monday . . .

Most affectionately yours

Gabriel

27

NEMESIS

In October 1871, *The Contemporary Review* published a damning review of Gabriel's *Poems* entitled 'The Fleshly School of Poetry'. It was signed by Thomas Maitland. Gabriel was already in a vulnerable state. His intake of chloral swallowed with large amounts of whisky had increased alarmingly and he reacted violently. Small wonder, for the review was vitriolic and he was consuming the equivalent of several large Mickey Finns a day. The basis of Mickey Finns, commonly known as knock-out drops, used for nefarious purposes in the late nineteenth and early twentieth centuries, particularly in Chicago, are chloral hydrate mixed with alcohol. Consumption of such a mixture may cause dreadful headaches, depression, dizziness and vomiting, and can be lethal. Rossetti's consumption outrivalled any victim of Chicago's most dubious bartenders. The only thing Rossetti and the frequenters of The Lone Star Saloon had in common was that the victims of Mickey Finns had no idea what they were drinking any more than Rossetti knew about the consequences of consuming so much chloral.

> Here is a full grown man [wrote Maitland], presumably intelligent and cultivated, putting on record for other full grown men to read, the most secret mysteries of sexual connection, and that with so sickening a desire to reproduce the sexual moods, so careful a choice of epithet to convey mere animal sensation, that we may shudder at the shameless nakedness. We are no purists in such matters . . . It is neither

poetic, nor manly, nor even human to obtrude such things as the theme of whole poems. It is simply nasty.

Females who bite, scratch, scream, bubble, munch, sweat, writhe, twist, wriggle, foam, and in a general way slaver over their lovers, must surely possess some extraordinary qualities to counteract their otherwise most offensive mode of conducting themselves. It appears, however, on examination, that their poet-lovers conduct themselves in a similar manner. They, too, bite, scratch, scream, bubble, munch, sweat, writhe, twist, wriggle, foam and slaver, in a style frightful to hear of.[1]

Like everyone, Maitland was entitled to his point of view, but on the whole, his article can scarcely be construed as constructive criticism and Gabriel took the line that it was just as nasty as anything Maitland accused him of. What Maitland specifically objected to were Rossetti's sonnets, *The Stream's Secret* and *Nuptial Sleep*. He also took objection to *Jenny*, a long and lyrical poem about a prostitute falling asleep in her lover's arms, which Gabriel's mother, a devout High Anglican, had particularly admired.

The effect of Maitland's review on Gabriel cannot be bettered by Bell Scott's testimony: 'The very first, I should say the only powerful attack upon his book knocked him over like the blow of the butcher's axe on the forehead of an ox.'[2]

In the summer of 1872, Gabriel suddenly learned that Maitland was none other than William Michael's old adversary, Robert Buchanan. The knowledge was later to drive him demented. Bell Scott, who was then living at Belle Vue, the house he named so quaintly, a few doors down from Tudor Lodge in Cheyne Walk, recalled Gabriel arriving late for a dinner party which the Bell Scotts were giving. 'At last we heard a tremendous peal on the bell, and knocking, a great noise ascended the stair, and he burst in upon us, shouting out the name of Robert Buchanan, who, it appeared, he had discovered to be the writer of the article in *The Contemporary Review* which was so distracting him. He was too excited to observe or to care who were present, and all the evening he continued unable to contain himself, or to avoid shouting out the name of his enemy. I was glad when the sitting came to an end . . . From this time he occupied himself in composing a long reply, which he read over a hundred times, till the lives of his friends became too heavy to bear. But in a very few weeks the crisis came.'[3]

It was a grizzly time for the Rossetti family. A short time before, on 14 May, Christina had collapsed and been diagnosed with a severe and altogether horrible form of Graves' disease, which changed the pigment of her skin and made her eyes bulge and seem hideous. Women who have been beautiful, and Christina indubitably had, can feel monstrous and altogether unfit to be seen when they suffer disfigurement. Given her determination, combined with her ardent faith in her conception of God, Christina, unlike Gabriel, didn't allow herself to indulge in self-pity.

The eldest of the siblings, Maria Rossetti, was preparing to join the Society of All Saints and to make her profession as a nun, which did nothing to cheer her immediate family. Gabriel wrote to Fanny Cornforth that she was going to be 'one of those old things whom you see going about in a sort of coal-scuttle and umbrella costume'. This was one of his last typically teasing observations for some time to come.

Long afterwards, William Michael recalled that the 2 June 1872, was 'one of the most miserable days of my life'. Gabriel was still living in Tudor House, more or less in consort with Fanny Cornforth, not seeing enough, for his liking, of Janey and employing Henry Treffry Dunn as his secretary assistant. Dunn became alarmed by Gabriel's evidently disturbed state. 'The deeply recessed windows,' he described of Gabriel's bedroom long after the event, 'were shrouded with curtains of heavy and sumptuously patterned velvet. On a fine summer's day, light was almost excluded from the room. The gloom of the room made one feel quite depressed and sad. Even the little avenue of lime trees outside the window helped to reduce the light and threw a sickly green over everything in the apartment.'[4]

Dunn sent for William Michael. 'From his wild way of talking –' he recalled, 'about conspiracies and what not – I was astounded to perceive that he was, past question, not entirely sane . . . I was dismayed to find my brother an actual monomaniac. I, who had known him since infancy, had never before seen or surmised the faintest seed of insanity in him . . . on that fatal 2 June, and for many days and months ensuing, I was compelled to regard my brother as partially insane, in the ordinary sense of that term.'[5]

Gabriel was suffering torments from paranoia, imagining he was the victim of various plots and conspiracies against him, hearing imaginary voices uttering menacing threats. If he was the victim of anything, it was of his intense dislike of any criticism combined with a sense of having been partly responsible for Lizzie's death and remorse for having been instrumental in her exhumation. As the actress Ellen Terry observed so astutely, he might not have suffered so terribly if he had dug her up himself.

William Michael turned up at Bell Scott's house, three doors down the road from Tudor House, early on the morning of 2 June. Bell Scott was alarmed by his agitation and gave him a cup of tea. Then they hurried back to Gabriel, who was growing more frantic by the hour.

By 7 June, he was in such a bad way that William Michael sent for Dr Hake, a retired doctor with a penchant for poetry, of whom both William Michael and Gabriel were fond. That William Michael sent for him instead of the Rossetti family practitioner indicates how anxious he was to keep Gabriel's state from his family and from wagging tongues and common gossip, which he rightly feared would only exacerbate Gabriel's condition. The only person William Michael alerted, apart from Bell Scott, Fanny and Dr Hake, was Ford Madox Brown, who proved, as always, to be the staunchest of friends. After much hesitation, William Michael agreed that Bell Scott should go round to Queen's Square to tell Janey. Neither he, nor Brown nor Bell Scott were particularly keen for Janey to visit Gabriel. They were under the mistaken impression that she was the cause of Gabriel's crisis. But the crucial question was what was to be done about Gabriel. Hake solved the problem by inviting Gabriel to convalesce under his care in his house at Roehampton, then a rural suburb of London. They were surprised but relieved by Gabriel's complicity in accepting Hake's kind invitation.

The cab rank was close by. Gabriel, a favourite with the cabbies, partly for his idiosyncratic charm and his commercially worthwhile nocturnal habits, climbed into the one sent for with the assistance of Hake and William Michael. The journey to Roehampton was a nightmare, Gabriel under the delusion that wild bells were ringing out portending chimes. Nobody else could hear anything at all except for the clip-clop of the horse's hooves upon the cobbles and the cabbie's chidings of 'Whoa, whoa', which might better have been uttered to Gabriel and his companions, for by now, William Michael, quite unusually, was near the end of his tether.

In the general confusion, they had all forgotten that it was Whitsun Week, when, by long tradition, a large fair was held at Roehampton on the green. Normally, Roehampton was one of the quietest of spots, which was mainly why William Michael, Bell Scott and Ford Madox Brown had taken up Hake's invitation so eagerly. But the funfair, though enchanting, made the most dreadful racket. There were the shrieks of chimpanzees and monkeys; organ-grinders; merry-go-rounds; the yells of pugilists; the whizz-bang reports of coconuts being shied at; the howls of men gawping at fat ladies demonstrating their tattoos; midgets demonstrating their diminutive proportions at the tops of their voices; and the natural and normally delightful mayhem of the caravansary. All were a serious cause of disturbance to Gabriel's peace of mind.

He could hardly be expected to countenance this unexpected hub-bub without it contributing to his delusions of persecution. In fact, he could hardly be expected to be answerable for anything by now. When Dr Hake and William Michael took him out for a short walk, Gabriel construed the silent shrieks of the goldfish, the beguiling tongues of the caged larks, the inexplicable messages tattooed on the fat ladies' flesh to be part of the imagined conspiracy against him – although what tongues the fish, the birds and the monkeys spoke in was beyond the comprehension of his companions. No one mentioned or tried to translate the significance of the hieroglyphs on the ladies' expansive flesh.

Unsurprisingly, Gabriel became involved in what might have become a public brawl, one of the outcomes of his insanity which his brother dreaded most, with a group of gypsies. With difficulty, Hake and William Michael managed to drag Gabriel away from the scene. Gabriel crumpled.

The following afternoon, Hake and William Michael became worried by Gabriel's continuing torpor. This wasn't negligence on their part, considering that Gabriel seldom woke before noon and was famous for his furies if aroused beforehand. But now, slap his jowls though they might, pour jugs of cold water over his face, spank his nether regions, they could not bring him back to his senses at all.

Gabriel was still breathing. Hake applied ammonia forte, a liquid closely allied to choral, to Gabriel's nostrils. Hake was a know-all. Gabriel didn't revive and Hake prophesied, possibly wagging his head, that even if Gabriel did recover, then he would never regain his wits. By now, William Michael was driven to distraction. At that point the doorbell rang to announce the arrival of the eminent surgeon, John Marshall.

It had probably been Ford Madox Brown's idea to call in Marshall. Marshall, who was well acquainted with the surviving members of the Pre-Raphaelite Brotherhood, dismissed the application of ammonia forte and insisted on dosing Gabriel with strong, black coffee. The only way in which this could be administered was by a tube of India rubber. It was an altogether sickening and exhausting business, likely to cause lung trouble and consequently brain damage, much worse than anything Hake had envisaged. Marshall struggled on. Thirty-six hours later, Gabriel revived and was furious.

If it appeared (which it did) to Bell Scott and to William

Michael, that Janey didn't care about Rossetti's collapse, they were mistaken. It would also be a grave error to believe that Bell Scott or William Michael underestimated Janey. Very few men ever appreciated her deep and genuine emotions which, for a multitude of reasons, she chose not to, or could not divulge. It is more than likely that at this time in Janey's strangely varied life, the only two men who truly understood her were her husband, William Morris, and her lover, Dante Gabriel Rossetti.

Janey definitely cared for Gabriel and, as far as she was capable of loving, she loved being adored by Gabriel who, like Morris, had already transformed her into many ideal images, none of which bore much resemblance to the woman whom she believed she was. That original Janey, the ostler's daughter, had vanished. It wasn't so much that she had reinvented herself as that she had been moulded by the men she inspired into a form they considered exquisite beyond compare. Malleable and complicit, she was part of the conspiracy. It was in her interest to play the part of Galatea, to sit sewing on the sofa, translating her husband's designs for embroidery into silks and Berlin wool of variegated colours, mainly shades of green, blue and yellow; sitting for Gabriel beneath the willows, sitting on cushions, sitting hither and thither; sitting for her portrait, for their inspiration.

The coffee, made in the pot Gabriel had bought in Paris for one of the earliest P. R. B. meetings, was 'growing cold'. Janey threw the coffee pot away. Later that day, taking an afternoon stroll along the river, that old magpie Holman Hunt, now married to Edith Waugh, his dead wife Fanny Waugh's sister, saw the coffee pot lying amongst the debris of the menagerie at Tudor House, pocketed it and gave it to his wife, who promptly labelled and placed it amongst her collection of curios – later, much later, to be catalogued by her perceptive granddaughter, Diana.*

*

---

*   Told to the author by the late Diana Holman-Hunt.

It was decided that Gabriel needed a change of scene. He agreed to go to Scotland in the care of George Hake, the son of Dr Hake, together with Madox Brown, Bell Scott and Allan, the alcoholic husband of one of Gabriel's more unreliable servants, Emma. They went first to William Graham's house near Perth. Graham was an ardent admirer and collector of Rossetti's paintings. He could only lend his house for a week, but afterwards he made available his fishing lodge, Stobhall, perched above the Tay. Bell Scott tried to stop Gabriel taking chloral and whisky with the almost inevitable result that Gabriel threatened to jump out of the window and hurl himself into the foaming waters of the Tay. Young Hake now proved an invaluable companion, watching over Gabriel and becoming responsible for his intake of drugs. He was in a lamentable state, hearing imaginary voices, believing that everywhere he was being spied on; that anyone they passed, even rabbits and watchdogs were all 'studied insults'. Once, while out walking by the banks of the Tay, they saw some seine fishermen casting wide their nets and drawing them in full of leaping, silvery fish. To Gabriel, it seemed that, 'It is an allegory of my state. My persecutions are narrowing the net round me . . .' He wasn't far wrong.

LOVE IS ENOUGH

Love is enough: though the World be a-waning,
And the woods have no voice but the voice of complaining,
Though the sky be too dark for dim eyes to discover
The gold-cups and daisies fair blooming thereunder
Though the hills be held shadows, and the sea a dark wonder,
And this day draw a veil over all deeds pass'd over,
Yet their hands shall not tremble, their feet shall not falter;
The void shall not weary, the fear shall not alter
These lips and these eyes of the loved and the lover.

WILLIAM MORRIS

Eventually, partly recovered by the end of the summer, Gabriel insisted on going to stay at Kelmscott. Janey and the girls had been there for the summer during his illness. Now, in the glory of the early autumnal weather, with red and green and golden apples hanging on the trees in the orchard, the blaze of the last of the summer flowers in the garden, the quiet, grey house was beautiful. Inside, Janey, whose natural taste and eye for beauty had been made much more acute through her marriage to Morris, had made the interior of the house yet more lovely and certainly more comfortable.

The addition of George Hake to the household was a brain-wave. His presence relieved Janey of the intolerable burden of being responsible for Gabriel. The girls, Jenny and May, took to Hake immediately. He took them on the river, accompanied them on pony rides, and made himself generally useful. When occasionally Morris came down for a Saturday to Monday, he and young Hake went fishing together.

The idyll between Gabriel and Janey was over. She could no longer see him in the same light as she had the previous summer, when all had seemed golden, illuminated by the haze of their love. Since his collapse, Gabriel was a changed man whose current dependency on her, despite Hake's care of him, was alarming. The consequent change in their relations was the end of the romance for Janey. Moreover, she had recovered some of her earlier attachment to her husband. Later, she recalled sadly, 'That Gabriel was mad is but too true; no one knows it better than myself.' As usual, she kept her thoughts to herself, showing Gabriel concern and deep affection, even though that earlier love had flickered out. Part of the problem was the fact that he was still taking chloral combined with whisky, even though it was doled out by the solicitous young George Hake.

Gabriel's continued presence at Kelmscott was now beginning to exasperate the usually tolerant Morris. He wrote to Aglaia Coronio that they hadn't quarrelled, but that Gabriel's presence spoilt his own enjoyment of being at Kelmscott and that it seemed as though he never meant to go away. 'Not only does that keep me away from that harbour of refuge (because it really is a farce our meeting when we can help it) but also he has all sorts of ways so unsympathetic with the sweet simple old place, that I feel his presence there as a kind of slur on it: this is very unreasonable though when one thinks why one took the place, and how this year it has really answered that purpose: nor do I think I should feel this about it if he had not been so unromantically discontented with it and the whole thing which made me very angry and disappointed.'

Matters were made worse by Gabriel's invitations to his friends and relations. He beseeched Ford Madox Brown to come down; he invited his mother, his sister Christina, Bell Scott and his brother William Michael. No one could help recognizing William Michael's evident goodness. Certainly, Gabriel was most appreciative of his brother's solid, reliable qualities. But he bored Morris stiff and Morris did not bother to disguise his boredom. When Gabriel taunted Morris about Sigurd (the character from his epic poem), whose brother happened to be a dragon, Morris retorted that it was better being brother to a dragon than to a bloody fool. It must be hoped that the absurdity of this exchange made them both burst out laughing – and in the old days, Gabriel certainly would have done so.

In spite of all this unpleasantness, Gabriel continued to paint. He painted Janey as Proserpine (often known as Persephone). While picking flowers in the meadow of Enna, Pluto, the King of the Underworld, saw Proserpine and was so entranced by her loveliness that he carried her off to Erebus, Proserpine thus becoming Queen of the land of the dead. But on being hoisted away by Pluto, Proserpine had screamed for her mother, Ceres, and, in her agitation, had spilt the flowers she had been gathering in the meadow. Ceres hunted high and low for her daughter and, when she learned of her fate, immediately went to Jove to implore him to intercede. He promised Proserpine's return to the upper world on condition that she ate nothing in Erebus and sent Mercury there, accompanied by Spring, to deliver his conditional promise. Proserpine had eaten some fleshy pomegranate seeds for

their juice, and so was only allowed out of Erebus for six months
of the year, in the spring, out into the light.

> *Not that fair field*
> *Of Enna where Proserpine gathering flowers,*
> *Herself a fairer flower, by gloomy Dis*
> *Was gathered, which cost Ceres all that pain to seek*
> *her through the world . . .*
> *. . . might with this Paradise*
> *Of Eden survive.*

MILTON, *Paradise Lost*, Book IV

The painting is a powerful one. Later, Rossetti made another seven
versions of it, but this one depicts Janey holding the seductively slit
pomegranate, from which she has eaten those fatal seeds, to her
throat. Her other hand grasps her wrist. He has changed the mane
of Janey's dark hair to that of Lizzie's golden-red and she wears a
bluish-green dress whose drapery is indeed marvellous. Since the
times of the ancient Greeks, the execution of drapery had long
occupied the artists of the Western world. In the nineteenth
century, the American sculptor based in Rome, William Wetmore
Story, had devoted years to emulating folds chiselled from marble
in his immense statues. In England, both G. F. Watts and Leighton
had become deeply involved in the same endeavour. No less so
had Rossetti. Every convoluted fold of Proserpine's robe is high-
lighted, the sleeves caught up from the wrist and then swirling
down again at the back. Quite where the light comes from to
create this effect is a mystery, known only to the painter and the
gods. In the background is a rectangle of light, presumably a
window to the Upper World, but it lets in scarcely more light than
the smouldering candle of the Underworld. On the left is a tendril
of ivy, signifying, in the language of flowers so popular with the
Victorians, memory. To the right, at the top of the canvas,
inscribed on gold, and only in this early version, is the sonnet
which Gabriel wrote to accompany the painting:

Afar away the light that brings cold cheer
Unto this wall, – one instant and no more
Admitted at my distant palace-door.
Afar the flowers from Enna from this drear
Dire fruit, which, tasted once, must thrall me here.
Afar those skies from this Tartarean gray
That chills me: and afar, how far away,
The nights shall be from the days that were.

Afar from mine own self I seem, and wing
Strange ways in thought, and listen for a sign:
And still some heart unto some soul doth pine,
O Whose sounds mine inner sense is fain to bring,
Continually together murmuring) –
'Woe's me for thee, unhappy Proserpine!'

Dwelling on the pain of separation, it seems that Gabriel, as sensitive as ever, knew as well as Janey did that, in spite of, or perhaps because of, her kindness to him, their idyll was over. When the time came for her and the girls to leave for London in the autumn of 1872, she was affectionate and promised to come back in the new year. Gabriel settled in to Kelmscott with George for the winter. It turned out to be one of the coldest winters imaginable. He sent word to Fanny to rummage about in Tudor House for a length of green velvet he had bought years before, to be made into curtains against the cold.

*

Janey was enjoying herself in Horrington House, the new house in Chiswick, then a pleasant suburb of fine old houses with gardens and a proximity to the river. She was preoccupied by decorating it, deciding to divide her bedroom, by means of a screen, into a sitting room. Morris kept on the workrooms and his own quarters at Queen's Square, but also had a studio at Horrington House full of pots of cow-gum, silver and gold leaf, paints of all description, coloured dyes and samples of the wool he intended to have woven

into tapestries and carpets. Meanwhile, he contented himself illuminating manuscripts and was delighted to have Janey and the
children back with him. Perhaps the most attractive of Janey's
qualities was her silent complicity; she avoided scenes or expla-
nations. She gave the impression, however much it was an illusion,
of life running seamlessly, uncomplicated by emotional tangles.
The girls were happy, and their friends, the Burne-Jones children,
fitted in very well. There were constant visitors. If Janey spent
an uncommon amount of time on the sofa with her embroidery,
everyone was used to it. It was a happy time.

After a short and not altogether agreeable visit to Italy with
Ned Burne-Jones, Morris set off once more to Iceland. Janey went
down to Kelmscott with the children. By spending the entire
winter there, Gabriel appeared to have dug his heels into Kelmscott. There were traces of him everywhere and it seemed, even to
Janey, to be much more his house than anyone else's. There was
no reason, according to the original agreement between Gabriel
and Morris, why he shouldn't be there as often as he liked, but it
was tacitly assumed that all parties should respect each other's
privacy. Not only had he acquired three dogs, which Janey knew
that her husband hated, a jet-black dog called Nero, Gabriel's
favourite black-and-tan terrier named Dizzy (after the Prime
Minister, Disraeli) and a mongrel of sorts, together with Hake's
deerhound Bess. Moreover, his friends flocked to the house without
any prior discussion with Janey. He still got up late, breakfasted off
quantities of eggs, refused lunch and went to bed extremely late.
He had grown remarkably stout. He was still dosing himself on
large amounts of chloral and drinking a great deal of whisky.

Sometimes his models, Alexa Wilding* in particular, came
down to pose for him. He had also somehow or other discovered

---

* Alexa Wilding (*c.*1845–84) was one of Gabriel's favourite models. He picked
her up in the Strand one evening in 1865. Among the portraits of her are *Lady
Lilith*, *Venus Verticordia* and *Sibylla Palmifera*. There is no evidence that her
relationship with Rossetti was anything but platonic.

a London girl in service locally, who had emancipated notions which simply meant that she was prepared to sit naked for him. Typically, Janey did not remonstrate but frequently went up to London leaving her daughters with Rossetti, young Hake and the servants at Kelmscott, blithely believing that they would be perfectly all right in the country. To some extent they were, but inevitably they suffered from lack of parental supervision and may well have felt abandoned, even though they spent time playing wild games of hide-and-seek in the attics with George Hake and, occasionally, Rossetti. May, who was becoming a budding beauty, sat for Rossetti several times. In spite of all his eccentricities she became noticeably fond of him. After all, she had known him all her life.

On Morris's return from Iceland, he seethed with irritation about Gabriel's prolonged occupancy of Kelmscott. Iceland had had a profound spiritual effect on him and although he confided to Aglaia Coronio that the place had invested him with a deeper insight and understanding of love, he was roused from his previous compliance with Rossetti's relations with his family and wrote Gabriel an uncharacteristically sharp letter: 'As to the future though I will ask you to look upon me as off my share, and not to look at me as shabby for that, since you have fairly taken to living at Kelmscott, which I suppose neither of us thought the other would do when we first began the joint possession of the house; for the rest I am both too poor and, by compulsion of poverty, too busy to be able to use it much in any case, and am very glad if you find it useful and pleasant to you.' This, in P. R. B. parlance, was a whammer. While it was true that Morris had lost a considerable amount of income from the shares he had inherited in the Devon copper mines, he was by no means as poor as his letter made out.

Gabriel made a half-hearted attempt to renew the lease but his efforts petered out. Shortly afterwards, Morris secured the lease in partnership with Ellis, his publisher. In July 1874, Gabriel left Kelmscott for good and returned to Cheyne Walk.

28

THE END OF THE FIRM

Iceland had wrought not only spiritual changes in Morris, enlightening his views on love, but had also made him radically much more of an overt socialist than he had been hitherto. Georgie, who, for a long time, had been under the influence of the vehemently socialist Rosalind Howard, shared his views with a deep passion. This shared attitude very much strengthened the bond between them. It is fair to say that Morris returned from Iceland a much more definitive man; his intentions more clearly outlined, his purpose clarified. One of the most resonant results of his *éclaircissement* was to fundamentally reorganize The Firm. After fierce and bitter arguments, he disbanded Morris, Marshall, Faulkner & Co., reinventing it as plain Morris & Co., under his own direction. He compensated Marshall, Ford Madox Brown and Rossetti to the tune of £1,000 each, which was an incontestably handsome sum. Charlie Faulkner and Ned refused to accept the compensation offered to them. This reshuffling resulted in a deal of ill-feeling, particularly on the part of Madox Brown. It was effectively the end of the second generation of the Pre-Raphaelite Brotherhood, but by no means the curtain call to either their creativity or the tangle of their personal relationships.

LOVE IS ENOUGH

Love is enough: draw near and behold me
Ye who pass by to your rest and your laughter,
And are full of the hope of the dawn coming after,

For the strong of the world have bought me and sold me
And my house is all wanted from threshold to rafter,
Pass by me, and hearken, and think of me not!

WILLIAM MORRIS

In July 1874, the same month that Rossetti finally left Kelmscott, Morris whisked his family, together with the Burne-Jones children, Pip and Margaret, off for a holiday in Belgium where, years before, he and Janey had spent their honeymoon. Morris was delighted to be reunited with Janey and, as always, took immense pleasure in being with his children. It was a sentimental journey and the family were reunited.

It was the first time that any of the children had been abroad and they never forgot being shown the wonders of Bruges with its myriad canals, the façades of the fine old houses with their quaint roofs reflected in the water, the old stone bridges, the immensity of the cobbled Burg Square, the churches and the astonishing carillon of the forty-odd bells being pulled in the thirteenth-century belfry. Morris was possessed of that rare gift of being able to make buildings, paintings and unforeseen absurdities come to life and he lent the children the enthusiasm of his own imagination. Unlike so many other children, trudging around beauty spots and art galleries, bored to stupefaction in the wake of their well-meaning parents, the Morris girls and the Burne-Jones siblings never suffered this in the company of Morris. When the children had gone to bed in the hotel, covered in quantities of feather quilts, their heads buzzing with the glories they had seen, Morris and Janey strolled through the city streets and squares and enjoyed drinking the good Flanders beer in a café. 'It would take a very crabbed grown-up or a particularly lumpish child not to be warmed and stimulated by my father's eager vision of the city of many memories,'[1] May wrote years later.

29

THE LAST JANEY PICTURE

By mid-October 1875, terrified that he might be subpoenaed in a libel case between Buchanan and Swinburne, Gabriel temporarily left Tudor House in Cheyne Walk for a drab villa in Bognor. Janey went down to visit him, taking May with her for a fortnight. She had agreed to model for *Astarte Syriaca*, one of the strangest and most powerful portraits Rossetti ever painted of her. Certainly, he thought it his finest. 'I think that my brother was always wont to regard this as his most exalted performance,'[1] William Michael wrote later.

Astarte was the powerful ancient Syrian goddess of love and fertility whom the Greeks identified as Venus. Most commonly, she was represented in a long tunic with medallions, and with a mantle swathed over the tunic and tucked beneath her left arm. Most often, one hand is stretched forth, while in the other she holds a staff in the shape of a cross. She is frequently associated with writhing snakes and is an object of both fascination and terror.

Rossetti depicts her, as personified by Janey, as a deity both compelling and unnerving; not a creature for the faint-hearted, the actual canvas on which Astarte is painted is over six feet tall. She looks and glowers. She is terrifying. Above her head rise the entwined circles of the sun and the moon. Astarte, or Janey, is portrayed full frontal, menacing in her sexuality, her right hand cupping her left breast, her left equally in the traditional pudicta position, beneath her golden girdle which encircles her sea-green half-transparent robes, her left thigh visible beneath the veil of her garment. All of Rossetti's portraits of Janey indicate her long, powerful arms and her elongated hands. None more so than this. Behind her, are two female torch-bearers. One of them, never specified, has always been attributed to a likeness of Janey's daughter, May. Since it is difficult to discern any dissimilarity between them, there is no reason to suppose that both the symmetrically placed torch-bearers are not both May, right and left. An immensely powerful painting, it is also possibly the most overtly sexual portrait that Rossetti ever painted of anyone. He must have known that he was bound to lose her. Lose her, he did.

As so often, he accompanied this picture with a sonnet he had written especially for it:

Mystery: lo! Betwixt the sun and moon
Astarte of the Syrians: Venus Queen
Ere Aphrodite was. In silver sheen
Her twofold girdle clasps the infinite boon
Of bliss whereof the heaven and earth commune:
And from her neck's inclining flower-stem lean
Love-freighted lips and the absolute eyes that wean
The pulse of hearts to the spheres' dominant tune.
Torch-bearing, her sweet ministers compel
All thrones of light beyond the sky and sea
The witnesses of Beauty's face to be:
That face, of Love's all-penetrative spell
Amulet, talisman, and oracle, –
Betwixt the sun and moon a mystery.

DANTE GABRIEL ROSSETTI

No other words summon Janey to life so compellingly. They reveal as much about Gabriel's passion for her as they do about Janey's hold on him. For she was mysterious, fascinating and alluring. She was, indeed, his ultimate muse.

As far as Janey was concerned, her visit to Gabriel at Bognor was a bore. The villa was dismal and suburban. The weather was so vile that there was no possibility of taking a walk: a fearsome gale blew up and tossed the ships over, scuppering them into the sea. Dizzy, Gabriel's favourite dog, went wild at this, his first sight of the ocean waves. Fish swam backwards; gulls mewed in panic. Sailors drowned.

It is possible that May might have got in the way. Janey might have been jealous of her increasingly lovely daughter. Ultimately, there is no telling. After a fortnight, Janey, shocked by Gabriel's intake of chloral, never thinking it might have something to do with her, left him. Later, she told her subsequent lover, Wilfrid Scawen Blunt,* that she had left him for the sake of her daughters. This is debatable. Whatever the reason, *Astarte Syriaca* was the last portrait Rossetti ever made of Janey directly.

The following Spring, 1876, Janey had an unfortunate reason to keep her at home. Her eldest daughter, Jenny, now aged sixteen, suffered from a seizure which was diagnosed as epilepsy clearly inherited from her father, whose sudden and unpredictable rages had been a source of constant amusement to his friends. Jenny was intelligent, witty and, like her father, dismissed other people's dimness without tolerance. She had done very well at school, had been commended for her proficiency in Latin and English literature, and was destined for Girton, the new college for female students at Cambridge. All of these well-founded hopes were dashed when she toppled overboard into the river on a boating accident when on a trip to Henley.

Georgie Burne-Jones never forgot how she learned of Jenny's illness. Many years later, she recalled how alarmed they had all been when she received a note from Janey imploring her to send a doctor because Jenny had fallen into a deep faint. Jenny did recover from her fainting fit, but not from her condition. In those days, epilepsy was an illness much feared and associated with adolescent hysteria in girls, and with madness, the victim being the host of evil spirits whose turmoil caused the fainting fits, the

---

* Wilfrid Scawen Blunt (1840–1922) was a diplomat, poet and essayist.

frothing at the mouth; the apparent craziness was thought to be the result of one possessed. From then on, despite her lucid intervals, Jenny's existence was swept to the fringes of acceptable society. For a while she was sent to a retreat during the week, coming home for holidays and weekends. As a result of either her condition or the drugs administered, she grew slower, more stolid, more torpid.

Janey found it difficult to cope with her daughter's malaise. It was Morris who transferred all the love and tenderness he had ever felt for Janey to his afflicted daughter. The more positive aspect of this lasting tragedy was that Georgie, who, for some time, had been somewhat aloof from Janey, now showed all her previous affection and proved a stalwart friend.

Even though Ned could not share Morris's increasingly socialist sympathies, he continued to enjoy Morris's companionship. The Sunday breakfasts at The Grange, with Morris guzzling enormous quantities of frazzled bacon, raised pies, eggs and black pudding, now became a fixed institution, the antics of Ally Sloper included as always, as well as discussions for further designs by Ned for stained-glass windows.

30

MORRIS AT LEEK

Unlike his colleagues, William Morris was not inspired by a female muse directly so much as by his ideals. Ardent as he was to live up to them (and this he did more than most of his fellow men), it's not surprising that on occasion his spirits sagged. It was work that was Morris's mistress.

In the 1850s, the commercial use of the German aniline dyes became widespread. The discovery of a synthetic mauve in 1856 was the first of a vast range of dyes such as fuchsine, a violent pink; safranin, a glaring yellow; and induline, which ranged from blue to black. The impact on ordinary domestic life was drastic. Suddenly, it felt as if, overnight, women who had previously worn muslin gowns patterned with the colours of subtly charming vegetable dyes, now sported mauves, purples, bright pinks and garish yellows in hues never seen before.

Their popularity was immediate. The effect was exaggerated because of the fashion of the day. Women's gowns took up an enormous amount of fabric – skirts were at least six yards in circumference, usually more, frequently looped over a brightly coloured underskirt. By now, the crinoline had slipped backwards. The cut of the dress remained the same, but the voluminous folds were looped into a bunch at the back, resulting in the bustle. These were frilled and flounced with *cascades*, *chûtes* and *ondulations*.

The French painter James Tissot, the son of a mantua maker and staying in London for political reasons, is probably one of the most reliable sources of the fashion of the time. Bodices were decorated with frogging, with bows, with ruffles, and were frequently frilled at the wrist and neck. For outdoor wear, women adopted a variety of jackets such as the polonaise and the bertha, trimmed with fur or velvet and often with short, pagoda sleeves. The poke bonnet, which had held sway for so long, now gave way to small, saucer-brimmed high hats set at a jaunty angle and trimmed with coloured ribbons which suddenly made women seem much taller than previously. In summer, straw hats fastened with wide satin ribbons as well as tulle bonnets were popular. In many ways, women's fashion resembled the complicated, ornate design of the furniture of the day, upholstered in ruches, swags, and buttoned for no good reason except ornamentation. The impact of the new, artificially produced colours, produced from coal tar mixed with chloride of lime and by treating indigo with caustic potash, was aggressive and, to someone with an eye as sensitive as Morris's, it was anathema.

The Pre-Raphaelite women adopted what was known as aesthetic dress. The effect was soft and flowing, very fine cashmere being much in use. They disdained the harsh, modern aniline dyes and favoured pastel shades, 'moon colour', which was a beautiful pearl grey, and, of course, sage green and drab yellow which led to their being lampooned as 'Greenery-Yallery/ Of the Grosvenor Gallery'. Their dresses were of a much simpler cut than those of mainstream fashion, quite plain and relatively narrow, with rounded necks which might be embroidered or enhanced with a ribboned collar or a string of amber beads. The sleeves were full and wide, drawn close at the wrist. They wore their hair either in a loose knot or bundled into a snood or net, often of silk and sometimes spangled with beads. Otherwise, they cut their hair short and wore it curly, as can be seen in many of Burne-Jones's paintings and Kate Greenaway's illustrations. George du Maurier, whose own wife, Emma, favoured aesthetic dress, did a series of wickedly funny cartoons for *Punch*, mocking the absurdities of exaggerated aesthetic dress.

I never met a man who knew so much about colours.

THOMAS WARDLE on William Morris

It is scarcely surprising that Morris began a crusade to bring
back the traditional colours made from vegetable dyes. This
campaign took him to Leek in Staffordshire, not far from Stoke-
on-Trent. An old-fashioned sleepy market town, mainly built of
brick and with low, whitewashed houses, Leek, situated in the
wild beauty of the Pennines, had always been a focal point of
importance in the Peak District when times had been sleepy and
old-fashioned. Now, in the nineteenth century, Leek became one of
the main European centres of the silk industry on account of the
quality of the local limestone sweet waters of the River Churnet,
on a distinct bend of which Leek is built. For the dyeing of
fabric, the quality of water available is of enormous importance,
which is why Lyon and Basle became famous in the dyeing trade.
There is usually a purely practical reason, such as the quality of
water or the minerals in the earth, to explain the springing up
of manufacture and, consequently, trade.

For Morris, the main attraction of Leek was the Hencroft
Works which specialized in the dyeing of tussore, a fabric of wild
silk imported from India. The manager of the Hencroft Works was
George Wardle; Thomas Wardle was his brother-in-law. Morris
had become acquainted with George, the manager of the works up
at Leek, through Philip Webb, who was part of Morris's own Firm.
George afforded the merciless gang of Pre-Raphaelites some
amusement, since, despite his northern earnestness, he had married
Madeleine Smith, the daughter of a well-known Glaswegian architect, David Hamilton. By her own account, she was infamous. In
1857, she had been charged with the murder of her lover, Emile
L'Angelier, by poisoning him with arsenic. He was a seed merchant
from Jersey, who was well intentioned, but probably bored her to
his ultimate death. To be put on trial on the charge of poisoning a
lover was scandalous enough – in Glasgow even to have a lover
with a French-sounding name was deemed depravity itself.

George's brother, Thomas Wardle, was steadier and more predictable than he was. Thomas had married his distant cousin, Elizabeth Wardle, who bore him fourteen healthy, yelling children. This kind of midland household was new to Morris: substantial polished furniture; pork pies; cabbage and mustard; cheddar cheese and pickles; and rhubarb and custard. It was an unknown land of common sense and no nonsense. Morris thrived. He thrived in the vats. Generally speaking, it may be observed that what men do is who they are: sculptors are men of mud, frequently covered in clay and sporting a dusty air; scholars incline to the ink pot and often have calluses, if right-handed, on the third finger of the right hand. As for gardeners and the like, no one knows what bunions, warts and other deformities their work may have induced. Morris once emerged bright blue from the vats of Leek: 'Mr Morris is in roaring health,' reported Georgie, 'and dined here the other day with two dark-blue hands bearing witness that he has plunged into work again.'

Mrs Wardle sat bolt upright on her horsehair settee and stitched, stabbing at her embroidery frame. She was already a skilled needlewoman and she understood Morris's intentions very well. In and out went her deft needle, threaded with blue and yellow silks, attacking the holes in the canvas. Lilies and worsted willows appeared from beneath her thimble. Thomas sent out for ale. The maid slammed the oven door and made sure that the pies for the fourteen children's high tea would be piping hot. Years later, when her children were settled, Mrs Wardle opened the Leek School of Embroidery. The students produced jewel-like embroideries based on designs by Morris and executed in dyed tussore silks for ecclesiastical and private commissions.

31

THE LAST PICTURE SHOW

I am broken, as a ship
Perishing of the song
Sweet, sweet and long,
The songs the sirens know.
The mariner forgets,
Voyaging in those straits,
And dies assuredly.

DANTE GABRIEL ROSSETTI

All the birds of the air
Fell a-sighing and a-sobbing
When they heard the bell toll
For poor Cock Robin

ANON, traditional ballad

When Gabriel died, Janey was startled by her own reaction, which was one of profound grief. She had not made her bereavement any easier by ignoring his last request to see her. He died at last, painfully, of Bright's disease at Birchington-on-Sea, near Hastings on Easter Sunday, 9 April 1882. His sister, Christina, had recovered sufficiently, though sallow and yellow after her own illness, to nurse him in his last weeks, together with her mother and William Michael. They were joined by Lucy Madox Brown and Gabriel's great-aunt, Charlotte Polidori, at his funeral. Maria had already succumbed to cancer and lay in her grave in Brompton Cemetery. Ford Madox Brown designed the cruciform cross for the headstone of Gabriel's grave but was in Manchester and could not attend the funeral. Others present included Vernon Lushington, Fred Stephens, Francis Hueffer, who had married Madox Brown's daughter Cathy, and the painter Fred Shields, who, for a time, had acted as Rossetti's studio assistant. The small churchyard was filled with other mourners, all old friends or connected in some professional capacity with Rossetti. Ned couldn't face it, saying he was too ill. Bell Scott was too lame. Neither Janey nor William Morris attended. Seagulls mewed. With Rossetti's death, the Pre-Raphaelite Brotherhood was finally disbanded, although the surviving members remained faithful to both art and friendship.

Holman Hunt married Fanny Waugh, and after she died in December 1886, leaving him with a son, Cyril Benone, Hunt married Fanny's sister Edith. This was considered scandalous for it was then illegal to marry your deceased wife's sister. To avoid illegality, Hunt and Edith married in Switzerland where the same law did not apply. In spite of this, the sculptor and poet Thomas Woolner, who had married another Waugh sister, Alice, refused to speak to Hunt or Edith or have anything to do with them ever again. Of all the Brotherhood, Hunt continued to paint in the early Pre-Raphaelite style for the rest of his life. Annie Miller, Hunt's first serious love, married Lord Ranelagh's cousin, Thomas R. Thomson, and lived in circumstances infinitely more prosperous than any she could have dreamed of in her early days.

Fanny Cornforth, Rossetti's old 'elephant', had been hounded out of Tudor House by Gabriel's relations while he had been ill in Herne Bay. Ever resourceful, she married a Mr Schott in 1879. Schott had vague and possibly nefarious connections with the art world. He and Fanny took over the premises of the Rose Tavern in Jermyn Street. When Rossetti realized that he couldn't bear anyone else to run his house except for Fanny, she returned to Tudor House, Schott proving tolerant of this arrangement. Whatever Fanny's moral shortcomings, she was a good friend to Rossetti until the end. After his death, she and Schott tried, unsuccessfully, to claim money Fanny insisted was owing to her from the Rossetti Estate. Undeterred by this failure, they opened a small gallery, the Rossetti Gallery, at 1a Old Bond Street, where they sold Pre-Raphaelite artwork, mainly by Rossetti, of dubious provenance. When Schott died, Fanny went to live with his sister in Hammersmith. Fanny died in Brighton in 1906 at the age of seventy-one.

For Ned and Georgie, nothing was ever quite the same again. They grew apart, maintaining appearances and retaining a degree of affection for one another. He achieved fame and riches by exhibiting in the Grosvenor Gallery when it was opened by Sir Coutts Lindsay in 1877. The opening of the Grosvenor was a milestone in the history of Victorian art. It was run by Sir Coutts with his wife Blanche, whose inherited Rothschild money funded the gallery. Charles Hallé and J. Comyns Carr, whose wife designed and made most of Ellen Terry's stage costumes at that time, were both directors. Previously, painters had the choice of being shown at the Royal Academy, or at one of the few small galleries, or opening their studios to the public. This last option was possible only for wealthy artists with imposing studios. The Grosvenor Gallery was a completely new concept and was an instant success in the fashionable art world. With a lavish Italianate interior, it was the first gallery to give its exhibits so much space and to hang each painter's works collectively. Ned had not shown his paintings to the public since the debacle at the Old Water-Colour Society. People were now amazed by the impact of his large and impressive canvases massed together. His reputation, and the prices he commanded, soared overnight.

Ned passed from Mary Zambaco into the hands of other, less important mistresses. Mary Gaskell, with whom he was in love, and Frances Graham, the daughter of William Graham, the art collector, whom he idealized. Georgie knew and pretended not to. She became increasingly involved with the swirl of social politics. In 1880, she and Ned bought a small whitewashed house on a cliff at Rottingdean in Sussex. Here, she put into practice what she and William Morris preached. She became a noticeably ardent if elegant member of the Socialist Party, descending upon unwary villagers, and was elected a parish councillor in Rottingdean. 'I want you to read Georgie's letter to the parish council electors of R'dean –' wrote Ned, 'I think it is so well done, so luminously put and so simple – all the crabbed legal hideousness got out of it and put into easy words of one syllable for simple people – so I send it by the same post as this . . . she is rousing the village – she is marching about – she is going like a flame through the village.' Their marriage, which had started blessed with a sprightly innocence, faded into a barely tolerable drabness. Yet, after Ned's death, Georgie, true to her memory as always, wrote to Val Prinsep, 'It was a good time for about three years, '56–'59, wasn't it?'

Of the Three Graces, Marie Spartali Stillman is best remembered for her much-admired paintings. She continued to paint seriously until the end of her life and her work can be seen in Delaware Art Museum in the Samuel and Mary Bancroft Collection, and in various other galleries and private collections. Her marriage to Stillman has been described as unhappy, but unconventional might be a more accurate way of describing it. She spent much of her life in Florence where Janey, who had always been intimate with her, frequently stayed. She died in 1927, still a woman of extraordinary beauty.

Aglaia Coronio, the close friend and confidante of William Morris, was noted for her skill both as a bookbinder and embroiderer. On the death of her daughter, Caliope, Aglaia committed suicide in 1906, stabbing herself repeatedly with a pair of sewing scissors.

Mary Zambaco continued her studies with Legros and later Rodin, for she was a serious sculptress and medallist, living between London, Paris and Athens. In 1891, she married a much younger man, a Greek named Sios, and spent her last years in Paris where she died in 1914.

After Rossetti's death, Janey had an affair with Wilfred Scawen Blunt, the poet, diplomat, writer and womanizer whom she met on a visit to Naworth Castle while staying with the Howards. It was an unlikely liaison. He came from a completely different background: aristocratic, worldly and sophisticated. His wife, Lady Anne, was Byron's granddaughter and together the Blunts had travelled in Arabia, later setting up a stud of Arab horses on their estate in Sussex. Janey knew that Blunt wasn't faithful to her and that he certainly wasn't in love with her, but he made her happier than she had been and she didn't seem to mind his infidelities. The intimacy between Janey and Blunt continued after Morris's death in 1896. Their relationship makes a bizarre coda to the story of the wives and stunners, the band of women who had inspired one of the most fascinating groups of English nineteenth-century artists to paint some of the most powerful portraits of their time, a legacy we still treasure today.

Acknowledgements

My very first thanks must go to my aunt, Anne Olivier Bell who, from the conception of this book, has been a source of constant encouragement, allowing me the run of my late uncle Quentin Bell's library, and affording me much generous hospitality as well as informative pleasure in discussing various aspects of some of the people in this book – the Pre-Raphaelites not being her particular cup of tea – with an air of amused tolerance.

I owe a particular debt of gratitude to the following: Adrian Glew and the staff of the Tate Gallery Archives for their remarkable generosity, help and support – Adrian went out of his way, far beyond the call of duty, to make my time at the Tate Archives as productive and pleasant as possible; Sir Geoffroy Millais, whose generous loan to the Tate Archives of papers pertaining to Millais, Effie and Ruskin, the Bowerswell Papers in particular, made my research possible; Richard and Jane Garnett for their moral support, with special thanks to Richard for his consistent practical help and for sharing his wealth of information with me; Oliver Garnett for his advice in the early stages; my late mother, Angelica Garnett, for her encouragement; Fanny Garnett for egging me on as only a sister can; Wenzle Gelpke, without whose generosity this book would never have seen the light of day; Julia and Jessica Gelpke for their encouragement and laughter; Sophie Partridge for her unfailing inspiration; Sophie Popham; Brian Hinton, whose combination of generosity in sharing his vast knowledge and quirkiness is tantamount to genius, as well as to everyone at Dimbola; the Julia Margaret Cameron Museum at Freshwater on the Isle of Wight; Richard Shone for his constant generosity, support, knowledge, wit and friendship; Evie Sulzmann for her perception and sparkle; Lulu Norman; Julian Bell for sharing his knowledge, sympathetic groans and cheering me in times of despondency; Mark Divall for sharing his botanical knowledge as well as for his humour and constant friendship; the Hon. Dog Dogan; Gill Metcalf for her practical help and consistent encouragement; Torquil Norman and family; Silvia MacRae Brown; Mr Bhupal Chitnavis, MBBS, FRCS, neurosurgeon, for taking his valuable time to discuss spinal curvatures and the consequences of taking too much laudanum and related opiates; Dr John Gaynor and his colleagues; the late Hugh Millais for many things, including his vivacious telling of Millais family anecdotes; the late Diana Holman-Hunt for her wit, friendship and knowledge; Bill and Juliet Alexander for their generous hospitality, encouragement and patience as well as an unforgettable excursion to Kelmscott with Juliet and an afternoon when Bill pointed out the puddle in a field in Gloucestershire which is the source of the Thames; my good friend and agent Maggie Hanbury of the Hanbury Agency and her staff, with special thanks to Henry de Rougemont and Catriona McDavid; Humphrey Price for putting the footnotes into some kind of order; Georgina Morley for her perspicacity and patience as well as everybody else at Macmillan, Kate Hewson, Tania Adams, Alison Menzies, Clare Sivell, Wilf Dickie and a special thanks to Kate Inship for the index; and an extra special thank you to my ex-sister-in-law Linda and her husband John Fawcett.

I am indebted to the following individuals for help, encouragement and inspiration of many kinds: my late father, David Garnett; Tony and Frances Bradshaw; Andrew Barrow; Matthew Sturgis; Willy and Josephine Landles; Sir Mark and Lady Palmer and Iris and Arthur Palmer; Jeremy Crowe; L'Abbé Hector Carissimo; the late Diana Gunn; Francis and Christina Kyle; Julian Lethbridge; Gill Lowe; Anne Chisholm; Clare Asquith; Alexa Gray; Magooshe Fielding; Philip and Frances Stevens; Katherine Fedden; Nicky Haslam; Annie Hole; Suzanne Nield; Georgia Tennant; the late Pauline, Lady Rumbold; Michael Barker; Georgia de Chamberet; Michael and Sue Fox, David and Martha Mlinaric; Jo Drayton; the late Frances Partridge; Sister Elizabeth of The Sisters of the Handmaids of the Holy Child Jesus; James Beechy; Michael Meredith;

Andrew McNeillie, Lord of the Footnotes, Archipelagos & Western Isles; Sarah Montagu; Colin and Sue Ford; Jo Drayton; the late John Couper; Michael Holroyd; Jonathan Gathorne-Hardy; Richard and Sally Morphet; Christopher Gibbs; Frances Spalding CBE; Lucinda Hawkesley; Herman Vinck; Sarah Knights; Gill Metcalfe; Christopher Mason; Cathy Brooks-Baker; Charles and Henrietta Nettlefold; Shruti Patel; Billy Aldington; Toby Salaman; Sue Snell; Spaska Stefanova Cristova; Shura Shivarg; Veronica Franklin-Gould; the late Charlie Thomas; the late Stanley Olson; Giovanni Calarco; Christian Soleil; Cathy Durand and Charlie de Bouillane; the Chairman and staff of the Chelsea Arts Club and many of its members for their benevolent encouragement; Simon and Harriet Frazer CBE; Domenic and Madeleine Aldiss; the late François Walter.

Among the many archivists, librarians and curators and others who have contributed to this book, I owe first and foremost an enormous debt of gratitude to the staff at the Victoria and Albert Museum; Inez Lynn, Librarian, and the staff of the London Library; the staff of John Sandoe (Books) Ltd; Bernard Horrocks and the staff of the National Portrait Gallery; the Syndics of the Fitzwilliam Museum, Cambridge; the British Museum and staff; the British Library and staff; the Geoffrey Museum and staff; Virginia Nicholson for allowing me to quote from *Blunderhead* by Quentin Bell; Julia Gelpke for photographing the exterior of Tudor House; the staff of the Watts Museum; Nottingham Art Gallery; the very helpful observations of the staff of the Lady Lever Art Gallery, Liverpool; the Walker Art Gallery and staff, Liverpool; Manchester City Art Gallery and staff; University of Leeds; Wightwick Manor; Birmingham Museums and Art Gallery; Cambridge University Library; King Edward VI Schools, Birmingham; l'Hôtel Meurice; the late Miriam Rothschild.

And last, BUT BY NO MEANS LEAST of this lengthy list of people to whom I am deeply indebted, my wholehearted love and thanks go to John Drane, to whom this book is dedicated in some small token of his extraordinary patience, humour, tolerance and knowledge. I could not possibly have finished *Wives and Stunners* on time without his practical help, both academic and domestic.

H.M.C.V.G., London 2012

Select Bibliography

Adburgham, Alison, *Shops and Shopping 1800–1914* (George Allen & Unwin Ltd, 1964; Barrie & Jenkins Ltd, 1984)

Allingham, H., ed. and Williams, E. B., *Letters to William Allingham* (Longmans, Green & Co, 1911)

Allingham, H., ed. and D. Radford, *A Diary 1911* (Penguin Books, 1985)

Angeli, Helen Rossetti, *Dante Gabriel Rossetti: His Friends and Enemies* (Hamish Hamilton, 1949)

Barnes, Rachel, *The Pre-Raphaelites and Their World* (Tate Gallery Publishing, 1998)

Batchelor, John, *Lady Trevelyan and the Pre-Raphaelite Brotherhood* (Chatto & Windus 2006)

Bell, Quentin, *A New and Noble School: The Pre-Raphaelites* (Macdonald, 1982)

—— *Ruskin* (Hogarth Press, 1978)

—— *On Human Finery*, revised edition (Hogarth Press, 1976)

Bell Scott, William, *Autobiographical Notes of the Life of William Bell Scott*, 2 vols (James R. Osgood, McIlvaine & Co, 1892)

Bignall, John, *Chelsea Seen From its Earliest Days* (Robert Hale Ltd, 1987)

Bryson, John and Camp Troxell, Janet, eds, *Dante Gabriel Rossetti and Jane Morris: Their Correspondence* (Clarendon Press, 1976)

Buckler, William E., *The Victorian Imagination: Essays in Aesthetic Exploration* (The Gotham Library, New York University Press, 1980)

Burne-Jones, Georgiana, *Memorials of Edward Burne-Jones*, 2 vols (Macmillan, 1904)

Cameron, Julia Margaret, *Annals of my Glass House: Photographs by Julia Margaret Cameron*, text by Violet Hamilton (Ruth Chandler Williamson Gallery, Scripps College with University of Washington Press, 1997)

———— *For My Best Beloved Sister, Mia: An Album of Photographs* (University of New Mexico Art Museum, 1994)

———— *The Herschel Album: An Album of Portraits*, with prefaces by John Hayes and Colin Ford (National Portrait Gallery, London, 1975)

———— *Victorian Photographs of Famous Men and Fair Women*, with introductions by Virginia Woolf and Roger Fry; Preface and Notes by Tristram Powell (Hogarth Press, 1973)

Cecil, David, *Visionary and Dreamer: Two Poetic Painters: Samuel Palmer and Edward Burne-Jones* (Princeton U. Pr., 1969)

Christiansen, Rupert, *The Victorian Visitors, Culture Shock in Nineteenth-Century Britain* (Atlantic Monthly Press, 2000)

Cook, E. T., ed. and Wedderburn, A., *The Works of John Ruskin*, 39 vols (George Allen, 1903)

Cooper, Suzanne Fagence, *The Model Wife: The Passionate Lives of Effie Gray, Ruskin and Millais* (Duckworth, 2010)

Cox, Julian and Ford, Colin, *Julia Margaret Cameron: The Complete Photographs* (Thames and Hudson, 2003)

Dakers, Caroline, *The Holland Park Circle: Artists and Victorian Society* (Yale University Press, 1999)

Davies, Agnes Maud, *A Book With Seven Seals (Victorian Childhood)* (The Cayme Press, 1928)

de la Motte Fouqué, Friedrich, with an introduction by Sir Edmund Gosse, *Undine and Other Stories from the German of La Motte Fouqué* (Oxford University Press, 1865)

———— *Aslauga's Knight* (1827)

———— *Sintram and His Companions* (James Burn, 1848)

Dish, Thomas M. & Naylor, Charles, *Neighbouring Lives: A Novel* (Charles Scribner's Sons, 1980)

Dorrell, Jane, ed., *Here is Chelsea: Reflections From the Chelsea Society*, Foreword by Tom Pocock (Elliot & Thompson Ltd, 2004)

Doughty, Oswald, ed. and Wahl, J. R., *The Letters of Dante Gabriel Rossetti*, 5 vols, (1953–67)

du Maurier, Daphne, ed., *The Young George du Maurier: A Selection of his Letters, 1860–67* (P. Davies, London, 1951)

du Maurier, George, *Trilby* (Osgood, McIlvaine & Co., 1895)

Edel, Leon, ed., *Letters of Henry James*, vols 2 and 3 (Macmillan, 1978)

Elliott, David B., *A Pre-Raphaelite Marriage: The Lives & Works of Marie Spartali Stillman & William James Stillman* (Antique Collectors Club, 2006)

Fitzgerald, Penelope, *A House of Air*, (Harper Perrenial, 2005)

Flanders, Judith, *A Circle of Sisters* (Viking, 2001)

Francatelli, Charles Elme, *The Modern Cook, A Practical Guide to the Culinary Art in all its Branches*, 29th edition (Richard Bentley and Son, 1896)

The Germ, 4 vols, printed for the P. R. B. (Tupper, 1850); republished 4 vols. (Thomas B. Misher, 1898)

Goldman, Paul, *Millais: Beyond Decoration* (Oak Knoll Press, 2005)

Hilton, Timothy, *John Ruskin* (Yale University Press, 2002)

——— *The Pre-Raphaelites* (Thames and Hudson, 1973)

Holman Hunt, Diana, *My Grandfather, His Wives and Loves* (Hamish Hamilton, 1969)

Holman-Hunt, William, *Pre-Raphaelitism and the Pre-Raphaelite Brotherhood*, 2 vols (Macmillan, 1905)

Hughes, Molly, *A Victorian Family 1870–1900* (Sidgwick & Jackson, 1990)

Hutchings, Elizabeth, *Discovering the Sculptures of George Frederick Watts O.M., R.A.* (Hunnyhill Publications, 1994)

Jalland, Pat, *Death in the Victorian Family* (Oxford University Press, 1990)

James, William, ed., *The Order of Release: the Story of John Ruskin, Effie Gray and John Everett Millais told for the first time in their unpublished letters*, (John Murray, 1947).

Kelmscott Manor (The Society of Antiquaries of London, 2004)

Lutyens, Mary, *The Ruskins and the Grays* (London, John Murray, 1972)

——— *Effie in Venice* (John Murray, 1965)

——— *Millais and the Ruskins* (London, John Murray, 1967)

Maas, Jeremy, Trimpe, Pamela White and Grere, Charlotte, et al. and

Martineau, Jane, ed., *Victorian Fairy Painting* (Royal Academy of Arts, 1997)

MacCarthy, Fiona, *William Morris* (Faber & Faber, 1994)

—— *The Last Pre-Raphaelite: Edward Burne-Jones and the Victorian Imagination* (Faber & Faber, 2011)

Mackenzie, John M., *The Victorian Vision* (V&A)

Madox Ford, Ford, *Your Mirror to My Times, The Selected Autobiographies and Impressions of Ford Madox Ford*, edited with an introduction by Michael Kiligrew (Holt, Rhinehart and Winston, 1971)

Marsh, Jan, *Dante Gabriel Rossetti: Painter and Poet* (Weidenfeld & Nicolson, 1999)

Millais, John Guille, *The Life and Letters of Sir John Everett Millais*, 2 vols (London, 1899)

Munro, Jane and Goddard, Linda, eds, *Literary Circles: Artist, Author, Word and Image in Britain 1800–1920* (Fitzwilliam Museum, Cambridge, 2006)

Ovenden, Graham, ed., *A Victorian Album: Julia Margaret Cameron and her Circle*, with an introduction by Lord David Cecil (Secker and Warburg, 1975)

Pedrick, Gale, *Life with Rossetti: or, No Peacocks Allowed* (Macdonald, 1964)

Prose, Francine, *The Lives of the Muses*, (Harper Perennial, 2003)

Roe, Sonia, ed., *Oil Paintings in Public Ownership in the Victoria and Albert Museum* (The Public Catalogue Foundation, 2008)

Rossetti, C. G., *Poetical Works with Memoir & Notes by William Michael Rossetti* (Macmillan, 1904)

Rossetti, William Michael, *Dante Gabriel Rossetti: His Family Letters*, vols 1 & 2 (Ellis and Elvey, 1895)

Severn, Arthur, ed. by James S. Dearden, *Professor Arthur Severn's Memoir of John Ruskin* (George Allen & Unwin, 1967)

Stansky, Peter, *William Morris and Bloomsbury* (Cecil Woolf, 1997)

Surtees, Virginia, ed., *Reflections of a Friendship: John Ruskin's Letters to Pauline Trevelyan 1848–1866*, Foreword by Raleigh Trevelyan (Allen & Unwin, 1979)

Thomas, Frances, *Christina Rossetti: A Biography* (Virago Press, 1995)

Thompson, F. M. L., *The Rise of Respectable Society: A Social History of Victorian Britain, 1830–1900* (Fontana Press, 1998)

Uglow, Jenny, *Elizabeth Gaskell: A Habit of Stories* (Faber & Faber, 1993)

Waugh, Evelyn, *The Earthly Paradise, Rossetti, His Life and Works* (Methuen, 1978)

Notes

Abbreviations

BP   Bowerswell Papers – the original Bowerswell Papers are in the Pierpoint Morgan Library. I have used the manuscript transcription made with annotations by Claire Stuart Wortley in 1937, currently on loan to the Tate Archives, courtesy of Sir Geoffrey Millais.

CSW   Claire Stuart Wortley

DGR   Dante Gabriel Rossetti

EG   Effie Gray

FMB   Ford Madox Brown

JGM   John Guille Millais

JJR   John James Ruskin (Ruskin's father)

JR   John Ruskin

ML   Mary Lutyens

Mrs G   Mrs Gray

WHM   William Holman Hunt

Introduction

1 Edward Walford, *Old and New London: A Narrative of Its History, Its People, and Its Places*. Vol. vi, (Cassell Petter & Galpin: London, Paris & New York) pp. 337–338.
2 Ibid.

1 ~ Formation of the P. R. B

1 William Bell Scott, *Autobiographical Notes of the Life of William Bell Scott*, (James R. Osgood, McIlvaine & Co, 1892) Edited by W. Minto vol. 1, pp. 310–319.

2 ~ Effie and the Ruskins

1 Anne Thackeray Ritchie, *Records of Tennyson, Ruskin and Browning*, (Macmillan, 1896) p. 108.
2 Ibid.
3 John Ruskin, *Praeterita, Outlines of Scenes and Thoughts Perhaps Worthy of Memory in my Past Life – The Autobiography of John Ruskin* with an introduction by Kenneth Clark, (Rupert Hart-Davis, London, 1949).
4 Letter from Effie Gray to Mrs Gray addressed to Mr Ruskin Wine Merchant/Biliter St. se [sic] 2nd 1840 from Avonbank, BP.
5 EG to Mrs G, 25 May 1841, Avonbank, BP.
6 *Praeterita*, vol. I, p. 348.
7 *Praeterita*, vol. I, p. 348.
8 Letter from Effie Gray to Mrs Gray, n.d.
9 BP, courtesy of Sir Geoffrey Millais and the Tate Gallery Archives.
10 EG to Mrs G, 15 June 1847, BP.
11 EG to Mrs G, 18 June 1847, BP.
12 EG to Mrs G, 18 June 1847, BP.
13 JR to Effie Gray, Tuesday morning, 9 November 1847, BP. Also quoted in Lutyens, *The Ruskins and the Grays*, p. 65.
14 JR to Effie Gray, Folkestone, 30 November 1847, BP.
15 JR to Effie Gray, Folkestone, 30 November 1847, BP.
16 JR to Effie Gray quoted in Phyllis Rose, *Parallel Lives*, (Penguin Books, 1985) p. 58.
17 JR to Effie Gray 30 November, Folkestone, BP.
18 EG to JR, BP.
19 Letter from Effie Gray to Mr Gray, Herne Hill, 7 March 1854 quoted in James, *The Order of Release* p. 219.
20 EG, Aberfeldy, 11 April 1848, see ibid. p. 98.
21 EG, Denmark Hill, 28 April 1848, see ibid. p. 101.

3 ~ Married Life

1 Mr Ruskin to Mr G, Denmark Hill, 24 May 1848, see ibid. p. 102.
2 EG to Mrs G, Denmark Hill, 29 April 1848, ibid, p. 104.

3 EG to Mrs G, BP, n.d.

4 EG to Mrs G, Denmark Hill, 24 May 1848.

5 EG to Mrs G, Denmark Hill, 24 May 1848, ibid.

6 EG to Mrs G, Bear Inn, Reading, 1 July 1848, ibid, p. 114.

7 EG to Mr G, Abbeville 9 August 1848, James, p. 121.

8 JR to Mr Ruskin, Lutyens, *The Ruskins and the Grays*, p. 86.

9 JR to Mr Ruskin, Mortain, September 4 1848, quoted in Lutyens, *The Ruskins and the Grays*, p. 140, partly quoted in Links, p. 41. Original in Yale.

10 EG to Mrs G, Bowerswell Papers.

11 Quoted from *Anny, A Life of Anny Thackeray Ritchie*, (Henrietta Garnett, Random House, Chatto and Windus, 2004) p. 198.

12 Quoted in *The Gentle Art of Cookery* by Mrs C. F Leyel and Miss Olga Hartley with an introduction by Elizabeth David, (Chatto and Windus, The Hogarth Press, 1983).

13 JR to EG, April 24 1849.

14 JR to EG, April 27 1849.

15 JJR to George Gray, 4 March 1849, quoted in ML *The Ruskins and the Grays*.

16 EG to Mrs G, BP.

17 EG to Mrs G, BP.

5 ~ *En Plein Air*

1 *Millais and the Hogsmill River*, Barbara C. L. Webb, ISBN 953007405. I am indebted to Richard Shone for bringing Miss Webb's research to my attention.

2 *The Life and Letters of Sir John Everett Millais*, John Guille Millais, vol. I, p. 121.

3 *Pre-Raphaelitism and the Pre-Raphaelite Brotherhood*, William Holman Hunt vol. I, p. 355.

4 *Pre-Raphaelitism and the Pre-Raphaelite Brotherhood*, William Holman Hunt.

5 *The Stones of Venice*, John Ruskin, Chapter iv, vol. 1.

6 ~ Lizzie Becomes Ophelia

1 *The Life and Letters of Sir John Everett Millais*, ed. John Guille Millais, 1899, vol. I, p. 144.

2 W. Holman Hunt *Pre-Raphaelitism and the Pre-Raphaelite Brotherhood* vol. I, p. 319.

3 Letter from John James Ruskin to Millais, quoted in JGM.

7 ~ Venice Regained

1 Mary Lutyens, *Effie in Venice* (John Murray, 1965) p. 206.
2 EG to Mrs G, 28 September 1851, BP.
3 BP and ML.
4 Letter from Elizabeth Gaskell to John Forster, 17 May 1854.
5 EG to Mrs G, 8 February 1852, BP.
6 JR to JJR quoted in John Ruskin, Tim Hilton (Yale University Press, 2002) p. 171.
7 BP.
8 BP.

8 ~ The Horror of Herne Hill

1 EG to Mr G, Sunday March 20 1853, BP.
2 Catalogue *Millais* by Jason Rosenfeld and Alison Smith (Tate Publishing, 2007), p. 76.
3 BP.

9 ~ At Glenfinlas

1 *Autobiographical Notes of the Life of William Bell Scott*, ed. W. Minto, vol. II, p. 3.
2 Pauline Trevelyan Journal quoted from John Batchelor, *Lady Trevelyan and the Pre-Raphaelite Brotherhood*.
3 Ibid.
4 JR to his father, 29 June, 1853.
5 John Guille Millais, *The Letters of John Everett Millais*, 2 vols, 1899, p. 109, vol. I.
6 Ibid.
7 *The Life and Letters of Sir John Everett Millais* by his son John Guille Millais, 1899, p. 211, vol. I.

10 ~ Consequences

1 JEM to Mrs G, 83 Gower Street, 19 December 1853 BP.
2 JR to JJR, 11 November 1853.
3 JEM to Mrs G, 83 Gower Street, 19 December 1853 BP.

11 ~ The Great Escape

1 Effie Ruskin to Mrs Gray, BP, n.d.
2 ER to Mrs G, 2 March 1854 BP.

3 JEM to Mrs G, Tuesday afternoon, 20 December 1853, Bedford Square, BP.

4 JR to JJR 6 November 1893, *Millais and the Ruskins*, Mary Lutyens pp. 107–8.

5 JEM to Mrs Comne, Dec 30 1853, quoted in *The Life and Letters of Sir John Everett Millais* by his son John Guille Millais, pp. 224–5.

6 Hunt, vol. I, p. 365.

7 Ibid.

8 ER to Mr G, 6 May [erroneously dated 7 May] 1854, BP.

9 See ML *Millais and the Ruskins*, p. 184.

10 Quoted in ML p. 219 also BP.

11 See ML *Millais and the Ruskins*, p. 188.

12 See ML *Millais and the Ruskins*, p. 188.

13 Derrick Leon, *Ruskin, The Great Victorian*, (Routledge & Kegan Paul, 1949) p. 197.

12 ~ The Dissolution of the P. R. B

1 *The Life and Letters of John Everett Millais*, John Guille Millais, vol. I, p. 216.

2 Ibid.

13 ~ Lizzie and Gabriel

1 W. M. Rossetti, *Memoirs*, 1906 vol. I, p. 137.

2 *The Diary of Ford Madox Brown* ed. Virginia Surtees, (Yale University Press, 1981) p. 197.

3 Quoted in Elizabeth Haldane, *Mrs Gaskell and her Friends*, (London, 1930) pp. 10–7. Also in Jenny Uglow, *Elizabeth Gaskell; A Habit of Stories*, (Faber & Faber, 1993) p. 455

14 ~ The Second Generation: The Revival of the P. R. B. and the Decline of Lizzie Siddal

1 Helen Angeli, *Dante Gabriel Rossetti*, p. 120, (Hamish Hamilton, 1949).

2 Georgiana Burne-Jones, *Memorials of Edward Burne-Jones*, p. 173, vol. I.

3 Quoted in *William Morris* by Fiona MacCarthy, (Faber & Faber, 1994) p. 133.

4 Georgiana Burne-Jones, *Memorials of Edward Burne-Jones*, vol. I p. 183.

15 ~ Weddings in the Wind

1 Georgiana Burne-Jones, *Memorials of Edward Burne-Jones*, vol. I, 1904, p. 203.
2 Ibid. p. 207.
3 Ibid. pp. 207–208.

16 ~ Red House

1 Georgiana Burne-Jones, *Memorials of Edward Burne-Jones*, vol. I, 1904, p. 203.
2 *William Morris on Art and Socialism*, ed. Norman Kelvin, 1999.
3 *Chapters from Some Memoirs*, Anne Thackeray Ritchie, (Macmillan & Co, 1894).

17 ~ Lizzie's Tragedy

1 Georgiana Burne-Jones, *Memorials of Edward Burne-Jones*, p. 238.

18 ~ Italian Interlude

1 Georgiana Burne-Jones, *Memorials of Edward Burne-Jones*, vol. I, p. 241.
2 Ibid. p. 245.

19 ~ Tudor House

1 Georgiana Burne-Jones, *Memorials of Edward Burne-Jones*, vol. I, pp. 220–221.
2 Ibid. p. 292.
3 Henry Treffry Dunn, quoted in *Life With Rossetti*, (Gale Pedrick Macdonald, London, 1964) p. 96.

20 ~ Mr and Mrs Burne-Jones

1 Georgiana Burne-Jones, *Memorials of Edward Burne-Jones* vol. I, p. 285.
2 Ibid. p. 286.
3 Ibid. pp. 235–236.
4 Georgiana Burne-Jones, *Memorials of Edward Burne-Jones* vol. I, p. 293.
5 William Michael Rossetti, *Some Reminiscences of William Michael Rossetti*, 2 vols, 1906.
6 *The Correspondence of Anna McNeill Whistler, 1829–1880*, edited by Georgia Toutziari (University of Glasgow, 2002).
7 Georgiana Burne-Jones, *Memorials of Edward Burne-Jones* vol I. p. 294.

21 ~ A Greek Tragedy

1 Daphne du Maurier, *The Young George du Maurier*, (Doubleday, 1952), p. 104.
2 *A Grandfather's Tale*, 1927, Alexander Constantine Ionides.
3 William Michael Rossetti, *Diary*, 1 March, 1880.
4 Penelope Fitzgerald, *A House of Air*, 2005, p. 135.
5 DGR to FMB, 23 January 1869, *Letters of Dante Gabriel Rossetti*, vol. I, p. 685. Browning's house was in Warwick Avenue opposite the Regent's Canal.
6 Rosalind Howard's *Diary*, 29 January 1869 CH, J22/27, quoted in *A Circle of Sisters*, Judith Flanders, (Viking, 2001).
7 G. B-J to Rosalind Howard, n.d. [Feb/March 1869], Castle Howard, see ibid.

24. Bad Ems

1 Morris to Philip Webb, quoted in *William Morris*, Fiona MacCarthy, (Faber and Faber, 1994) p. 234.
2 DGR to Jane Morris.

25 ~ Cracking Up

1 William Bell Scott *Autobiographical Notes*, vol. II, p. 112.
2 Ibid.

26 ~ Kelmscott

1 Quoted in *A House of Air*, p. 120, Harper Perennial, 2005.
2 Suzanne Shonfield, *The Precariously Privileged: A Professional Family in Victorian London*, (Oxford University Press, 1978) p. 117.

27 ~ Nemesis

1 'The Fleshly School of Poetry' article written under the pseudonym of Thomas Maitland (Robert Buchannan) August-November, *The Contemporary Review*, 1871.
2 William Bell Scott, *Autobiographical Notes*, vol. II, p. 171, (James R. Osgood, McIlvaine & Co. London MDCCCXCII).
3 Ibid. pp. 171–172.
4 *Recollections of Rossetti and His Circle* by H.T. Dunn, London 1904.
5 Ibid.

28 ~ The End of the Firm

1 May Morris, *The Introductions to the Collected Works of William Morris*, II vols, (Oriole Editions, 1973).

29 ~ The Last Janey Picture

1 William Michael Rossetti, *Dante Gabriel Rossetti, His Family Letters with a Memoir*, (Ellis & Elvey, 1895).

Index

Illustration Acknowledgements